THE PELICAN CLASSICS

THE THEORY OF POLITICAL ECONOMY

WILLIAM STANLEY JEVONS (1835–82) has long been recognized as one of the key figures in the development of English economic thought. Born in Liverpool, he entered University College, London, in 1852, but left before completing his degree to become, at the age of nineteen, Assayer in the newly formed Royal Mint at Sydney. During his years in Australia his interests moved from chemistry and meteorology towards social science, and he returned to complete his studies in London, taking a gold medal in the M.A. examinations in 1862. In 1866 he became professor of logic, mental and moral philosophy and political economy at Owens College, Manchester, and ten years later he was made professor of political economy at University College, London. He became a Fellow of the Royal Society and in 1876 was awarded an honorary LL.D. by the University of Edinburgh.

In his short life Jevons introduced a wealth of new ideas not only in economics but also in logic and the philosophy of science. The 'logical machine' which he designed and built in 1865 was in some respects a fore-runner of modern computers, and his pamphlet of 1863, *A Serious Fall in the Value of Gold Ascertained*, is recognized as a landmark in the development of index-number techniques. His bold use of mathematical methods and insistence on the importance of utility in the explanation of value have made *The Theory of Political Economy* his best-known work.

R. D. COLLINSON BLACK was born in Dublin. He completed his under-graduate and postgraduate training at Trinity College, Dublin, and began his academic career there as deputy for the Professor of Political Economy. In 1950–51 he went to the United States as a Rockefeller Fellow and studied under Professor Jacob Viner at Princeton University. Having been succes-sively Assistant Lecturer, Lecturer, Senior Lecturer and Reader in Econo-mics at Queen's University, Belfast, he became Professor there in 1962. In 1964–5 he was Visiting Professor of Economics at Yale University.

His interest in the relation of thought to policy led to his study of *Economic Thought and the Irish Question 1817–1870* (1960). He is currently com-pleting an edition of the unpublished letters and papers of W. S. Jevons for the Royal Economic Society. Professor Black is married and has a son and a daughter.

D0378033

W. STANLEY JEVONS

The Theory of Political Economy

EDITED
WITH AN INTRODUCTION BY
R. D. COLLISON BLACK

PENGUIN BOOKS

Penguin Books Ltd, Harmondsworth, Middlesex, England
Penguin Books Inc., 7110 Ambassador Road, Baltimore, Maryland, 21207, U.S.A.
Penguin Books Australia Ltd, Ringwood, Victoria, Australia

—

First published 1871
Published in Pelican Books 1970

—

Introduction and notes copyright © R. D. Collison Black, 1970

—

Made and printed in Great Britain
by Richard Clay (The Chaucer Press), Ltd
Bungay, Suffolk
Set in Monotype Times

This book is sold subject to the condition
that it shall not, by way of trade or otherwise,
be lent, re-sold, hired out, or otherwise circulated
without the publisher's prior consent in any form of
binding or cover other than that in which it is
published and without a similar condition
including this condition being imposed
on the subsequent purchaser

CONTENTS

INTRODUCTION

I

THE *Theory of Political Economy* has been described as 'one of the four or five great books of nineteenth-century English political economy'[1] and its author as 'one of the most genuinely original economists who ever lived'.[2] It is now very nearly a century since it was first published and for more than half that century the book has been recognized as a landmark in the development of economic ideas. Its publication date has been taken by many historians of such ideas as heralding the replacement of classical political economy, as founded by Adam Smith and developed by Ricardo and J. S. Mill, by neo-classical economics. This process, begun by Jevons's *Theory*, has frequently been described as a revolution.[3]

What was the nature of this revolution, if indeed it was a revolution, and what was the peculiarly original contribution of Jevons's *Theory* towards it?

An answer to these questions requires, first of all, some sketch of the characteristics of classical political economy and neo-classical economics.

Classical political economy began in the eighteenth century as a branch of moral philosophy, combining observation of facts with deductive analysis of cause and effect relationships in an essentially literary manner to explain the workings of the economic system in which men lived. The recognition that there was a *system* capable of logical explanation was the starting point for the later development of political economy as a separate discipline, but, as its very name implies, its practitioners did not make any very sharp distinction between the analysis of the workings of the system and the discussion of the policy problems which arose in it.

A political economist of the early nineteenth century asked to define his subject would almost certainly have replied that it was concerned with 'the production, distribution, exchange and consumption of wealth', meaning by wealth mainly material goods. The topics on which interest centred, however, were the changes in the production and distribution of wealth over time – especially the relative rates of growth of population and material resources and the consequences of this for economic progress and the welfare of individuals and society.

Now the material goods which constitute wealth clearly are a heterogeneous collection and any attempt to examine changes in the amount and distribution of wealth therefore requires some measuring rod or common denominator for the elements of wealth – in other words some form of *valuation*. From its earliest stages, then, the analysis of value has been one of the key subjects in economic thought.

Classical economists were concerned to find both a measure of the value of goods and services and an explanation of the causes of their value – not so much of the short-term movements of market prices, but of long-term changes in the relative values of goods. Adam Smith, the acknowledged master of the classical school, had sought both the source and the measure of value in labour – 'the first price, the original purchase money that was paid for all things'. Smith himself allowed that only in a primitive society would goods exchange in proportion to the quantities of labour used in producing them, but contended that in all stages of society cost of production determined the normal value (or 'natural price') of goods.[4] This was accepted by most of his followers, many of whom also paid lip service at least to the idea of labour as the most real (if not invariable) measure of value.

Such an approach to valuation problems was natural in writers whose main concern was with changes in the wealth of society *through time*. Similarly, to classical economists a 'theory of distribution' meant mainly an attempt to explain the proportion of the total real income of society received by labourers, landlords and capitalists, and the causes of changes in these proportions, again over time.

What has come to be called neo-classical economics developed in the last quarter of the nineteenth century and the change in the name of the subject reflects a considerable shift in its content and character. The questions with which neo-classical economists dealt were often given the same names which classical writers had used, but it does not therefore follow that they were the same questions. Value and the distribution of income, in particular, remained major concerns of the new economics as they had been of the old political economy, but now they were no longer treated as incidental to the great question of the growth of wealth but as central in themselves. The basic question which the neo-classical economists asked was – 'given an economy with a certain population having given tastes, and certain resources and techniques, how can these resources be allocated through a market system so as to maximize the satisfaction of consumers?' To answer this question it was necessary to show how consumers and producers would react to the stimuli of given prices, attempting to maximize their own satisfaction or profits, and how their actions in turn would influence prices to bring about a redistribution of resources until an equilibrium position was reached – a position from which, so long as tastes and resources remained unchanged, any movement would be disadvantageous.

Thus the neo-classical economists central concern when they talked about a 'theory of value' was first those very phenomena of market price which their classical predecessors had tended to disregard, and when they talked about a 'theory of distribution' they referred to the influences determining the prices of productive services (of land, labour, capital and so on) and so really made this another facet of the analysis of price.

These changes in the content of economic analysis could be characterized as a shift of interest from macro-analysis, or the treatment of major aggregates (such for example as the share of labour in the national product) to micro-analysis or the treatment of individual variables (such as the weekly wage of a fitter). The shift was from what has been well described as the 'magnificent dynamics'* of economic growth to the precise statics of the optimum allocation of given resources. With this shift in content came a corresponding shift in method. Neo-classical economics,

---

*See Baumol, *Economic Dynamics*, New York, 1951. It should be emphasized that the discussion here relates to pre-Keynesian economics. Keynesian theory, often thought of as the essence of modern economics, is essentially of a 'macro' character. See Jan Pen, *Modern Economics*, London, 1965, ch. I.

more interested in individuals than aggregates, had to consider individual behaviour and adopted a simple – some might say naïve – definition of rational behaviour as maximizing or minimizing in the appropriate circumstances – for example, maximizing satisfaction (utility) or minimizing costs.

Combine this concept with the idea of price and demand or supply as functionally related, and it becomes clear that many of these economic problems allow of a simple and elegant mathematical treatment with the aid of the differential calculus. Economists thus began to follow the methods of the natural rather than the moral philosopher, often using mathematics to express the relations between the variables they studied.

Accompanying this move towards a more scientific type of economic theorizing was a greater emphasis on the distinction between analysis and policy, evidenced directly by the change in the name of the subject from political economy to economics. The neo-classical economists made a sharper distinction than their predecessors had done between the explanation of 'what is' in an economic system and the consideration of 'what ought to be'. While there was no lack of writing on questions of economic policy and the role of the state these tended to be separated, under the name of welfare economics, from the pure analysis of the price system.

Such, in outline, was the nature of the revolution in economic thought which began just about a century ago. In one respect the term revolution is certainly a misnomer, for the change did not take place violently or in a short space of time; nevertheless it was a fundamental change, producing ultimately the emergence of the first true social *science*. And undoubtedly historians of economic thought have been right in pointing to Jevons's *Theory of Political Economy* as the herald of this fundamental change.

The *Theory* was published at a time when no major innovations in the core of economic analysis had been made for almost a generation. John Stuart Mill, perhaps the most influential and respected social thinker of mid-Victorian England, had published his *Principles of Political Economy* in 1848 and it had been received, as its author intended, as a definitive summing-up of the accepted principles of classical orthodoxy. In this, the most widely-read economic text of its time, Mill had declared, 'Happily there is nothing in the laws of value which remains for the present or any future writer to clear up; the theory of the subject is complete'[5] – and up to 1871 this statement had not been contradicted.

Jevons took up the question of value, the key question of political economy, on the very first page of his book and at once proceeded to lay down a proposition about it – 'value depends entirely upon utility' – which was almost diametrically opposed to classical orthodoxy. It shifted the focal point of value theory from long-run 'normal' values determined by cost of production to short-run exchange-ratios determined by the psychology of the parties making the exchange.

Almost every other feature which was to become characteristic of neo-classical economics is to be found in Jevons's book. The 'mathematical character of the science' is boldly asserted, and substantiated by the employment of the techniques of calculus – a disagreeable novelty at the time to almost every English economist. And, although as Jevons himself said 'I make hardly any attempt to employ statistics in this work, and thus I do not pretend to any numerical precision'[6] he showed himself fully conscious of the desirability of quantifying the variables with which he dealt *. Again, if the limits of his subject are not too precisely defined at the beginning of the book, it emerges clearly in the 'Concluding Remarks' of Chapter VIII[7] that Jevons viewed 'the problem of economics' not as the growth or distribution of the wealth of nations but essentially as the problem of allocating given resources to obtain maximum satisfaction.

---

* This is evidenced particularly by the sections in ch. IV of the *Theory* on the 'Numerical Determination of the Laws of Utility' and 'Variation of the Price of Corn' (pp. 174, 178 below). The combination of economic theory with statistical analysis has led today to the fast-growing subject of econometrics. While it is not in the field of value theory that most progress has so far been made with econometric techniques, the fact that almost a century ago Jevons should so clearly have anticipated the trends of modern thinking is another proof of the continuing freshness and relevance of his *Theory*.

Why should Jevons have chosen to state 'the problem of economics' in this way and to tackle it by these methods? He was not employing any lightly chosen phrase when he wrote of his approach as being the outcome of 'repeated reflection and inquiry'. In order to understand this it is necessary to know something of the background to Jevons's career up to the time of his publishing the *Theory*.

Jevons was born in 1835, the ninth child of Thomas Jevons, who was well placed in the iron trade in Liverpool. In 1850 young William Stanley entered University College School, London, and in 1852 matriculated into the University of London with honours in chemistry and botany.

Before he had completed his degree he was offered a lucrative post as assayer at the new branch of the Royal Mint in Sydney, and accepted it in order to help the financial circumstances of his family, straitened since the crisis of 1848 had forced his father into bankruptcy. So in 1854 Jevons emigrated to Australia; his duties there left him time for study and travel in the new colony. Though he devoted himself mainly to meteorology (in which he maintained a lifelong interest) it was at this period also that he became interested in social and economic questions.

As early as 1858 he wrote to one of his sisters, who was also reading political economy,

'You will perceive that *economy*, scientifically speaking, is a very contracted science; it is in fact a sort of vague mathematics which calculates the causes and effects of man's industry, and shows how it may best be applied. There are a multitude of allied branches of knowledge connected with man's condition; the relation of these to political economy is analogous to the connexion of mechanics, astronomy, optics, sound, heat, and every other branch more or less of physical science, with pure mathematics.'[8]

The working-out of this idea – a remarkable piece of prescience for a young man of twenty-three, working alone – to its fruition in the *Theory of Political Economy* can be clearly traced through the events of the intervening years, as recorded in Jevons's letters and papers. In 1859 Jevons returned to England and enrolled again as an undergraduate at University College, London. On 1 June 1860 he wrote to his brother

During the last session I have worked a good deal at political economy; in the last few months I have fortunately struck out what I have no doubt is *the true Theory of Economy*, so thorough-going and consistent, that I cannot now read other books on the subject without indignation. While the theory is entirely mathematical in principle, I show, at the same time, how the data of calculation are so complicated as to be for the present hopeless. Nevertheless, I obtain from the mathematical principles all the chief laws at which political economists have previously arrived, only arranged in a series of definitions, axioms, and theories almost as rigorous and connected as if they were so many geometrical problems. One of the most important axioms is, that as the quantity of any commodity, for instance, plain food, which a man has to consume, increases, so the utility or benefit derived from the last portion used decreases in degree. The decrease of enjoyment between the beginning and end of a meal may be taken as an example. And I assume that on an average, the *ratio of utility* is some continuous mathematical function of the quantity of commodity. This law of utility has, in fact, always been assumed by political economists under the more complex form and name of the Law of Supply and Demand. But once fairly stated in its simple form, it opens up the whole of the subject. Most of the conclusions are, of course, the old ones stated in a consistent form; but my definition of capital and law of the interest of capital are, as far as I have seen, quite new. I have no idea of letting these things lie by till somebody else has the advantage of them, and shall therefore try to publish them next spring.[9]

It was actually not until the autumn of 1862 that Jevons did publish his 'Notice of a General Mathematical Theory of Political Economy', read as a paper to the British Association for the Advancement of Science 'and received without a word of interest or belief'.[10]

Hence it is clear that the concept of the 'true theory of economy' as a 'contracted science' is one which Jevons had worked out more than ten years before he published the *Theory of Political Economy*. And it is not difficult to see why Jevons should have conceived the subject in this way – it is an approach such as could only come from an original mind trained primarily in the natural sciences and secondarily in mathematics. After graduation Jevons went on to develop a considerable reputation not only as an economist but also as a logician. As such he had a special interest in scientific method[11] and although he never wrote at length on the methods of the social sciences his studies in this field must have tended to confirm and strengthen his early views on the approach to economic theory.

After the failure of his first paper on a general mathematical theory of political economy to attract attention, Jevons devoted his energies to studies in applied economics and statistics as well as logic. He went to Manchester in 1863 as a general tutor to the undergraduates of what was then Owens College (later to become the Victoria University of Manchester) and in 1866 became professor of logic and Cobden lecturer on political economy there.

By 1870 Jevons had established a considerable reputation through his book *The Coal Question*, which raised the issue of Britain's industrial supremacy being lost as her supplies of cheap coal became exhausted, and through his papers on monetary questions. According to his son he might well have postponed further writings on economic theory for some years 'had it not been for the appearance in 1868 and 1870 of articles by Professor Fleeming Jenkin [then professor of mechanical engineering at Edinburgh] which are distinctly mathematical in method and contain a number of very ingenious geometrical diagrams illustrating the laws of supply and demand'.[12]

Jevons and Fleeming Jenkin were certainly in correspondence in March 1868[13] about problems in the theory of exchange. It was apparently not until after the publication of Jenkin's paper on 'The Graphic Representation of the Laws of Supply and Demand' in 1870 that Jevons decided to produce his own results in book form. He submitted the manuscript of the *Theory of Political Economy* to Macmillan on 28 March 1871 and it was published in October of that year. From these facts we can reasonably infer not only the reason for the *Theory of Political Economy* being published when it was but also the reasons why it assumed the shape which it has. Jevons was anxious to establish his priority by publishing his ideas in a form which would ensure wider circulation and greater permanence, and he was able to write the book in a remarkably short space of time because the

essentials of it had long been clear in his mind. In fact it represented an expansion and development of the ideas of his 1862
paper – and this in turn accounts for the comparative brevity and
limited scope of the volume. For all that Jevons had set out to
give in that paper was an outline of a general theory of economy –
that 'very contracted science' of which he had written to his
sister in 1858. In his 'Concluding Remarks' to the *Theory* he
indicated 'the branches of economic doctrine which have been
passed over' and in the preface to the second edition his precise
and limited purpose is made even clearer:

> But as all the physical sciences have their basis more or less obviously
> in the general principles of mechanics, so all branches and divisions of
> economic science must be pervaded by certain general principles. It is
> to the investigation of such principles – to the tracing out of the
> mechanics of self-interest and utility, that this essay has been devoted.
> The establishment of such a theory is a necessary preliminary to any
> definite drafting of the superstructure of the aggregate science.[14]

To other branches and divisions of economics, such as monetary and trade cycle theory, Jevons made notable contributions.
In 1875 he left Manchester to become professor at his old college,
University College, London, where his teaching duties were lighter
and left more time and opportunity for his writing. In 1880 he
began what might have been the 'definite drafting of the superstructure of the aggregate science', a large book under the title of
Principles of Economics. After his resignation from the London
chair in 1880 he hoped to complete this book within two or three
years, but comparatively little of it had been finished at the time
when Jevons died in a drowning accident in 1882. It was not
until 1905 that the chapters which he had left were published[15]
but though not without interest these are not at all comparable
to the *Theory of Political Economy* for originality and certainly
did not in any way supersede it.

III

The *Theory of Political Economy* contained so many of the ideas
which won general acceptance among economists within the

ensuing twenty-five years and foreshadowed so many of the trends which actually developed in economics that commentators have usually tended to judge it by the standards of neo-classical analysis in its most mature form.

In that form economic theory centred around a model of a system in which the allocation of resources to consumer satisfaction was achieved through competitive market processes, and made extensive use of the technique of marginal analysis. Indeed the change over from classical to neo-classical thinking has been characterized as 'the marginal revolution' – and the characterization is sound, for certainly the concept of the margin had hardly been present in classical thinking, but was being exploited to the full at the end of the nineteenth century. In essence the technique consists of considering the effect of a small increment or decrement of a good or service on consumption or production and thence on price determination.

On the consumption side it involves merely an elaboration of that axiom which Jevons had stated in 1860: '. . . as the quantity of any commodity, for instance, plain food, which a man has to consume, increases, so the utility or benefit derived from the last portion decreases in degree.'

In other words, consumption of successive units yields an increasing *total* utility, but each additional unit consumed adds a smaller amount to that total; we can say that *marginal* utility, the utility of an increment to the consumer's stock, is diminishing. It can then be shown how this marginal utility will serve to determine the quantity of the good which the consumer will demand at a given price.

Similarly, in the case of a productive service, or factor of production, it can be shown that if successive increments of one such factor are employed, while the stock of others used in combination with it is held fixed, these increments will, after a point, yield successively smaller and smaller additions to the total product. Again the relation of this to the quantity of the service employed at a given price for it can be readily shown – and this theory can be generalized to apply to all productive services. Hence marginal analysis can be used to produce a consistent explanation of the determination of all prices in a market system, and this can perhaps be regarded as the crowning achievement of neo-classical economics.

The most obvious claim which Jevons's *Theory of Political Economy* has to originality is that the concepts of marginal alterations in the utility of commodities and in the productiveness of factors are clearly set out in it – though not in exactly the terminology which later neo-classical writers used. Jevons refers to the 'final degree of utility' rather than 'marginal utility'* and to the 'final rate of production' rather than 'marginal productivity' – but these are differences in form rather than in the substance of the ideas. The book therefore contains all the necessary materials required to build a complete and symmetrical 'theory of value and distribution' with all the prices of both consumer and producer goods and services explained by marginal analysis. Yet Jevons does not take the apparently simple step of putting his materials together in this way and so has often been criticized for this failure to do so by those who wrote from the viewpoint of later neo-classicism.

Thus Professor (now Lord) Robbins wrote in 1936.

He [Jevons] nowhere shows any real appreciation of the interdependence of the various elements determining the prices of the factors of production. Time and time again he seems to be on the brink of the modern theory. ... But he does not develop a general productivity theory. ... All of which is very disappointing. For the idea that the value of ultimate commodities comes from their utility leads directly, as Menger emphasized, to the idea that the value of factors of production depends on the value of their products. All that is needed is the development of a technique for identifying marginal products.[16]

These are the strengths and weaknesses in the *Theory of Political Economy* as they appeared to a distinguished exponent of neo-classical price theory at the time when that approach to economics had perhaps reached the zenith of its sophistication. Five years later Jevons's book received a similar, but even less sympathetic, interpretation from Professor G. J. Stigler.[17] Treating

---

* If we denote utility by u, and write x for the good or service from which that utility is derived, then final degree of utility $= \dfrac{du}{dx}$, whereas marginal utility $= \dfrac{du}{dx} \delta x$.

Jevons's chapters not in the order in which the author wrote them, but in the order which a modern economist would expect, Stigler concludes that 'Jevons' theories of distribution contribute little to the solution of the problem of distribution, although they contain the germs of some important later developments'.[18]

All such criticism starts from the premiss that Jevons either was attempting or should have attempted to build up a theory of value and distribution (or a theory of prices) along the lines which became familiar and accepted among economists in the first half of the twentieth century. Hence there has emerged a stereotyped view of the *Theory of Political Economy* as a pioneering, but incomplete, exposition of this sort of analysis – but this, like most stereotypes, does not give a true picture of the book or of its author's intentions.

What Jevons's intentions were in writing the book is stated plainly enough in the preface to the first edition: 'In this work I have attempted to treat Economy as a Calculus of Pleasure and Pain, and have sketched out, almost irrespective of previous opinions, the form which the science, as it seems to me, must ultimately take.'[19] It is, in fact, an application of Bentham's utilitarian philosophy to the economic problem. This may seem a paradoxical assertion in view of Jevons's declared opposition to Ricardo, whom Bentham claimed as his 'spiritual grandson', and John Stuart Mill, who had modified but never entirely abandoned the utilitarian creed by which he had been reared. Classical political economy, however, contained very little that was specifically utilitarian. As Professor T. W. Hutchison has said 'Bentham's economic ideas, both as regards theory and policy, run on fundamentally different lines from those of Ricardo' – and on the specific question of value Hutchison argues that 'if Bentham had ever got down to formulating precisely a general theory of value his approach would have differed fundamentally from the classical analysis of Smith and Ricardo. He would have continued in the tradition of Galiani, Pufendorf and the Schoolmen.'[20]

This task which Bentham himself never undertook was the one which Jevons set himself. When this point is borne in mind, the layout of the *Theory of Political Economy* can be seen as clear and logical. Having discussed method in his Introduction, Jevons goes on to set out the basic Theory of Pleasure and Pain. Then comes the Theory of Utility, which explains how pleasure is derived from the consumption of commodities. This brings us to the centre-piece of the work, the Theory of Exchange, with its demonstration of how utility is increased by exchange, and how the parties to exchange can maximize utility. The Theory of Labour is then to be seen as the correlative of the Theory of Utility; 'Labour is the painful exertion which we undergo to ward off pains of greater amount, or to procure pleasures which leave a balance in our favour.'[21] What this chapter affords is not a theory of wages but a theory of cost of production in terms of disutility.

So far the structure is perfectly symmetrical, and perfectly Benthamite. But there remain two further chapters – Theory of Rent, and Theory of Capital – before Jevons winds up with his 'Concluding Remarks'. Where do these fit in? It is tempting to take them, as many commentators have done, along with the Theory of Labour as constituting a typical tripartite theory of distribution or factor pricing. Viewed in this way they appear, as we have seen, irritatingly untidy to those who, with the benefit of hindsight, know how easily and elegantly the marginal productivity theory can be generalized instead of being developed only for the case of capital, as Jevons appears to do.

There is, however, an alternative explanation which fits the circumstances of the case very much better. Chapters I to V develop the theory of economy as a calculus of pleasures and pains – which can only be felt by human beings. Yet in the production of commodities to satisfy wants, man must have the help of non-human agents, and so a discussion of the role of land and capital is essential.

The careful reader will note that there is a certain asymmetry in the treatment here – Jevons does not give a Theory of Land and a Theory of Capital, or a Theory of Rent and a Theory of Interest, but a Theory of Rent followed by a Theory of Capital. The Theory of Rent is in fact an essential corollary of the Theory of Labour designed to explain how, when labour and land are combined, a surplus over and above the 'necessary recompense' for the pain of labour can emerge. On the other hand, the Theory of Capital is formally separate from the rest of the work, for Jevons argues that 'there is no close or necessary connexion between the employment of capital and the processes of exchange' – since capital might benefit, for example, an isolated man. Exchange and capital are both seen as means of increasing the sum of utility – with the result that 'Economics, then, is not solely the science of Exchange or value: it is also the science of Capitalization'.[22]

IV

The reader has now been offered an interpretation of the problem with which the *Theory of Political Economy* is concerned and the manner in which Jevons tackled it. Such is the freshness and lucidity of his style that for the rest he may well be left to speak for himself. The reader who is acquainted with modern economics but not with the work of Jevons may nevertheless find interest in a more detailed commentary on some parts of the analysis – which may serve to throw light on the development of economic theory towards its present shape.

In recent times economists have debated the question of the measurability of utility at some length, and it is therefore interesting to see how Jevons treats this point. He nowhere attempts to define a unit of utility and the diagrams which he uses to illustrate the law of the variation of utility do not have any units marked on the vertical axis. In one passage in the Introduction he treats the question in a way which is reminiscent of Marshall's later appeals to 'the measuring rod of money': 'A unit of pleasure or of pain is difficult even to conceive; but it is the amount of these feelings which is continually prompting us to buying and selling . . . and it is from the quantitative effects of the feelings that we must estimate their comparative amounts'.[23] When he goes on to say 'The will is our pendulum, and its oscillations are minutely registered in the price lists of the markets' we may almost be tempted to hail him as an anticipator of revealed preference doctrines.

In other passages, however, Jevons does not hesitate to refer to 'quantity of utility' and his whole analysis involves treating this (and its correlative, *disutility*) *as if* it could be measured. There have been distinguished economists of recent times, notably D. H. Robertson, prepared to contend for the essential sanity of this approach[24]; but whether we accept or reject Jevons's views on the measurement of feelings we must give him credit for his pioneering attempts to deal specifically with the dimensions of economic quantities, and particularly to point out the pervasive character of the time dimension.

While Jevons might be accused of equivocating on the question of utility measurement, he is certainly quite unequivocal on the question of personal comparisons – 'the reader will find . . . that there is never in any single instance, an attempt made to compare the amount of feeling in one mind with that in another. I see no means by which such comparison can be accomplished'.[25] It may be that this, by excluding social welfare considerations, prevented Jevons from building bridges between his pure theory and his work in applied economics – but in any case questions of economic policy are entirely excluded from the *Theory of Political Economy*.

On passing from the Theory of Utility to the Theory of Exchange the modern student of economics will find himself confronted with a curious blend of the familiar and the strange. For value Jevons substitutes 'the wholly unequivocal expression Ratio of Exchange' and conducts the whole discussion in these terms – which gives those accustomed to thinking in terms of price a problem of translation, though no more. Later authors having followed the convenient example of Walras in adopting one commodity as a common denominator, or *numéraire*, in terms of which all the ratios can be expressed, Jevons's technique now appears clumsy and unfamiliar but it is nevertheless perfectly correct.

The present-day reader will find himself more at home with the ensuing definition of a market, the development of the notion of a perfect market, and the statement of what Jevons calls the 'law of indifference' that 'in the same open market at any one moment, there cannot be two prices for the same kind of article'. Nevertheless Jevons's treatment of these matters cannot be regarded as satisfactory. Although his references to a perfect market seem to imply the existence of a large number of buyers and sellers (as well as complete information) he does not appear to realize that this is a necessary condition for the establishment of the single determinate price. Instead he uses the concept of a trading body to comprise both individuals and groups of buyers and sellers. Now exchange between two individuals can be conducted within a wide range of ratios of exchange, rather that at one determinate one, and exchange between trading bodies (e.g., two governments or corporations) would have the same characteristic, as later writers, notably Edgeworth, demonstrated. Jevons has been accused of failing to recognize this, and the charge cannot really be dismissed; but in fairness to him it can be said that his intention when introducing the trading body concept seems to have been not so much to reduce the complex case of large groups to the simple one of two individuals as to invest this simple case with the sophisticated characteristics of the large group – notably continuity of the variables. Even so, it is hard to be satisfied with such a statement as 'the principles of exchange are the same in nature, however wide or narrow may be the market considered'.[26]

The equations of exchange which Jevons then proceeds to build up are probably the best-known part of his work. In effect they state one fundamental condition for equilibrium in exchange – that for each party, final degrees of utility (marginal utilities) must be proportionate to prices.

As Professor Blaug has pointed out, the Jevonian equation

$$\frac{\varphi_1 (a - x)}{\psi_1 y} = \frac{y}{x} = \frac{\varphi_2 x}{\psi_2 (b - y)}$$

can be immediately translated into modern terms by introducing a *numéraire* whose price = 1, thus:

$$\frac{MUx}{MUy} = \frac{px}{py} = \frac{y}{x}. \quad [27]$$

In fact Jevons does himself translate the argument into price terms at a later stage, and writes the equation

$$\frac{y}{x} = \frac{p_1}{p_2}$$

where p_1 is the unit price of x and p_2 the unit price of y.[28]

From this first simple case, in which a ratio of exchange of 1 for 1 is assumed, Jevons proceeds to develop a number of the propositions which have since become accepted as fundamental in the theory of consumer behaviour. He generalizes his analysis to deal with the case of a consumer spending his income on a range of commodities available at different prices, and points out that 'the theory thus represents the fact that a person distributes his income in such a way as to equalize the utility of the final increments of all commodities consumed'.[29]

This leads on to the question of 'the utility of money, or of that supply of commodity which forms a person's income' and here Jevons shows that what Marshall was later to call 'the marginal utility of money' is lower for a rich than for a poor family. In view of all that has subsequently been written about the income effects of price changes it is noteworthy that when Jevons later sketches out his ideas for the empirical determination of utility he makes the assumption 'that the general utility of a person's income is not affected by the changes of price of the commodity: so that ... we may treat ... the utility of money as a constant'.

At this point Jevons goes as far as he ever does in the direction of formulating general welfare propositions when he argues that 'so far as is consistent with the inequality of wealth in every community, all commodities are distributed by exchange so as to produce the maximum benefit'. In view of his insistence, as noticed above, on the impossibility of inter-personal comparisons of satisfaction it is rather disconcerting to find that in the ensuing section on 'The Gain by Exchange' Jevons applies utility analysis to the gains from international trade, referring blithely to such concepts as wool's 'total utility to Australia' without considering any of the problems involved in summing together the utilities derived from wool by individual Australians. His criticism of Mill's use of the commodity terms of trade as a measure of the gain from trade, on the ground that these relate to the final degree of utility whereas the benefit from exchange must be considered in terms of total utility, is nevertheless well founded. The different concepts of the terms of trade introduced by Professor Jacob Viner and now well-known to economists, were developed in an attempt to meet this criticism.*

It has been a frequent criticism of the *Theory of Political Economy* that it contains an inadequate treatment of supply and costs, and if attention is confined to the section on 'The Origin of Value' at the end of Chapter IV this criticism seems to be justified. Here, despite his assertion that 'labour once spent has no influence on the future value of any article', Jevons admits that 'it is in a large proportion of cases the determining circumstance' because 'labour affects supply, and supply affects the degree of utility, which governs value'.[30] Marshall justly criticized this chain of reasoning on the ground that 'it does not represent supply price, demand price and amount produced as mutually determining one another (subject to certain other conditions) but as determined one by another in a series'[31]; but this is not all that Jevons has to say on the subject. In Chapter V there is much that is relevant and interesting, but which seems largely to have escaped the attention of commentators.

The best-known part of this chapter is the first few pages in which the theory of disutility of labour is developed, and the diagram showing 'pleasure gained' balanced against labour endured has often been reproduced, but the ensuing section headed 'Balance between Need and Labour' is perhaps of greater interest now, for it will be found to foreshadow much of what has been said in modern discussions of the choice between income and leisure.

It is surprising that the second half of this chapter has been so much less noticed for in it Jevons brings together his theories of labour and exchange, pointing out that they 'lead directly to the well-known law . . . that value is proportional to the cost of production'. It is unnecessary to summarize the argument of this and the ensuing section, in which Jevons translates his equations into the more familiar terms of cost and price per unit, for he sets

---

*Viner, *Studies in the Theory of International Trade*, New York and London, 1937, pp. 557–64. Viner points out that Jevons's suggestion that Mill's argument that the gain increased with the cheapening of imports relative to exports was less likely to be true than its converse itself involves a disregard of the total utility aspects of the problem.

it out with lucid economy – nevertheless some comments may usefully be made.

First of all it must be emphasized that here Jevons is concentrating on production by labour, and while he does not explicitly face the question of whether there can be production by labour alone he certainly gives minimal attention to the role of cooperating factors. This accounts for the absence of anything like a theory of the firm. Jevons is in fact dealing with the case of what Karl Marx called 'simple commodity production' in which the problems of organization and entrepreneurship do not arise.* Secondly, it should be noted that Jevons almost implicitly assumes an increasing cost function – 'But as the increment of labour considered is always the final one, our equation also expresses the truth, that articles will exchange in quantities inversely as the costs of production of the most costly portions, i.e. the last portions added.'[32] This produces symmetry with the diminishing utility function of the theory of exchange, but it is not possible to say whether Jevons had this in mind, or was merely making the further assumption that his simple production process was an agricultural process, involving only fixed land and variable labour inputs. This interpretation is consistent with the statement which immediately follows the passage quoted above: 'This result will prove of great importance in the theory of rent.' However this may be, Jevons certainly does not examine the possibilities of constant or increasing returns.

In the 'various cases of the theory' which he examines, Jevons seems mainly concerned to find 'new proofs that value depends not upon labour but upon the degree of utility'. The most interesting and important case considered is that of joint production, but Jevons is unable to show how a separate supply price can be assigned to each product in this case – for he takes as normal the situation which Marshall regarded as exceptional and considers the two goods as being always produced in fixed proportions.[33]

Clearly at this point in the analysis the question of distribution of a joint product has not really arisen; it deserves to be

* Marx, *Capital*, vol. I, part I, ch. III. I owe this approach to discussions with the late Professor H. D. Dickinson and Professor W. Jaffé, who pointed out to me that the work of Walras is similarly oriented.

emphasized that Chapter V contains what the title says, a theory of labour and not a theory of wages. The question of distribution does arise in Chapter VI, which at first glance seems to contain little more than an orthodox restatement of the Ricardian theory of rent; but it has often been pointed out that the Ricardian theory was a form of marginal analysis, and Jevons did not fail to see its implications. He considers the application of increments of labour to different grades of land first, and shows how it will be applied so as to equate the 'final ratios of produce to labour'; then follows his treatment of the 'intensive case' of application of increments of labour to a fixed quantity of land. The diagram on page [223] clearly shows labour's share of the product as determined by its marginal productivity, with rent as the residual.* Thus we are taken to the very brink of the idea that in a two-factor case the reward to both factors is determined by marginal productivity; certainly the common assertion that Jevons had only a produce-less-deductions theory of wages must result from reading his section on the relation of wages and profit in Chapter VIII (pp. [255–8]) without regard to these earlier passages.

In this connexion the section in his preface to the second edition (pp. 69–71), where Jevons treats of the relation between wages and rent, is noteworthy. Arguing that wages, like rent, 'are clearly the effect not the cause of the value of the produce' he comments that 'the parallelism between the theories of rent and wages is seen to be perfect in theory. Precisely the same view may be applied, *mutatis mutandis*, to the rent yielded by fixed capital, and to the interest of free capital.'

Professor Stigler has argued that in these pages 'Jevons arrives at a substantive statement of the alternative cost doctrine'[34] and it is indeed clearly enough set out here in relation to the pricing of products and services. Yet it would be impossible to regard Jevons as accepting 'foregone alternatives' as explaining the ultimate nature of costs. It is clear from many passages in his theory of labour, such as his acceptance of Adam Smith's idea that 'the real price of everything . . . is the toil and trouble of

* Jevons himself speaks of the 'final rate of production'; his son, editing the 4th edition in 1911, commented that this is 'now generally known as marginal productiveness or productivity': see p. 269, below.

acquiring it', that costs to him are in the last analysis painful efforts and sacrifices, real costs in the old classical sense.

The relationship of the chapter on the theory of capital to the rest of the book has already been explained above, but it is perhaps worth emphasizing again that Jevons's main purpose is to explain the functions of capital in 'increasing the sum of utility' and only secondarily to explain the phenomenon of interest. The keynote of the chapter is struck in the heading of its second section: 'Capital is concerned with Time'. When he characterizes the function of capital as being 'to put an interval between the beginning and the end of an enterprise' Jevons anticipates the work of Austrian writers, notably Eugen von Böhm-Bawerk,[35] who stressed the 'superior productivity of roundabout methods of production'. Nevertheless the germ of this idea was to be found in the work of Ricardo, and Jevons does not fail to recognize this.

In one respect at least Jevons seems to go further in the Ricardian direction than Ricardo himself in defining capital as 'the aggregate of those commodities which are required for sustaining labourers' and refusing to draw any sharp distinction between fixed and circulating capital. This amounts to making all capital into a wages fund, which may seem surprising in view of Jevons's insistence on the connexion between wages and product rather than wages and capital. There is, however, nothing wrong with the concept of a wages fund as such, provided it is not conceived as fixed and unrelated to the produce of labour. Jevons himself sees this and sets it out correctly in his 'Concluding Remarks' where he says that 'the wage-fund theory acts in a wholly temporary manner'.[36]

One of the main causes which led classical economists into the fallacy of regarding the wages-fund as fixed was the tendency to take the period of production as fixed, usually at one year, the natural period of agriculture. In this respect Jevons makes an important advance for he specifically treats the period as variable. His use of the concept of dimensions in economics enables him to show that 'amount of investment of capital' is 'a quantity of two dimensions, namely, the quantity of capital, and the length of time during which it remains invested'.[37] Jevons argues that

27

every lengthening of the period of production involves an increased use of capital, and his whole presentation of the subject appears to involve acceptance of the converse – that increased use of capital necessarily results in a lengthening of the time period of production, which is not necessarily the case. All his 'illustrations of the investment of capital' are of this time-consuming character, but clearly this is not the only form which investment might take.

Similarly when Jevons comes to make the necessary and important distinction between 'free and invested capital' he assumes that it is only in the support of labour over time that free capital can be invested, which is certainly not a necessary or realistic assumption.[38] In these respects Jevons's theory of capital is closer to the classical tradition of Ricardo and Mill than most of his other analyses.

The concept of free capital naturally leads on to that of a uniform rate of interest thereon, and the theory by which Jevons explains the determination of this rate is one of his best-known contributions to economic analysis. It has become customary to classify theories of interest as real or monetary and on this basis Jevons's theory must be regarded as real in an unusually strong sense. It is in fact more a theory of the marginal productivity of capital than a fully rounded account of interest determination. Marshall characterized it as a 'bold and subtle' attempt to give 'an account of interest independent of any theory of wages or value' and summed up its essence in an example: 'Suppose that A and B employ the same capital in producing hats by different processes. If A's process occupies a week longer than B's, the number of hats he obtains in excess of the number obtained by B must be the interest for a week on the latter number.'[39]

Marshall objected that Jevons's reasoning served only to express the rate of interest rather than to determine it, and that he had neglected to recognize the existence and mutual interaction of many other factors in the problem. To this the author's son, H. S. Jevons, writing in 1911, admitted that

> in writing of Interest, my father has followed the unfortunate practice of the Ricardian school by abstracting for treatment certain ideas, and assuming that his readers are familiar with their relations, and take his

point of view. . . . I think a study of his examples, especially in the sections on the *Tendency of Profits to a Minimum* and on the *Advantage of Capital to Industry* (pp. 245–9), makes it clear that he well understood that his formula for 'rate of interest' may also be taken as an expression for the *final rate of yield*, or *marginal productivity*, of capital, a quantity which, in practice, is adjusted to the rate of interest at which capital can be obtained.[40]

Jevons had indeed grasped the essential concept of marginal productivity of capital, but presented it only for a special case in which the time element could be isolated clearly. He makes only incidental, if suggestive, references to the sources of supply of free capital and, as his son said, 'probably he tacitly assumed that supply of capital remained constant'. In fact in the theory of capital we have an outstanding example of the way in which Jevons's major ideas were, as Keynes said, 'chiselled in stone where Marshall knitted in wool'.[41] In detail the theory may be open to criticism but the essentials are firmly blocked out and they are, as Marshall conceded, bold and subtle.

V

The closing pages of the *Theory of Political Economy* leave the reader in no doubt that Jevons saw himself as something of a crusader against established doctrines in the subject. His paragraphs on 'The Noxious Influence of Authority' are more highly charged than was then – or, for that matter, is now – customary in a scientific monograph. When these are read in conjunction with the comments in the preface to the first edition, there is no room for doubt that when Jevons spoke of the hurtful tendency to allow opinions to crystallize into creeds, manifesting itself especially 'when some eminent author, with the power of clear and comprehensive exposition, becomes recognized as an authority upon the subject' he had John Stuart Mill in mind.

Much, probably too much, has been made of what Keynes called Jevons's 'violent aversion' to Mill, 'pursued almost to the point of morbidity'.[42] Jevons had no personal aversion to Mill, with whom his only contact was one polite exchange of letters in 1866, but he was a frequent and outspoken critic both of Mill's logic and of his political economy. He certainly saw the great authority of Mill as presenting a barrier to new ideas, and on the whole this view was quite justified. Even Marshall, ever respectful towards his predecessors, admitted that Mill's assertion about the laws of value was 'unfortunate'.[43]

To Marshall, Jevons seemed 'perversely to twist his own doctrines so as to make them more inconsistent with Mill's and Ricardo's than they really were'.[44] This again perhaps overstates the case, but there is no doubt that Jevons did present his work in such a way as to stress the break which he was trying to make with classical doctrine, and particularly the doctrines of Ricardo and Mill. In this respect we can see quite a close resemblance between Jevons and Keynes, who in his *General Theory of Employment* of 1936 deliberately stressed the differences between that theory and the classical theory as he conceived it.

Anyone who sets out to challenge an orthodoxy is almost bound to overstate the distinction between his own work and what has gone before; inevitably, also, those who look at it in the perspective of history are likely to perceive many links between the two. So now Jevons's *Theory* can be regarded as manifesting an evolutionary rather than a revolutionary change in the economic thought of the nineteenth century. In one respect it could be argued that J. S. Mill was the revolutionary and Jevons the traditionalist for, as is well known, Mill rebelled against the Benthamite philosophy in which his father has so relentlessly schooled him[45] whereas Jevons founded his economic analysis upon it in a most thorough-going fashion. Apart from this, other elements of continuity not merely with classical political economy, but even with Mill and Ricardo, can be found in the writings of Jevons. The outstanding example is the theory of rent, which Jevons characterizes as 'a theory of a distinctly mathematical character which seems to give a clue to the correct mode of treating the whole science'. In the theory of capital, as has already been pointed out above, there is much which derives from Ricardo, and the clear distinction of statics and dynamics which is in one sense the basis of Jevons's theory is to be found in Mill's *Principles*.[46]

All this can be said without detracting from the substantial originality of Jevons's book, or denying that it helped to usher in a new era in economic thought – just as one can recognize the links between Keynes and his predecessors without denying the importance of the *General Theory* as a landmark in economics.

If Jevons was reluctant to acknowledge any filiation between his work and that of Ricardo and Mill, he was more than willing to pay homage to those whom he considered 'had a far better comprehension of the true doctrines ... but ... were driven out of the field by the unity and influence of the Ricardo–Mill school', notably T. R. Malthus and Nassau Senior.[47] He was also careful to acknowledge all those who had preceded him in using the mathematical method in economic studies, and between the appearance of the first and second editions of the *Theory* he undertook an extensive search for what he called mathematico-economic writings.[48]

It is difficult to see that Jevons owed much to Malthus, whose theory of population he accepted but whose other doctrines he does not examine at all in the *Theory*. He clearly owed somewhat more to Senior, whose law of variety he quotes approvingly, and to some of the lesser-known writers he mentions, particularly Jennings and Banfield.[49] Nevertheless it is beyond dispute that the essential features of his theories were evolved by Jevons quite independently. He was unaware of the fact that similar theories were being developed at this same period by Carl Menger, Léon Walras and Alfred Marshall and the great majority of mathematico-economic writings pre-dating his own came to his notice only after the first edition of the *Theory* had been published. Of these the work of Gossen contained the most complete anticipation of Jevons's ideas but the 'disagreeable incident' of its discovery by his successor in the chair of political economy at Owens College, Robert Adamson, did not occur until the summer of 1878.

In a very natural mood of depression at this time Jevons confided to his brother Tom: 'There are, in fact, a whole series of books, hitherto quite unknown, even on the Continent, in which the principal ideas of my theory have been foreshadowed. I am, therefore, in the unfortunate position that the greater number of people think the theory nonsense, and do not understand it, and the rest discover that it is not new'.[50] Jevons had indeed more reason to be discouraged by the slowness with which his theories gained acceptance than by the fact that others working independently had reached similar results.

There was certainly little in the early reception of the *Theory of Political Economy* which gave any indication of its future status and influence. J. E. Cairnes, commonly regarded as the last of the classical economists, reviewed the book in a way which revealed his own complete lack of sympathy with Jevons's approach[51] and he made this manifest again in his own treatise, *Some Leading Principles of Political Economy newly expounded*, published in 1874. The only other British economist to write a signed review of the first edition of Jevons's book was Marshall, whose piece on it in the *Academy* was his first published work. As might have been expected from a young man who was to become the leader of his profession, Marshall displayed a clear grasp of the ideas in the book, but was strongly critical of many of them and disposed to minimize their originality. The few other anonymous reviews which appeared mostly displayed that lack of understanding of which Jevons complained, and none were enthusiastic.

Indeed for some time Jevons seemed to be cast in the proverbial role of the prophet without honour in his own country. His theory was at first much better received on the Continent than in England. It was enthusiastically taken up by a young Dutch economist, Johann d'Aulnis de Bourouill (afterwards professor of economics at Utrecht), who incorporated it into a doctoral thesis submitted at Leiden in 1874. In that same year Jevons received from Walras a copy of his first memoir, *Principe d'une théorie mathématique de l'échange*, and this led to an exchange of letters which Walras persuaded the well-known French economist Joseph Garnier to publish in the *Journal des Économistes*.[52] Walras was also able to give Jevons a considerable list of names of Italian authorities who would receive his theory favourably, but Jevons in return could give Walras only a few names of people in Britain who might be interested.

Of these only Leonard Courtney and W. B. Hodgson of Edinburgh were the holders of chairs of political economy. The others were Fleeming Jenkin and G. H. Darwin, son of the famous naturalist and himself a mathematician. Jevons himself endeavoured to call attention in England to the work of Walras by means of the paper on 'The Mathematical Theory of Political Economy' which he gave to the Manchester Statistical Society. Although this provoked a sneering review in the *Examiner*, upholding the orthodoxy of Mill and Cairnes,[53] it also brought a much more sympathetic response from Marshall, and Jevons was able to tell Walras: '... I think that a considerable change of opinion is taking place in England. Various correspondents express their acquiescence, and some of the professors are beginning to bring the theory before their students.'[54] The preface to the second edition of the *Theory*, dated May 1879, still plainly seems to be the work of a man who feels himself contending for a doctrine which is far from having won general acceptance, but in 1881 Jevons was prepared to say that 'the mathematical view of economics is making much progress in England, and is fully recognized by those competent to judge'.[55] He might have added that it had also received some recognition in the United States, notably from Simon Newcomb and Henry Carter Adams.[56]

Even at this time Jevons had not attracted around him any considerable group of pupils or disciples. His closest friend among the English economists of his day was undoubtedly H. S. Foxwell, who succeeded him in the chair at University College, London; but Foxwell's interests in economics did not lie in the area covered by the *Theory of Political Economy* and he published nothing which built on Jevons's ideas. These ideas may have had more influence on F. Y. Edgeworth, Drummond Professor of Political Economy at Oxford from 1891 to 1922 and first editor of the *Economic Journal*, who in his earlier years lived near Jevons in Hampstead. Edgeworth acknowledged the encouragement and 'peculiar intellectual sympathy' which Jevons gave him, and certainly Edgeworth's approach to economics and the social sciences generally was very much after Jevons's own heart. His first two books were concerned with the application of mathematical methods to utilitarianism,[57] but in later life he became more sceptical of the value of the

Benthamite philosophy and in matters of economic theory came more under the influence of Marshall.

Of Marshall, Foxwell could say, even in 1888, that 'half the economic chairs in the United Kingdom are occupied by his pupils, and the share taken by them in general economic instruction in England is even larger than this'.[58] He was indeed the dominant influence in English academic economics from that time until his death in 1924, and consequently his relations with Jevons are of special interest. We have already seen that his review of the *Theory of Political Economy* was reserved and critical, where as a representative of the younger generation of economists and an accomplished mathematician he might have been expected to be understanding and enthusiastic. It is true that in later years he did try to make amends for this and ultimately 'reverenced him [Jevons] as among the very greatest of economists'.[59] Jevons did examine for Marshall at Cambridge in 1874–5 and professed himself much impressed by the answers given by Marshall's pupils (including Mary Paley, afterwards Mrs Marshall, and J. N. Keynes). Apart from this, relations between the two men were confined to brief and infrequent letters and, as J. M. Keynes said many years later, 'Marshall was extraordinarily reluctant to admit that he owed anything to Jevons'.[60]

There seem to have been a number of reasons for this. The one which Marshall himself stressed was the fact that Jevons attacked Ricardo and Mill whom Marshall particularly revered, and this certainly set a gulf between them. Another was that Marshall had been lecturing on economic theory at Cambridge since 1868 and independently developing ideas and techniques similar to those of Jevons. He therefore felt piqued when Jevons anticipated him by publishing so rapidly in 1871 – though not with very good reason, since Jevons's original paper on the subject dated from 1862. It is hard to escape the feeling that there may have been less worthy elements in Marshall's attitude as well, such as the contempt of the second wrangler for the self-taught mathematician. Whatever the reason, Marshall cannot be regarded as in any sense a disciple of Jevons.

If Jevons had a true disciple it was P. H. Wicksteed (1844–

1927), a many-sided Unitarian cleric who contrived also to be a Dante scholar and an outstanding economist. Wicksteed was acquainted with Jevons and helped to revise the third edition of the *Theory* for Mrs Jevons and the fourth for H. S. Jevons. Perhaps no one ever knew and understood the book better[61] and the articles which he wrote for Palgrave's *Dictionary of Political Economy* on 'Dimensions of Economic Quantities' and 'Final Degree of Utility' show how thoroughly he had absorbed Jevonian ideas. Himself an original thinker of a very high order, Wicksteed carried marginal analysis far beyond the point at which Jevons had left it, and he also drew much from other sources, notably the Austrian economists of the time. Nevertheless Wicksteed undoubtedly qualified for, and would happily have accepted, the title of a thorough-going follower of Jevons.

This discussion of the relation of Jevons to his predecessors and successors naturally prompts the question – to what school of economists, if any, did Jevons belong? The standard answer of the textbooks is that he was one of the founders, if not the founder, of the neo-classical school; but such an answer must be interpreted with care if it is not to prove misleading. The term 'neo-classical school' can be given various connotations; it is perhaps most often used to describe the whole set of English economists who contributed to the development of orthodox theory between about 1870 and 1914, although it is sometimes extended to cover the Austrian and Lausanne economists of this same period as well. That Jevons was a member of this set is unquestionable, but it should be equally clear that he was not the leader or acknowledged master of the school. That role belonged to Marshall, if it belonged to anyone – for in fact the neo-classical school in the sense given here was not a unified whole.[62] The Cambridge school under Marshall's leadership was certainly the most unified group within it, but Wicksteed's comment that 'the school of economists of which Professor Marshall is the illustrious head may be regarded from the point of view of the thorough-going Jevonian as a school of apologists'[63] shows that its leadership was far from being un-challenged. Wicksteed, 'thorough-going Jevonian' that he was, felt unable to accept Marshall's attempts to play down the distinction between the old classical and the marginalist approach which Wicksteed felt must be applied with greater completeness along the lines suggested by the Austrian economists. But although a distinctive approach can be traced here, continuing to and culminating in Lionel Robbins's *Nature and Significance of Economic Science* in the nineteen-thirties, it would be putting matters too strongly to suggest that the English neo-classical school divided into a 'Cambridge school' headed by Marshall and a 'London school' stemming from Jevons.

On the other hand neo-classical economics can be looked at as a particular line of approach to the subject rather than a particular group of personalities. The characteristics of this line of approach have already been outlined above. Comparing this outline with the outline of Jevons's *Theory* subsequently given, the resemblance between the two is evidently close but not complete: the mature neo-classical approach included many features not to be found in the *Theory of Political Economy*. Among these are the concept of the entrepreneur who maximizes profits by equating marginal cost with price, incurring these costs by hiring the factors of production and paying each of them in accordance with the value of its marginal product. Here again the appropriate point cannot be put better than in the words of Wicksteed: 'It is clear to the careful reader of Jevons that the universal application of the theory of margins was rather felt by him as a presentiment than carried out and realized in its details'.[64]

It would indeed be quite wrong to think of Jevons as the founder and acknowledged master of the neo-classical school as Adam Smith was of the classical, or of his *Theory of Politica Economy* as a monumental treatise like the *Wealth of Nations* from which all the doctrines of his followers could be seen to stem. Jevons realized that economic studies in his time were in need of 'reform and reconstruction' and foresaw with great clarity and acuteness that this would come through subdivision of the science; in this realization he attempted merely to outline the basic principles as he saw them.

Like Keynes, sixty-five years later, Jevons addressed himself primarily to his fellow-economists, and his influence on their ways of thinking, if immediately slight, was ultimately profound.

Unlike Keynes, on the other hand, his new theory carried with it no implications for policy. It was an exercise in what would today be called positive economics, concerned to analyse and not to prescribe, to bring light rather than to bear fruit.

Yet because he based his theory on the utilitarian philosophy, Jevons has sometimes been accused of advocating a crude hedonism or a gross materialism, and it is intriguing to find that within the last few years one writer has traced the *malaise* of present-day Western man to its source in the *Theory of Political Economy*. In his challenging book *The Decline of Pleasure*, Mr Walter Kerr, the well-known American dramatic critic, has this to say

> Jevons was the man who made the unqualified pronouncement that *'value depends entirely upon utility'*, and though some men still professed shock at so absolute an assertion, and though Jevons is thought to have considered modifying its phrasing, the phrase continued to fly, banner-bright, at the head of his *Theory of Political Economy*. The phrase became, as it were, the last word, the conclusive word in a philosophical debate that had preoccupied one century and was about to occupy, in an almost military sense, the next.
>
> Jevons had won; the utilitarian theory of value, in its strictest and most uncompromising sense, had won. 'Value,' as everyone knows whether he has consulted a dictionary or not, refers to worth, moral or monetary; it signifies whatever men hold to be estimable, important, worth doing or having. What twentieth-century man holds to be important and worth-while is usefulness, the profit that may be extracted from an experience or a possession. This is no crude justification he has made for his own greedy conduct. It is an ethic that has been handed to him, imposed on him, in the guise of 'clarity', 'correctness', 'reason', and 'light' – and as an infallible guide in the pursuit of 'pleasure'. It is the truth in which he believes – not simply an economic truth, calculated to fill his home and his bank account with treasures, but a moral truth, calculated to fill his heart with a high sense of rectitude. When he does not put his every waking hour to useful pursuits, he is, socially, a poor citizen. When he wastes his time on acts that 'rest in the understanding merely', he is, morally, guilty.[65]

If this is what twentieth-century man believes, he has no warrant from Jevons for doing so, as a study of the section on the 'Relation of Economics to Ethics' at the end of the Introduction to the *Theory* should make clear. Here Jevons divides feelings into 'various grades' and assigns 'a proper place to the pleasures and pains with which the economist deals' as the lowest rank of feelings. He was not indifferent to or unaware of higher grades of feeling, but considered that they fell outside the scope of the 'very contracted science' of which his book treats. Jevons in 1871 did not set out to write a tract for his times or ours; neither did he attempt to build the complete structure of modern economics. What he attempted was to clear the ground and lay the foundations for a central part of it, and in this he can be seen to have succeeded.

Notes

1. Allyn A. Young, 'Jevons's *Theory of Political Economy*', *American Economic Review*, vol. V, 1912.
2. J. A. Schumpeter, *History of Economic Analysis*, London, 1954, p. 826.
3. See, for example, Gide & Rist, *History of Economic Doctrines*, 7th ed., 1947, p. 485; Roll, *A History of Economic Thought*, 1951 ed., pp. 368–9; Blaug, *Economic Theory in Retrospect*, 2nd ed., London, 1968, ch. 8.
4. *Wealth of Nations*, Book I, chs. IV & VI. The reader who wishes for a fuller account of Smith's work and its relation to classical analysis generally should refer to William J. Barber, *A History of Economic Thought*, London, 1967, part I.
5. Mill, *Principles of Political Economy*, Book III, ch. I, §1.
6. *T. P. E.*, ch. I, p. 90, below.
7. *T. P. E.*, p. 254, below.
8. Letter to Henrietta Jevons, 28 February 1858, *Letters and Journal of W. Stanley Jevons*, edited by his wife, London, 1886, p. 101.
9. Loc. cit., pp. 151–2. See also J. A. La Nauze, 'The Conception of Jevons's Utility Theory', *Economica*, vol. 20, November 1953, pp. 356–8.
10. Journal of W. S. Jevons, 31 December 1862, *Letters & Journal*, p. 175. The paper was first printed in full in the *Journal of the* [Royal] *Statistical Society*, vol. XXIX, 1866, but attracted little or no attention at this stage either.
11. Cf. his monumental *Principles of Science*, London, 1874. Also W. Mays: 'Jevons's Conception of Scientific Method', *Manchester School*, vol. XXX, September 1962, pp. 223–50.
12. H. S. Jevons, Preface to the 4th edition of the *Theory of Political Economy*, p. lvii.
13. For a full account of the circumstances see R. D. C. Black, 'W. S. Jevons and the Economists of his Time', *Manchester School*, vol. XXX September 1962, pp. 206–7.

14. *T. P. E.*, p. 50, below.
15. *The Principles of Economics, a Fragment of a Treatise on the Industrial Mechanism of Society*, London, 1905.
16. Robbins, 'The Place of Jevons in the History of Economic Thought', *The Manchester School*, vol. VII, 1936, pp. 1–17.
17. In his *Production and Distribution Theories*, New York, 1941.
18. Stigler, op. cit., p. 35.
19. *T. P. E.*, preface to first ed., p. 44, below.
20. T. W. Hutchison, 'Bentham as an Economist', *Economic Journal*, vol. LXVI, June 1956, pp. 306, 291.
21. *T. P. E.*, ch. V, p. 188, below.
22. *T. P. E.*, ch. VII, p. 225, below.
23. *T. P. E.*, Introduction, p. 83, below. Cf. Marshall, *Principles of Economics*, Book I, ch. II, 1.
24. See, for example, D. H. Robertson, *Utility and All That*, London, 1952. For a valuable survey of the problems involved in this question, see T. Majumdar, *The Measurement of Utility*, London, 1958.
25. *T. P. E.*, Introduction, p. 85, below.
26. *T.P.E.*, ch. IV, p. 135, below.
27. Blaug, *Economic Theory in Retrospect*, 2nd ed., London, 1968, p. 310. For explanation of symbols see text of *T. P. E.*, p. 142, below.
28. *T. P. E.*, ch. V, p. 204, below.
29. ibid., ch. IV, p. 170, below.
30. *T. P. E.*, ch. IV, p.187, below.
31. Marshall, *Principles of Economics*, Appendix I, §3, 9th ed., vol. I, pp. 818–19.
32. *T. P. E.*, ch. V, p. 202, below.
33. *T. P. E.*, pp. 208–12, below. Cf. Marshall, *Principles of Economics*, Book V, ch. VI, §5, 9th ed., p. 390.
34. *Production and Distribution Theories*, pp. 15–16.
35. *Positive Theory of Capital*, 1889.
36. *T. P. E.*, p. 258, below. On this whole issue, see Taussig, *Wages and Capital*, New York, 1896.
37. *T. P. E.*, p. 229, below.
38. Cf. Fellner, *Emergence and Content of Modern Economic Analysis*, New York, 1960, p. 264.
39. *The Academy*, vol. III, no. 45, April 1, 1872, p. 130. (Reprinted in Pigou, *Memorials of Alfred Marshall*, London, 1925, p. 94.)
40. H. S. Jevons, Appendix I to fourth edition, *T. P. E.*, p. 280.
41. Keynes, *Essays in Biography*, 1961 ed., p. 284.
42. Keynes, *Essays in Biography*, 1961 ed., p. 291.
43. Quoted above, page 77, *Memorials of Alfred Marshall*, p. 95. For a fuller account of Mill's influence on economic thought in the period 1848–68, see S. G. Checkland 'Economic Opinion in England as Jevons found it', *Manchester School*, vol. 19, 1951, pp. 143–69.
44. *Memorials of Alfred Marshall*, p. 99.

45. See John M. Robson, *The Improvement of Mankind: the Social and Political Thought of John Stuart Mill*, Toronto, 1968, chs. 1 & 2.
46. J. S. Mill, *Principles of Political Economy*, Book IV, ch. I.
47. *T. P. E.*, preface to the second edition, p. 72, below. See also p. 261 below, and *Letters and Journal*, p. 344.
48. An annotated bibliography of these appeared as Appendix I to the second edition.
49. On this see Ross M. Robertson 'Jevons and his Precursors', *Econometrica*, vol. 19, 1951, pp. 229–49.
50. *Letters and Journal of W. S. Jevons*, p. 387.
51. *Fortnightly Review*, New Series, vol. XI, 1872, pp. 72–7.
52. *Journal des Économistes*, vol. XXXIV, 15 June 1874. See also W. Jaffé, *Correspondence of Léon Walras and Related Papers*, Amsterdam, 1965, vol. I, p. 409.
53. *The Examiner*, 28 November 1874, pp. 1294–5.
54. Jevons to Walras, 14 February 1875, printed in *Letters and Journal*, p. 332.
55. Jevons to Walras, 20 July 1881, printed in *Letters and Journal*, p. 431.
56. Simon Newcomb, professor of mathematics at Johns Hopkins University, reviewed the first edition of *T. P. E.* in the *North American Review*, 1872. H. C. Adams, professor at Cornell and Michigan Universities, presented Jevons's theory of value in his *Outline of Lectures on Political Economy*, 1881.
57. *New and Old Methods of Ethics*, Oxford, 1877, *Mathematical Psychics*, London, 1881.
58. Foxwell, 'The Economic Movement in England', *Quarterly Journal of Economics*, vol. II, p. 92.
59. *Memorials of Alfred Marshall*, p. 99.
60. *Essays in Biography*, p. 287.
61. See, for example, his article 'On Certain Passages in Jevons's *Theory of Political Economy*', *Quarterly Journal of Economics*, vol. III, 1889, pp. 293–314.
62. Cf. A. W. Coats, 'Sociological Aspects of British Economic Thought (ca. 1880–1930)', *Journal of Political Economy*, vol. 75, no. 5, Oct. 1967 pp. 706–29.
63. Wicksteed, 'Jevons's Economic Work' *Economic Journal*, vol. XV, 1905, p. 435.
64. Wicksteed, loc. cit., p. 435.
65. Kerr, *The Decline of Pleasure*, New York, 1962, p. 64.

THE

THEORY OF POLITICAL ECONOMY.

BY

W. STANLEY JEVONS, M.A. (Lond.)

PROFESSOR OF LOGIC AND POLITICAL ECONOMY
IN OWENS COLLEGE, MANCHESTER.

London and New York

MACMILLAN AND CO.

1871.

[All rights reserved]

PREFACE TO THE FIRST EDITION
(1871)

THE contents of the following pages can hardly meet with ready acceptance among those who regard the science of political economy as having already acquired a nearly perfect form. I believe it is generally supposed that Adam Smith laid the foundations of this science; that Malthus, Anderson and Senior added important doctrines; that Ricardo systematized the whole; and, finally, that Mr J. S. Mill filled in the details and completely expounded this branch of knowledge. Mr Mill appears to have had a similar notion, for he distinctly asserts that there was nothing in the laws of value which remained for himself or any future writer to clear up. Doubtless it is difficult to help feeling that opinions adopted and confirmed by such eminent men have much weight of probability in their favour. Yet in the other sciences this weight of authority has not been allowed to restrict the free examination of new opinions and theories, and it has often been ultimately proved that authority was on the wrong side.

There are many portions of economical doctrine which appear to me as scientific in form as they are consonant with facts. I would especially mention the theories of population and of rent, the latter a theory of a distinctly mathematical character, which seems to give a clue to the correct mode of treating the whole science. Had Mr Mill contented himself with asserting the unquestionable truth of the laws of supply and demand, I should have agreed with him. As founded upon facts, those laws cannot be shaken by any theory, but it does not therefore follow that our conception of value is perfect and final. Other generally accepted doctrines have always appeared to me purely delusive, especially the so-called wage fund theory. This theory pretends to give a solution of the main problem of the science – to determine the wages of labour – yet, on close examination, its conclusion is found to be a mere truism, namely that the average rate of wages is found by dividing the whole amount appropriated to the payment of wages by the number of those between whom it is divided. Some other supposed conclusions of the science are of a less harmless character, as, for instance, those regarding the advantage of exchange (see the section on 'The Gain by Exchange', p. 171).

In this work I have attempted to treat economy as a calculus of pleasure and pain, and have sketched out, almost irrespective of previous opinions, the form which the science, as it seems to me, must ultimately take. I have long thought that as it deals throughout with quantities, it must be a mathematical science in matter if not in language. I have endeavoured to arrive at accurate quantitative notions concerning utility, value, labour, capital, etc., and I have often been surprised to find how clearly some of the most difficult notions, especially that most puzzling of notions *value*, admit of mathematical analysis and expression. The theory of economy, thus treated, presents a close analogy to the science of statical mechanics, and the laws of exchange are found to resemble the laws of equilibrium of a lever as determined by the principle of virtual velocities. The nature of wealth and value is explained by the consideration of indefinitely small amounts of pleasure and pain, just as the theory of statics is made to rest upon the equality of indefinitely small amounts of energy. But I believe that dynamical branches of the science of economy may remain to be developed, on the consideration of which I have not at all entered.

Mathematical readers may perhaps think that I have explained some elementary notions, that of the degree of utility for instance, with unnecessary prolixity. But it is to the neglect of economists to obtain clear and accurate notions of quantity and degree of utility that I venture to attribute the present difficulties and imperfections of the science, and I have purposely dwelt upon the point at full length. Other readers will perhaps think that the occasional introduction of mathematical symbols obscures instead of illustrating the subject. But I must request all readers to remember that, as mathematicians and political economists have hitherto been two nearly distinct classes of persons, there is no slight difficulty in preparing a mathematical work on economy with which both classes of readers may not have some grounds of complaint.

It is very likely that I have fallen into errors of more or less importance, which I shall be glad to have pointed out, and I may say that the cardinal difficulty of the whole theory is alluded to in the section of chapter IV on the 'Ratio of Exchange', beginning at p. 91 (that on the 'Law of Indifference', p. 136 of this edition). So able a mathematician as my friend Professor Barker, of Owens College, has had the kindness to examine some of the proof-sheets carefully; but he is not, therefore, to be held responsible for the correctness of any part of the work.

My enumeration of the previous attempts to apply mathematical language to political economy does not pretend to completeness even as regards English writers; and I find that I forgot to mention a remarkable pamphlet, 'On Currency', published anonymously in 1840 (London, Charles Knight and Co.) in which a mathematical analysis of the operations of the money market is attempted. The method of treatment is not unlike that adopted by Dr Whewell, to whose memoirs a reference is made; but finite or occasionally infinitesimal differences are introduced. On the success of this anonymous theory I have not formed an opinion, but the subject is one which must some day be solved by mathematical analysis. Garnier, in his treatise on political economy, mentions several continental mathematicians who have written on the subject of political economy; but I have not been able to discover even the titles of their memoirs.

PREFACE TO THE SECOND EDITION
(1879)

In preparing this second edition certain new sections have been added, the most important of which are those treating of the *dimensions of economic quantities* (pp. 117–21, 131–2, 195–6, 232–4). The subject, of course, is one which lies at the basis of all clear thought about economic science. It cannot be surprising that many debates end in logomachy, when it is still uncertain how many meanings the word *value* has, or what kind of a quantity *utility* itself is. Imagine the mental state of astronomers if they could not agree among themselves whether *Right Ascension* was the name of a heavenly body, or a force or an angular magnitude. Yet this would not be worse than failing to ascertain clearly whether by value we mean a numerical ratio, or a mental state, or a mass of commodity. John Stuart Mill tells us explicitly * that 'The value of a thing means the quantity of some other thing, or of things in general, which it exchanges for.' It might of course be explained that Mill did not intend what he said; but as the statement stands it makes value into a thing, and is just as philosophic as if one were to say, 'Right Ascension means the planet Mars, or planets in general.'

These sections on the dimensions of economic quantities have caused me great perplexity, especially as regards the relation between utility and time (pp. 118–21). The theory of capital and interest also involves some subtleties. I hope that my solutions of the questions raised will be found generally correct; but where they do not settle a question, they may sometimes suggest one which other writers may answer. A correspondent, Captain Charles Christie, R.E., to whom I have shown these sections after they were printed, objects reasonably enough that commodity should not have been represented by M, or Mass, but by some symbol, for instance Q, which would include quantity of space or time or force, in fact almost any kind of quantity. Services

---

* *Principles of Political Economy*, Book III, ch. VI, sec. i 1. This definition occurs at the beginning of a carefully prepared summary of the principles of the theory of value.

often involve time, or force exerted, or space passed over, as well as mass. In this objection, I quite concur, and I must therefore request the reader either to interpret M with a wider meaning than is given to it in p. 118, or else mentally to substitute another symbol.

In treating the dimensions of interest, I point out the curious fact that so profound a mathematician as the late Dean Peacock went quite astray on the subject (pp. 243–5). Other new sections are those in which I introduce the idea of negative and approximately zero value, showing that negative value may be brought under the forms of the equations of exchange without any important modification. Readers of Mr Macleod's[1] works are of course familiar with the idea of negative value, but it was desirable for me to show how important it really is, and how naturally it falls in with the principles of the theory. I may also draw attention to the section (pp. 144–7) in which I illustrate the mathematical character of the equations of exchange by drawing an exact analogy between them and the equations applying to the equilibrium of the lever.

Two or three correspondents, especially Herr Harald Westergaard[2] of Copenhagen, have pointed out that a little manipulation of the symbols, in accordance with the simple rules of the differential calculus, would often give results which I have laboriously argued out. The whole question is one of maxima and minima, the mathematical conditions of which are familiar to mathematicians. But, even if I were capable of presenting the subject in the concise symbolic style satisfactory to the taste of a practised mathematician, I should prefer in an essay of this kind to attain my results by a course of argument which is not only fundamentally true, but is clear and convincing to many readers who, like myself, are not skilful and professional mathematicians. In short, I do not write for mathematicians, nor as a mathematician, but as an economist wishing to convince other economists that their science can only be satisfactorily treated on an explicitly mathematical basis. When mathematicians recognize the subject as one with which they may usefully deal, I shall gladly resign it into their hands. I have expressed a feeling in more than one place that the whole theory might probably have been put in a more general form by treating labour as a negative utility, and thus bringing it under the ordinary equations of exchange. But the fact is there is endless occupation for an economist in developing and improving his science, and I have found it requisite to reissue this essay, as the bibliopoles say, 'with all faults'. I have, however, carefully revised every page of the book, and have reason to hope that little or no real error remains in the doctrines stated. The faults are in the form rather than the matter.

Among minor alterations, I may mention the substitution for the name political economy of the single convenient term *economics*. I cannot help thinking that it would be well to discard, as quickly as possible, the old troublesome double-worded name of our science. Several authors have tried to introduce totally new names, such as plutology, chrematistics, catallactics, etc. But why do we need anything better than economics? This term, besides being more familiar and closely related to the old term, is perfectly analogous in form to *mathematics, ethics, æsthetics*, and the names of various other branches of knowledge, and it has moreover the authority of usage from the time of Aristotle. Mr MacLeod is, so far as I know, the re-introducer of the name in recent years, but it appears to have been adopted also by Mr Alfred Marshall at Cambridge. It is thus to be hoped that *economics* will become the recognized name of a science, which nearly a century ago was known to the French economists as *la science économique*. Though employing the new name in the text, it was obviously undesirable to alter the title-page of the book.

When publishing a new edition of this work, eight years after its first appearance, it seems natural that I should make some remarks upon the changes of opinion about economic science which have taken place in the interval. A remarkable discussion has been lately going on in the reviews and journals concerning the logical method of the science, touching even the question whether there exists any such science at all. Attention was drawn to the matter by Mr T. E. Cliffe Leslie's remarkable article * 'On

* *Hermathena*, no. iv, 1876, pp. 1–32. Republished in Mr Leslie's collected *Essays in Political and Moral Philosophy*, Dublin, 1879, pp. 216–42.

the Philosophical Method of Political Economy', in which he endeavours to dissipate altogether the deductive science of Ricardo. Mr W. T. Thornton's writings have a somewhat similar tendency.[3] The question has been further stirred up by the admirable criticism to which it was subjected in the masterly address of Professor J. K. Ingram at the last meeting of the British Association.[4] This address has been reprinted in several publications * in England, and has been translated into the chief languages of Western Europe. It is evident, then, that a spirit of very active criticism is spreading, which can hardly fail to overcome in the end the prestige of the false old doctrines. But what is to be put in place of them? At the best it must be allowed that the fall of the old orthodox creed will leave a chaos of diverse opinions. Many would be glad if the supposed science collapsed altogether, and became a matter of history, like astrology, alchemy and the occult sciences generally. Mr Cliffe Leslie would not go quite so far as this, but would reconstruct the science in a purely inductive or empirical manner. Either it would then be a congeries of miscellaneous disconnected facts, or else it must fall in as one branch of Mr Spencer's sociology. In any case, I hold that *there must arise a science of the development of economic forms and relations.*

But as regards the fate of the deductive method, I disagree altogether with my friend Mr Leslie; he is in favour of simple deletion; I am for thorough reform and reconstruction. As I have previously explained† the present chaotic state of economics arises from the confusing together of several branches of knowledge. Subdivision is the remedy.

We must distinguish the empirical element from the abstract theory, from the applied theory and from the more detailed art of finance and administration. Thus will arise various sciences, such as commercial statistics, the mathematical theory of

* *Journal of the London Statistical Society*, December 1878, vol. XLI, pp. 602–29. *Journal of the Statistical and Social Inquiry Society of Ireland*, August 1878, vol. VII, Appendix. Also as a separate publication, Longmans, London, 1878.

† 'The Future of Political Economy', *Fortnightly Review*, November 1876, vol. VIII, N. S., pp. 617–31. Translated in the *Journal des Économistes*, March 1877, 3me série, vol. XLV, p. 325.

economics, systematic and descriptive economics, economic
sociology and fiscal science. There may even be a kind of cross
subdivision of the sciences; that is to say, there will be division
into branches as regards the subject, and division according to the
manner of treating the branch of the subject. The manner may
be theoretical, empirical, historical or practical; the subject may
be capital and labour, currency, banking, taxation, land tenure,
etc. – not to speak of the more fundamental division of the
science as it treats of consumption, production, exchange and
distribution of wealth. In fact, the whole subject is so extensive,
intricate and diverse, that it is absurd to suppose it can be treated
in any single book or in any single manner. It is no more one
science than statics, dynamics, the theory of heat, optics, magneto-
electricity, telegraphy, navigation and photographic chemistry
are one science.

But as all the physical sciences have their basis more or less
obviously in the general principles of mechanics, so all branches
and divisions of economic science must be pervaded by certain
general principles. It is to the investigation of such principles –
to the tracing out of the mechanics of self-interest and utility,
that this essay has been devoted. The establishment of such a
theory is a necessary preliminary to any definite drafting of the
superstructure of the aggregate science.

Turning now to the theory itself, the question is not so much
whether the theory given in this volume is true, but whether there
is really any novelty in it. The exclusive importance attributed in
England to the Ricardian school of economists has prevented
almost all English readers from learning the existence of a series
of French, as well as a few English, German or Italian economists,
who had from time to time treated the science in a more or less
strictly mathematical manner. In the first edition (pp. 14–18) I gave
a brief account of such writings of the kind as I was then acquainted with; it is from the works there mentioned, if from any,
that I derived the idea of investigating economics mathematically.
To Lardner's *Railway Economy* I was probably most indebted,
having been well acquainted with that work since the year
1857. Lardner's book has always struck me as containing a very
able investigation, the scientific value of which has not been

sufficiently estimated; and in chapter XIII (pp. 286–96, etc.) we find the laws of supply and demand treated mathematically and illustrated graphically.

In the preface to the first edition (p. xi),* I remarked that in his treatise on political economy M. Joseph Garnier mentioned several continental mathematicians who had written on the subject of economics, and I added that I had not been able to discover even the titles of their memoirs. This, however, must have been the result of careless reading or faulty memory, for it will be found that Garnier himself † mentions the titles of several books and memoirs. The fact is that, writing as I did then at a distance from any large library, I made no attempt to acquaint myself with the literature of the subject, little thinking that it was so copious and in some cases so excellent as is now found to be the case. With the progress of years, however, my knowledge of the literature of political economy has been much widened, and the hints of friends and correspondents have made me aware of the existence of many remarkable works which more or less anticipate the views stated in this book. While preparing this new edition, it occurred to me to attempt the discovery of all existing writings of the kind. With this view I drew up a chronological list of all the mathematico-economic works known to me, already about seventy in number, which list, by the kindness of the editor, Mr Giffen, was printed in the *Journal of the London Statistical Society* for June 1878 (vol. XLI. pp. 398–401), separate copies being forwarded to the leading economists, with a request for additions and corrections. My friend, M. Léon Walras, Rector of the Academy of Lausanne, after himself making considerable additions to the list, communicated it to the *Journal des Économistes* (December 1878), to the editor of which we are much indebted for its publication. Copies of the list were also sent to German and Italian economical journals. For the completion of the bibliographical list I am under obligations to Professor W. B. Hodgson, Professor Adamson, Mr W. H. Brewer, M.A., H.M. Inspector of Schools, the Baron d'Aulnis de Bourouill, Professor of Political Economy at Utrecht, M. N. G. Pierson of Amsterdam,

* See p. 45 of this edition.
† *Traité d'économie politique*, 5me éd., Paris, 1863, pp. 700–702.

M. Vissering of Leiden, Professor Luigi Cossa of Pavia, and others.[5]

All reasonable exertions have thus been made to render complete and exhaustive the list of mathematico-economic works and papers, which is now printed in the first [now fifth] appendix to this book.[*] It is hardly likely that many additions can be made to the earlier parts of the lists, but I shall be much obliged to any readers who can suggest corrections or additions. I shall also be glad to be informed of any new publications suitable for insertion in the list. On the other hand, it is possible that some of the books mentioned in the list ought not to be there. I have not been able in all cases to examine the publications myself, so that some works inserted at the suggestion of correspondents may have been named under misconception of the precise purpose of the list. Economic works, for instance, containing numerical illustrations and statistical facts numerically expressed, however abundantly, have not been intentionally included, unless there was also mathematical method in the reasoning. Without this condition the whole literature of numerical commercial statistics would have been imported into my list. In other cases only a small portion of a book named can be called mathematico-economic; but this fact is generally noted by the quotation of the chapters or pages in question. The tendency, however, has been to include rather than to exclude, so that the reader might have before him the whole field of literature requiring investigation.

To avoid misapprehension it may be well to explain that the ground for inserting any publication or part of a publication in this list, is its containing *an explicit recognition of the mathematical character of economics, or the advantage to be attained by its symbolic treatment*. I contend that all economic writers must be mathematical so far as they are scientific at all, because they treat of economic quantities, and the relations of such quantities, and all quantities and relations of quantities come within the scope of the mathematics. Even those who have most strongly and clearly protested against the recognition of their own method, continually betray in their language the quantitative character of their reasonings. What, for instance, can be more

* Omitted in this Pelican edition.

clearly mathematical in matter than the following quotation from Cairnes's chief work *

We can have no difficulty in seeing how cost in its principal elements is to be computed. In the case of labour, the cost of producing a given commodity will be represented by the number of average labourers employed in its production – regard at the same time being had to the severity of the work and the degree of risk it involves – multiplied by the duration of their labours. In that of abstinence, the principle is analogous: the sacrifice will be measured by the quantity of wealth abstained from, taken in connexion with the risk incurred, and multiplied by the duration of the abstinence.

Here we deal with computation, multiplication, degree of severity, degree of risk, quantity of wealth, duration, etc., all essentially mathematical things, ideas or operations. Although my esteemed friend and predecessor has in his preliminary chapter expressly abjured my doctrines, he has unconsciously adopted the mathematical method in all but appearance.

We might easily go farther back and discover that even the father of the science, as he is often considered, is thoroughly mathematical. In the fifth chapter of the First Book of the *Wealth of Nations*, for instance, we find Adam Smith continually arguing about 'quantities of labour', 'measures of value', 'measures of hardship', 'proportion', 'equality', etc.; the whole of the ideas in fact are mathematical. The same might be said of almost any other passages from the scientific parts of the treatise, as distinguished from the historical parts. In the first chapter of the Second Book (29th paragraph) we read: 'The produce of land, mines and fisheries, when their natural fertility is equal, is in proportion to the extent and proper application of the capitals employed about them. When the capitals are equal, and equally well applied, it is in proportion to their natural fertility.' Now every use of the word *equal* or *equality* implies the existence of a mathematical equation; an equation is simply an equality; and every use of the word proportion implies a ratio expressible in the form of an equation.

* *Some Leading Principles of Political Economy Newly Expounded*, pt 1, ch. III, p. 97.

I hold, then, that to argue mathematically, whether correctly or incorrectly, constitutes no real differentia as regards writers on the theory of economics. But it is one thing to argue and another thing to understand and to recognize explicitly the method of the argument. As there are so many who talk prose without knowing it, or, again, who syllogize without having the least idea what a syllogism is, so economists have long been mathematicians without being aware of the fact. The unfortunate result is that they have generally been bad mathematicians, and their works must fall. Hence the explicit recognition of the mathematical character of the science was an almost necessary condition of any real improvement of the theory. It does not follow, of course, that to be explicitly mathematical is to ensure the attainment of truth, and in such writings as those of Canard and Whewell, we find plenty of symbols and equations with no result of value, owing to the fact that they simply translated into symbols the doctrines obtained, and erroneously obtained, without their use. Such writers misunderstood and inverted altogether the function of mathematical symbols, which is to guide our thoughts in the slippery and complicated processes of reasoning. Ordinary language can usually express the first axioms of a science, and often also the matured results; but only in the most lame, obscure and tedious way can it lead us through the mazes of inference.

The bibliographical list, of which I am speaking, is no doubt a very heterogeneous one, and may readily be decomposed into several distinct classes of economic works. In a first class may be placed the writings of those economists who have not at all attempted mathematical treatment in an express or systematic manner, but who have only incidentally acknowledged its value by introducing symbolic or graphical statements. Among such writers may be mentioned especially Rau (1868), Hagen (1844), J. S. Mill (1848) and Courcelle-Seneuil (1867). Many readers may be surprised to hear that John Stuart Mill has used mathematical symbols; but, on turning to Book III, chapters XVII and XVIII, of the *Principles of Political Economy*, those difficult and tedious chapters in which Mill leads the reader through the theory of international trade and international values, by means of yards of linen and cloth, the reader will find that Mill at last yields, and expresses himself concisely and clearly * by means of equations between m, n, p and q. His mathematics are very crude; still there is some approach to a correct mathematical treatment, and the result is that these chapters, however tedious and difficult, will probably be found the truest and most enduring parts of the whole treatise.

A second class of economists contains those who have abundantly employed mathematical apparatus, but, misunderstanding its true use, or being otherwise diverted from a true theory, have built upon the sand. Misfortunes of this kind are not confined to the science of economics, and in the most exact branches of physical science, such as mechanics, molecular physics, astronomy etc., it would be possible to adduce almost innumerable mathematical treatises, which must be pronounced nonsense. In the same category must be placed the mathematical writings of such economists as Canard (1801), Whewell (1829, 1831 and 1850), Esmenard du Mazet (1849 and 1851) and perhaps Du Mesnil-Marigny (1860).

The third class forms an antithesis with the second, for it contains those authors who, without any parade of mathematical language or method, have nevertheless carefully attempted to reach precision in their treatment of quantitative ideas, and have thus been led to a more or less complete comprehension of the true theory of utility and wealth. Among such writers Francis Hutcheson, the Irish founder of the great Scottish school, and the predecessor of Adam Smith at Glasgow, probably stands first. His employment of mathematical symbols † seems rather crude and premature, but the precision of his ideas about the estimation of quantities of good and evil is beyond praise. He thoroughly anticipates the foundations of Bentham's moral system, showing that the 'moment of good or evil' is, in a compound proportion of the 'duration' and 'intenseness', affected also by the 'hazard' or uncertainty of our existence.‡ As to Bentham's ideas, they are adopted as the starting-point of the theory given in this work, and are quoted at the beginning of

* Book III, ch. XVIII, sec. vii.
† 1720, Hutcheson, *An Inquiry*, 1729, etc., pp. 186–98.
‡ 1728, Hutcheson, *An Essay*, etc., pp. 34–43, and elsewhere.

chapter II (p. 94). Bentham has repeated his statement as to the mode of measuring happiness in several different works and pamphlets, as for instance in that remarkable one called 'A Table of the Springs of Action' (London, 1817, p. 3)[6]; and also in the 'Codification Proposal, Addressed by Jeremy Bentham to All Nations Professing Liberal Opinions' (London, 1822, pp. 7–11). He here speaks explicitly of the application of *arithmetic* to questions of utility, meaning no doubt the application of mathematical methods. He even describes (p. 11) the four circumstances governing the value of a pleasure or pain as the *dimensions* of its value, though he is incorrect in treating *propinquity* and *certainty* as dimensions.

It is worthy of notice that Destutt de Tracy, one of the most philosophic of all economists, has in a few words recognized the true method of treatment, though he has not followed up his own idea. Referring to the circumstances which, in his opinion, render all economic and moral calculations very delicate, he says* '*On ne peut guère employer dans ces matières que des considérations tirées de la théorie des limites.*' So well-known an English economist as Malthus has also shown in a few lines his complete appreciation of the mathematical nature of economic questions. In one of his excellent pamphlets † he remarks, 'Many of the questions, both in morals and politics, seem to be of the nature of the problems *de maximis et minimis* in fluxions; in which there is always a point where a certain effect is the greatest, while on either side of this point it gradually diminishes.' But I have not thought it desirable to swell the bibliographical list by including all the works in which there are to be found brief or casual remarks of the kind.

I may here remark that all the writings of Mr Henry Dunning Macleod exhibit a strong tendency to mathematical treatment. Some of his works or papers in which this mathematical spirit is

**Élémens d'ideologie*, 4me et 5me Parties. *Traité de la volonté et de ses effets*, Paris, 1815, 8vo, p. 499. Edition of 1826, p. 335. American Edition, *A Treatise on Political Economy, Translated from the Unpublished French Original*. Georgetown, D.C., 1817, p. xiii.

† *Observations on the Effects of the Corn Laws, and of a Rise or Fall in the Price of Corn on the Agriculture and General Wealth of the Country*. London, 1814, p. 30; 3rd ed., 1815, p. 32.

most strongly manifested have been placed in the list. It is not my business to criticize his ingenious views, or to determine how far he really has created a mathematical system. While I certainly differ from him on many important points, I am bound to acknowledge the assistance which I derive from the use of several of his works.

In the fourth and most important class of mathematico-economic writers must be placed those who have consciously and avowedly attempted to frame a mathematical theory of the subject, and have, if my judgement is correct, succeeded in reaching a true view of the science. In this class certain distinguished French philosophers take precedence and priority. One might perhaps go back with propriety to Condillac's work, *Le Commerce et le gouvernement*, first published in the year 1776, the same year in which the *Wealth of Nations* appeared.[7] In the first few chapters of this charming philosophic work we meet perhaps the earliest distinct statement of the true connexion between value and utility. The book, however, is not included in the list because there is no explicit attempt at mathematical treatment. It is the French engineer Dupuit who must probably be credited with the earliest perfect comprehension of the theory of utility. In attempting to frame a precise measure of the utility of public works, he observed that the utility of a commodity not only varies immensely from one individual to another, but that it is also widely different for the same person according to circumstances. He says, '*nous verrions que l'utilité du morceau de pain peut croître pour le même individu depuis zéro jusqu'au chiffre de sa fortune entière*' (1849, Dupuit, *De l'influence des péages*, etc., p. 185). He establishes, in fact, a theory of the *gradation of utility*, beautifully and perfectly expounded by means of geometrical diagrams, and this theory is undoubtedly coincident in essence with that contained in this book. He does not, however, follow his ideas out in an algebraic form. Dupuit's theory was the subject of some controversy in the pages of the *Annales des ponts et chaussées*, but did not receive much attention elsewhere, and I am not aware that any English economist ever knew anything about these remarkable memoirs.

The earlier treatise of Cournot, his admirable *Recherches sur*

les principes mathématiques de la théorie des richesses (Paris,
1838), resembles Dupuit's memoirs in being, until within the
last few years, quite unknown to English economists. In other
respects Cournot's method is contrasted to Dupuit's. Cournot
did not frame any ultimate theory of the ground and nature of
utility and value, but, taking the palpable facts known concerning
the relations of price, production and consumption of commodities, he investigated these relations analytically and diagraphically
with a power and felicity which leaves little to be desired. This
work must occupy a remarkable position in the history of the
subject. It is strange that it should have remained for me among
Englishmen to discover its value. Some years since (1875), Mr
Todhunter wrote to me as follows

I have sometimes wondered whether there is anything of importance
in a book published many years since by M. A. A. Cournot, entitled
Recherches sur les principes mathématiques de la théorie des richesses[8].
I never saw it, and when I have mentioned the title, I never found any
person who had read the book. Yet Cournot was eminent for mathematics and metaphysics, and so there may be some merit in this book.

I procured a copy of the work as far back as 1872, but have
only recently studied it with sufficient care to form any definite
opinion upon its value. Even now I have by no means mastered
all parts of it, my mathematical power being insufficient to enable
me to follow Cournot in all parts of his analysis. My impression
is that the first chapter of the work is not remarkable; that the
second chapter contains an important anticipation of discussions
concerning the proper method of treating prices, including an
anticipation (p. 21) of my logarithmic method of ascertaining
variations in the value of gold; that the third chapter, treating of
the conditions of the foreign exchanges, is highly ingenious if not
particularly useful; but that by far the most important part of the
book commences with the fourth chapter on the '*Loi du Débit*'.
The remainder of the book, in fact, contains a wonderful analysis
of the laws of supply and demand, and of the relations of prices,
production, consumption, expenses and profits. Cournot starts
from the assumption that the *débit* or demand for a commodity
is a function of the price, or $D = F(p)$; and then, after laying

down empirically a few conditions of this function, he proceeds to work out with surprising power the consequences which follow from these conditions. Even apart from its economic importance, this investigation, so far as I can venture to judge it, presents a beautiful example of mathematical reasoning, in which knowledge is apparently evolved out of ignorance. In reality the method consists in assuming certain simple conditions of the functions as conformable to experience, and then disclosing by symbolic inference the implicit results of these conditions. But I am quite convinced that the investigation is of high economic importance, and that, when the parts of political economy to which the theory relates come to be adequately treated, as they never have yet been, the treatment must be based upon the analysis of Cournot, or at least must follow his general method. It should be added that his investigation has little relation to the contents of this work, because Cournot does not recede to any theory of utility, but commences with the phenomenal laws of supply and demand.

Discouraged apparently by the small amount of attention paid to his mathematical treatise, Cournot in a later year (1863) produced a more popular non-symbolic work on economics;[9] but this later work does not compare favourably in interest and importance with his first treatise.

English economists can hardly be blamed for their ignorance of Cournot's economic works when we find French writers equally bad. Thus the authors of Guillaumin's excellent *Dictionnaire de l'économie politique*, which is on the whole the best work of reference in the literature of the science, ignore Cournot and his works altogether, and so likewise does Sandelin in his copious *Répertoire général d'économie politique*. M. Joseph Garnier in his otherwise admirable textbook * mixes up Cournot with far inferior mathematicians, saying; '*Dans ces derniers temps M. Esmenard du Mazet, et M. du Mesnil-Marigny ont aussi fait abus, ce nous semble, des formules algébriques; les Recherches sur les Principes Mathématiques des Richesses de M. Cournot, ne nous ont fourni aucun moyen d'élucidation*.' MacCulloch of course knows nothing of Cournot. Mr H. D. Macleod has the merit at least of mentioning Cournot's work, but he misspells the name

Traité d'économie politique, 5me ed., p. 701.

of the author, and gives only the title of the book, which he had probably never seen.

We now come to a truly remarkable discovery in the history of this branch of literature. Some years since my friend Professor Adamson had noticed in one of Kautz's works on political economy* a brief reference to a book said to contain a theory of pleasure and pain, written by a German author named Hermann Heinrich Gossen. Although he had advertised for it, Professor Adamson was unable to obtain a sight of this book until August 1878, when he fortunately discovered it in a German bookseller's catalogue, and succeeded in purchasing it. The book was published at Brunswick in 1854; it consists of 278 well-filled pages, and is entitled, *Entwickelung der Gesetze des menschlichen Verkehrs, und der daraus fliessenden Regeln für menschliches Handeln*, which may be translated – 'Development of the laws of human commerce, and of the consequent rules of human action'. I will describe the contents of this remarkable volume as they are reported to me by Professor Adamson.

Gossen evidently held the highest possible opinion of the importance of his own theory, for he commences by claiming honours in economic science equal to those of Copernicus in astronomy. He then at once insists that mathematical treatment, being the only sound one, must be applied throughout; but, out of consideration for the reader, the higher analysis will be explicitly introduced only when it is requisite to determine maxima and minima. The treatise then opens with the consideration of economics as the theory of pleasure and pain, that is as the theory of the procedure by which the individual and the aggregate of individuals constituting society, may realize the maximum of pleasure with the minimum of painful effort. The natural law of pleasure is then clearly stated, somewhat as follows: *Increase of the same kind of consumption yields pleasure continuously diminishing up to the point of satiety*. This law he illustrates geometrically, and then proceeds to investigate the conditions under which the total pleasure from one or more objects may be raised to a maximum.

The term *werth* is next introduced, which may, Professor

* *Theorie und Geschichte der National-Oekonomik*, 1858, vol. I, p. 9.

Adamson thinks, be rendered with strict accuracy as *utility*, and Gossen points out that the quantity of utility, material or immaterial, is measured by the quantity of pleasure which it affords. He classifies useful objects as: (1) those which possess pleasure-giving powers in themselves; (2) those which only possess such powers when in combination with other objects; (3) those which only serve as means towards the production of pleasure-giving objects. He is careful to point out that there is no such thing as absolute utility, utility being purely a relation between a thing and a person. He next proceeds to give the derivative laws of utility somewhat in the following manner: that separate portions of the same pleasure-giving object have very different degrees of utility, and that in general for each person only a limited number of such portions has utility; any addition beyond this limit is useless, but the point of uselessness is only reached after the utility has gone through all the stages or degrees of intensity. Hence he draws the practical conclusion that each person should so distribute his resources as to render the final increments of each pleasure-giving commodity of equal utility for him.

In the next place Gossen deals with labour, starting from the proposition that the utility of any product must be estimated after deduction of the pains of labour required to produce it. He describes the variation of the pain of labour much as I have done, exhibiting it graphically, and inferring that we must carry on labour to the point at which the utility of the product equals the pain of production. In treating the theory of exchange he shows how barter gives rise to an immense increase of utility, and he infers that exchange will proceed up to the point at which the utilities of the portions next to be given and received are equal. A complicated geometrical representation of the theory of exchange is given. The theory of rent is investigated in a most general manner, and the work concludes with somewhat vague social speculations, which, in Professor Adamson's opinion, are of inferior merit compared with the earlier portions of the treatise.

From this statement it is quite apparent that Gossen has completely anticipated me as regards the general principles and method of the theory of economics. So far as I can gather, his treatment of the fundamental theory is even more general and thorough than what I was able to scheme out. In discussing the book, I lie under the serious difficulty of not being able to read it; but, judging from what Professor Adamson has written or read to me, and from an examination of the diagrams and symbolic parts of the work, I should infer that Gossen has been unfortunate in the development of his theory. Instead of dealing, as Cournot and myself have done, with undetermined functions, and introducing the least possible amount of assumption, Gossen, assumed, for the sake of simplicity, that economic functions follow a linear law, so that his curves of utility are generally taken as straight lines. This assumption enables him to work out a great quantity of precise formulas and tabular results, which fill many pages of the book. But, inasmuch as the functions of economic science are seldom or never really linear, and usually diverge very far from the straight line, I think that the symbolic and geometric illustrations and developments introduced by Gossen must for the most part be put down among the many products of misplaced ingenuity.[10] I may add, in my own behalf, that he does not seem really to reach the equations of exchange as established in this book; that the theory of capital and interest is wanting; and that there is a total absence of any resemblance between the working out of the matter, except such as arises from a common basis of truth.

The coincidence, however, between the essential ideas of Gossen's system and my own is so striking that I desire to state distinctly, in the first place, that I never saw nor so much as heard any hint of the existence of Gossen's book before August 1878, and to explain, in the second place, how it was that I did not do so. My unfortunate want of linguistic power has prevented me, in spite of many attempts, from ever becoming familiar enough with German to read a German book. I once managed to spell out with assistance part of the logical lecture notes of Kant, but that is my sole achievement in German literature. Now this work of Gossen has remained unknown even to most of the great readers of Germany. Professor Adamson remarks that the work seems to have attracted no attention in Germany. The eminent and learned economist of Amsterdam, Professor

N. G. Pierson, writes to me: 'Gossen's book is totally unknown to me. Roscher does not mention it in his very laborious *History of Political Economy in Germany*. I never saw it quoted; but I will try to get it. It is very curious that such a remarkable work has remained totally unknown even to a man like Professor Roscher, who has read everything.' Mr Cliffe Leslie, also, who has made the German economists his special study, informs me that he was quite unaware of the existence of the book.* Under such circumstances it would have been far more probable that I should discover the theory of pleasure and pain, than that I should discover Gossen's book, and I have carefully pointed out, both in the first edition and in this, certain passages of Bentham, Senior, Jennings and other authors, from which my system was, more or less consciously, developed. I cannot claim to be totally indifferent to the rights of priority; and from the year 1862, when my theory was first published in brief outline, I have often pleased myself with the thought that it was at once a novel and an important theory. From what I have now stated in this preface it is evident that novelty can no longer be attributed to the leading features of the theory. Much is clearly due to Dupuit, and of the rest a great share must be assigned to Gossen. Regret may easily be swallowed up in satisfaction if I succeed eventually in making that understood and valued which has been so sadly neglected.

Almost nothing is known to me concerning Gossen; it is uncertain whether he is living or not. On the title-page he describes himself as 'königlich preussischem Regierungs-Assessor ausser Dienst', which may be translated 'Royal Prussian Government Assessor, retired'; but the tone of his remarks here and there seems to indicate that he was a disappointed if not an injured man. The reception of his one work can have lent no relief to these feelings; rather it must much have deepened them. The book seems to have contained his one cherished theory, for I can find under the name of Gossen no trace of any other publication or scientific memoir whatever. The history of these forgotten works is, indeed, a strange and discouraging one, but the

* A copy of Gossen's book will be found in the library of the British Museum (press mark 8408. cc. 16). It was not acquired by that institution until 24 May 1865, as shown by the date stamped upon the copy.

day must come when the eyes of those who cannot see will be opened. Then will due honour be given to all who like Cournot and Gossen have laboured in a thankless field of human knowledge, and have met with the neglect or ridicule they might well have expected. Not indeed that such men do really work for the sake of honour; they bring forth a theory as the tree brings forth its fruit.

It remains for me to refer to the mathematico-economic writings of M. Léon Walras, the Rector of the Academy of Lausanne. It is curious that Lausanne, already distinguished by the early work of Isnard (1781), should recently have furnished such important additions to the science as the memoirs of Walras. For important they are, not only because they complete and prove that which was before published elsewhere in the works described above, but because they contain a third or fourth independent discovery of the principles of the theory. If we are to trace out 'the filiation of ideas' by which M. Walras was led to his theory, we should naturally look back to the work of his father, Auguste Walras, published at Paris in 1831, and entitled *De la nature de la richesse, et de l'origine de la valeur*. In this work we find, it is true, no distinct recognition of the mathematical method, but the analysis of value is often acute and philosophic. The principal point of the work moreover is true, that value depends upon *rarity* – '*La valeur*', says Auguste Walras, '*dérive de la rareté.*' Now it is precisely upon this idea of the degree of rarity of commodities that Léon Walras bases his system. The fact that some four or more independent writers such as Dupuit, Gossen, Walras and myself should in such different ways have reached substantially the same views of the fundamental ideas of economic science, cannot but lend great probability, not to say approximate certainty, to those views. I am glad to hear that M. Walras intends to bring out a new edition of his mathematico-economic memoirs, to which the attention of my readers is invited. The titles of his publications will be found in the Appendix I·[V of this edition].*

The works of Von Thünen and of several other German economists contain mathematical investigations of much interest and importance. A considerable number of such works will be

* Omitted in this Pelican edition.

found noted in the list, which, however, is especially defective as regards German literature. I regret that I am not able to treat this branch of the subject in an adequate manner.

My bibliographical list shows that in recent years, that is to say since the year 1873, there has been a great increase in the number of mathematico-economic writings. The names of Fontaneau, Walras, Avigdor, Lefèvre, Petersen, Boccardo, recur time after time. In such periodicals as the *Journal des actuaires français*, or the *National-Oekonomisk Tidsskrift* – a journal so creditable to the energy and talent of the Danish economic school – the mathematical theory of economics is treated as one of established interest and truth, with which readers would naturally be acquainted. In England we have absolutely no periodical in which such discussions could be conducted. The reader will not fail to remark that it is into the hands of French, Italian, Danish or Dutch writers that this most important subject is rapidly passing. They will develop that science which only excites ridicule and incredulity among the followers of Mill and Ricardo. There are just a few English mathematicians, such as Fleeming Jenkin, George Darwin, Alfred Marshall or H. D. Macleod, and one or two Americans like Professor Simon Newcomb, who venture to write upon the obnoxious subject of mathematico-economic science.[11] I ought to add, however, that at Cambridge (England) the mathematical treatment of economics is becoming gradually recognized owing to the former influence of Mr Alfred Marshall, now the Principal of University College, Bristol, whose ingenious mathematico-economic problems, expounded *more geometrico*, have just been privately printed at Cambridge.

If we overlook Hutcheson, who did not expressly write on economics, the earliest mathematico-economic author seems to be the Italian Ceva, whose works have just been brought to notice in the *Giornale degli Economisti* (see 1878, Nicolini). Ceva wrote in the early part of the eighteenth century, but I have as yet no further information about him. The next author in the list is the celebrated Beccaria, who printed a very small, but distinctly mathematical, tract on taxation as early as 1765.[12] Italians were thus first in the field. The earliest English work of the kind yet discovered is an anonymous *Essay on the Theory of*

Money, published in London in 1771, five years before the era of the *Wealth of Nations*. Though crude and absurd in some parts, it is not devoid of interest and ability, and contains a distinct and partially valid attempt to establish a mathematical theory of currency. This remarkable essay is, so far as I know, wholly forgotten and almost lost in England. Neither MacCulloch nor any other English economist known to me, mentions the work. I discovered its existence a few months ago by accidentally finding a copy on a bookseller's stall. But it shames an Englishman to learn that English works thus unknown in their own country are known abroad, and I owe to Professor Luigi Cossa, of the University of Pavia, the information that the essay was written by Major-General Henry Lloyd, an author of some merit in other branches of literature.[13] Signor Cossa's excellent *Guido alla studio di economia politica*, a concise but judiciously written text-book, is well qualified to open our eyes as to the insular narrowness of our economic learning. It is a book of a kind much needed by our students of economics, and I wish that it could be published in an English dress.[14]

From this bibliographical survey emerges the wholly unexpected result, that the mathematical treatment of economics is coeval with the science itself. The notion that there is any novelty or originality in the application of mathematical methods or symbols must be dismissed altogether. While there have been political economists there has always been a certain number who with various success have struck into the unpopular but right path. The unfortunate and discouraging aspect of the matter is the complete oblivion into which this part of the literature of economics has always fallen, oblivion so complete that each mathe matico-economic writer has been obliged to begin almost *de novo*. It is with the purpose of preventing for the future as far as I can such ignorance of previous exertions, that I have spent so much pains upon this list of books.

I should add that in arranging the list I have followed, very imperfectly, the excellent example set by Professor Mansfield Merriman, of the Sheffield Scientific School of Yale College, in his 'List of writings relating to the method of least squares'.*

* *Transactions of the Connecticut Academy*, 1877, vol. IV, pp. 151–232.

Such bibliographies are of immense utility, and I hope that the time is nearly come when each student of a special branch of science or literature will feel bound to work out its bibliography, unless, of course, the task shall have been already accomplished. The reader will see that, in Appendix II [IV of this edition],* I have taken the liberty of working out also a part of the bibliography of my own writings.

Looking now to the eventual results of the theory, I must beg the reader to bear in mind that this book was never put forward as containing a systematic view of economics. It treats only of the theory, and is but an elementary sketch of elementary principles. The working out of a complete system based on these lines must be a matter of time and labour, and I know not when, if ever, I shall be able to attempt it. In the last chapter, I have, however, indicated the manner in which the theory of wages will be affected. This chapter is reprinted almost as it was written in 1871; since then the wage-fund theory has been abandoned by most English economists, owing to the attacks of Mr Cliffe Leslie, Mr Shadwell, Professor Cairnes, Professor Francis Walker, and some others. Quite recently more extensive reading and more careful cogitation have led to a certain change in my ideas concerning the superstructure of economics – in this wise:

Firstly, I am convinced that the doctrine of wages, which I adopted in 1871, under the impression that it was somewhat novel, is not really novel at all, except to those whose view is bounded by the maze of the Ricardian economics. The true doctrine may be more or less clearly traced through the writings of a succession of great French economists, from Condillac, Baudeau and Le Trosne, through J.-B. Say, Destutt de Tracy, Storch and others, down to Bastiat and Courcelle-Seneuil.[15] The conclusion to which I am ever more clearly coming is that the only hope of attaining a true system of economics is to fling aside, once and for ever, the mazy and preposterous assumptions of the Ricardian school. Our English economists have been living in a fool's paradise. The truth is with the French school, and the sooner we recognize the fact, the better it will be for all the world,

*Omitted in this Pelican edition.

except perhaps the few writers who are too far committed to the old erroneous doctrines to allow of renunciation.

Although, as I have said, the true theory of wages is not new as regards the French school, it is new, or at any rate renewed, as regards our English schools of economics. One of the first to treat the subject from the right point of view was Mr Cliffe Leslie, in an article first published in *Fraser's Magazine* for July 1868, and subsequently reprinted in a collection of essays.* Some years afterwards Mr J. L. Shadwell independently worked out the same theory of wages which he has fully expounded in his admirable *System of Political Economy*.† In Hearn's *Plutology* however, as pointed out in the text of this book (pp. 258–9), we find the same general idea that wages are the share of the produce which the laws of supply and demand enable the labourer to secure. It is probable that like ideas might be traced in other works were this the place to attempt a history of the subject.[16]

Secondly, I feel sure that when, casting ourselves free from the wage-fund theory, the cost of production doctrine of value, the natural rate of wages, and other misleading or false Ricardian doctrines, we begin to trace out clearly and simply the results of a correct theory, it will not be difficult to arrive at a true doctrine of wages. This will probably be reached somewhat in the following way: we must regard labour, land, knowledge and capital as conjoint conditions of the whole produce, not as causes each of a certain portion of the produce. Thus in an elementary state of society, when each labourer owns all the three or four requisites of production, there would really be no such thing as wages, rent or interest at all. Distribution does not arise even in idea, and the produce is simply the aggregate effect of the aggregate conditions. It is only when separate owners of the elements of production join their properties, and traffic with each other, that distribution begins, and then it is entirely subject to the principles of value and the laws of supply and demand. Each labourer must be regarded, like each landowner and each capitalist, as bringing into the common stock one part of the component elements, bar-

* 'Land Systems and Industrial Economy of Ireland, England, and Continental Countries', London, 1870. Appendix, pp. 357–79.
† London, 1877, Trübner.

gaining for the best share of the produce which the conditions of the market allow him to claim successfully. In theory the labourer has a monopoly of labour of each particular kind, as much as the landowner of land, and the capitalist of other requisite articles. Property is only another name for monopoly. But when different persons own property of exactly the same kind, they become subject to the important law of indifference, as I have called it (pp. 136–9), namely, that in the same open market, at any one moment, there cannot be two prices for the same kind of article. Thus *monopoly is limited by competition*, and no owner, whether of labour, land or capital, can, theoretically speaking, obtain a larger share of produce for it than what other owners of exactly the same kind of property are willing to accept.

So far there may seem to be nothing novel in this view; it is hardly more than will be found stated in a good many economic works. But as soon as we begin to follow out this simple view, the consequences are rather startling. We are forced, for instance, to admit that rates of wages are governed by the same formal laws as rents. This view is not new to the readers of Storch,[17] who in the third book of his excellent *Cours d'économie politique* has a chapter * 'De la Rente des talens et des qualités morales'. But it is a very new doctrine to one whose economic horizon is formed by Mill and Fawcett, Ricardo and Adam Smith. Even Storch has not followed out the doctrine thoroughly, for he applies the idea of rent only to cases of *eminent* talent. It must be evident, however, that talent and capacity of all kinds are only a question of degree, so that, according to the law of continuity, the same principle must apply to all labourers.

A still more startling result is that, so far as cost of production regulates the values of commodities, wages must enter into the calculation on exactly the same footing as rent. Now it is a prime point of the Ricardian doctrines that rent does not enter into cost of production. As J. S. Mill says,† 'Rent, therefore, forms no part of the cost of production which determines the value of agricultural produce.' And again,‡ 'Rent is not an element in

* Ch. V, vol. I, p. 304.
† *Principles of Political Economy*, Book III, ch. V, sec. ii, paragraph 3.
‡ Ibid., Book III, ch. VI, sec. i, article 9.

the cost of production of the commodity which yields it; except in the cases' etc. Rent in fact is represented as the effect not the cause of high value; wages on the contrary are treated as the cause, not the effect. But if rent and wages be really phenomena subject to the same formal laws, this opposite relation to value must involve error. The way out of the difficulty is furnished by the second sentence of the paragraph from which the last quotation was taken. Mill goes on to say, 'But when land capable of yielding rent in agriculture is applied to some other purpose, the rent which it would have yielded is an element in the cost of production of the commodity which it is employed to produce.' Here Mill edges in as an exceptional case that which proves to be the rule, reminding one of other exceptional cases described as 'some peculiar cases of value' (see p. 208, below), which I have shown to include almost all commodities.

Now Mill allows that when land capable of yielding rent in agriculture is applied to some other purpose, the rent which would have been produced in agriculture is an element in the cost of production of other commodities. But wherefore this distinction between agriculture and other branches of industry? Why does not the same principle apply between two different modes of agricultural employment? If land which has been yielding £2 per acre rent as pasture be ploughed up and used for raising wheat, must not the £2 per acre be debited against the expenses of the production of wheat? Suppose that somebody introduced the beetroot culture into England with a view to making sugar; this new branch of industry could not be said to pay unless it yielded, besides all other expenses, the full rents of the lands turned from other kinds of culture. But if this be conceded, the same principle must apply generally; a potato-field should pay as well as a clover-field, and a clover-field as a turnip-field; and so on. The market prices of the produce must adjust themselves so that this shall in the long run be possible. The rotation of crops, no doubt, introduces complication into the matter, but does not modify the general reasoning. The principle which emerges is that *each portion of land should be applied to that culture or use which yields the largest total of utility, as measured by the value of the produce*; if otherwise applied there will be loss. Thus the rent of land is determined by the excess of produce in the most profitable employment.

But when the matter is fully thought out it will be seen that exactly the same principle applies to wages. A man who can earn six shillings a day in one employment will not turn to another kind of work unless he expects to get six shillings a day or more from it. There is no such thing as absolute cost of labour; it is all matter of comparison. Every one gets the most which he can for his exertions; some can get little or nothing, because they have not sufficient strength, knowledge or ingenuity; others get much, because they have, comparatively speaking, a monopoly of certain powers. Each seeks the work in which his peculiar faculties are most productive of utility, as measured by what other people are willing to pay for the produce. Thus wages are clearly the effect not the causes of the value of the produce. But when labour is turned from one employment to another, the wages it would otherwise have yielded must be debited to the expenses of the new product. Thus the parallelism between the theories of rent and wages is seen to be perfect in theory, however different it may appear to be in the details of application. Precisely the same view may be applied, *mutatis mutandis*, to the rent yielded by fixed capital, and to the interest of free capital. In the last case, the law of indifference peculiarly applies, because free capital, loanable for a certain interval, is equally available for all branches of industry; hence, at any moment and place, the interest of such capital must be the same in all branches of trade.

I ought to say that Mill, as pointed out to me by Professor Adamson, has a remarkable section at the end of chapter V of Book III of the *Principles*, in which he explains that all inequalities, artificial or natural, give rise to extra gains of the nature of rent. This section is a very satisfactory one inasmuch as it tends to support the view on which I am now insisting; a view, however, which, when properly followed out, will overthrow many of the principal doctrines of the Ricardo–Mill economics. Those who have studied Mill's philosophical character as long and minutely as I have done, will not for a moment suppose that the occurrence of this section in Mill's book tends to establish its consistency with other portions of the same treatise.

But of course I cannot follow out the discussion of this matter in a mere preface. The results to be expected are partly indicated in my *Primer of Political Economy*, but in that little treatise my remarks upon the origin of rent (p. 94), as originally printed in the first edition, were erroneous, and the section altogether needs to be rewritten.[18] When at length a true system of economics comes to be established, it will be seen that that able but wrong-headed man, David Ricardo, shunted the car of economic science on to a wrong line – a line, however, on which it was further urged towards confusion by his equally able and wrong-headed admirer, John Stuart Mill. There were economists, such as Malthus and Senior, who had a far better comprehension of the true doctrines (though not free from the Ricardian errors), but they were driven out of the field by the unity and influence of the Ricardo–Mill school. It will be a work of labour to pick up the fragments of a shattered science and to start anew, but is a work from which they must not shrink who wish to see any advance of economic science.

The Chestnuts,
Hampstead Heath, N.W.
   May, 1879.

CONTENTS

73

CONTENTS

CHAPTER IV

Theory of Exchange

CHAPTER V

Theory of Labour

CONTENTS

CHAPTER VI

Theory of Rent

CHAPTER VII

Theory of Capital

CONTENTS

CHAPTER VIII

Concluding Remarks

CHAPTER I

Introduction

—

THE science of political economy rests upon a few notions of an apparently simple character. Utility, wealth, value, commodity, labour, land, capital, are the elements of the subject; and whoever has a thorough comprehension of their nature must possess or be soon able to acquire a knowledge of the whole science. As almost every economic writer has remarked, it is in treating the simple elements that we require the most care and precision, since the least error of conception must vitiate all our deductions. Accordingly, I have devoted the following pages to an investigation of the conditions and relations of the above-named notions.

Repeated reflection and inquiry have led me to the somewhat novel opinion, that *value depends entirely upon utility*. Prevailing opinions make labour rather than utility the origin of value; and there are even those who distinctly assert that labour is the *cause* of value. I show, on the contrary, that we have only to trace out carefully the natural laws of the variation of utility, as depending upon the quantity of commodity in our possession, in order to arrive at a satisfactory theory of exchange, of which the ordinary laws of supply and demand are a necessary consequence. This theory is in harmony with facts, and, whenever there is any apparent reason for the belief that labour is the cause of value, we obtain an explanation of the reason. Labour is found often to determine value, but only in an indirect manner, by varying the degree of utility of the commodity through an increase or limitation of the supply.

These views are not put forward in a hasty or ill-considered manner. All the chief points of the theory were sketched out ten years ago; but they were then published only in the form of a brief paper communicated to the Statistical or Economic Section of the British Association at the Cambridge Meeting, which took place in the year 1862. A still briefer abstract of that paper was inserted in the Report of the Meeting,* and the paper itself was not printed until June 1866.† Since writing that paper, I have, over and over again, questioned the truth of my own notions, but without ever finding any reason to doubt their substantial correctness.

Mathematical Character of the Science

It is clear that economics, if it is to be a science at all, must be a mathematical science. There exists much prejudice against attempts to introduce the methods and language of mathematics into any branch of the moral sciences. Many persons seem to think that the physical sciences form the proper sphere of mathematical method, and that the moral sciences demand some other method – I know not what. My theory of economics, however, is purely mathematical in character. Nay, believing that the quantities with which we deal must be subject to continuous variation, I do not hesitate to use the appropriate branch of mathematical science, involving though it does the fearless consideration of infinitely small quantities. The theory consists in applying the differential calculus to the familiar notions of wealth, utility, value, demand, supply, capital, interest, labour and all the other quantitative notions belonging to the daily operations of industry. As the complete theory of almost every other science involves the use of that calculus, so we cannot have a true theory of economics without its aid.

To me it seems that *our science must be mathematical, simply because it deals with quantities*. Wherever the things treated are capable of being *greater or less*, there the laws and relations must be mathematical in nature. The ordinary laws of supply and demand treat entirely of quantities of commodity demanded or supplied, and express the manner in which the quantities vary in connexion with the price. In consequence of this fact the laws *are* mathematical. Economists cannot alter their nature by denying them the name; they might as well try to alter red light by calling it blue. Whether the mathematical laws of economics

* *Reports of Sections*, p. 158.
† *Journal of the Statistical Society*, vol. XXIX, p. 282.

are stated in words, or in the usual symbols, x, y, z, p, q, etc., is an accident, or a matter of mere convenience. If we had no regard to trouble and prolixity, the most complicated mathematical problems might be stated in ordinary language, and their solution might be traced out by words. In fact, some distinguished mathematicians have shown a liking for getting rid of their symbols, and expressing their arguments and results in language as nearly as possible approximating to that in common use. In his *Système du monde*, Laplace attempted to describe the truths of physical astronomy in common language;[19] and Thomson and Tait interweave their great *Treatise on Natural Philosophy* with an interpretation in ordinary words, supposed to be within the comprehension of general readers.*

These attempts, however distinguished and ingenious their authors, soon disclose the inherent defects of the grammar and dictionary for expressing complicated relations. The symbols of mathematical books are not different in nature from language; they form a perfected system of language, adapted to the notions and relations which we need to express. They do not constitute the mode of reasoning they embody; they merely facilitate its exhibition and comprehension. If, then, in economics, we have to deal with quantities and complicated relations of quantities, we must reason mathematically; we do not render the science less mathematical by avoiding the symbols of algebra – we merely refuse to employ, in a very imperfect science, much needing every kind of assistance, that apparatus of appropriate signs which is found indispensable in other sciences.

Confusion between Mathematical and Exact Sciences

Many persons entertain a prejudice against mathematical language, arising out of a confusion between the ideas of a mathematical science and an exact science. They think that we

*The large-type or non-symbolic portion of the *Treatise* has been reprinted in a separate volume, under the title *Elements of Natural Philosophy*, by Professors Sir W. Thomson and P. G. Tait, part I, Oxford, Clarendon Press, 1873. But the authors appear to me to be inaccurate in describing this work, in the preface, as *non-mathematical*. It is comparatively *non-symbolic*, but equally mathematical with the complete *Treatise*.

must not pretend to calculate unless we have the precise data which will enable us to obtain a precise answer to our calculations; but, in reality, there is no such thing as an exact science, except in a comparative science. Astronomy is more exact than other sciences, because the position of a planet or star admits of close measurement; but, if we examine the methods of physical astronomy, we find that they are all approximate. Every solution involves hypotheses which are not really true: as, for instance, that the earth is a smooth, homogeneous spheroid. Even the apparently simpler problems in statics or dynamics are only hypothetical approximations to the truth.*

We can calculate the effect of a crowbar, provided it be perfectly inflexible and have a perfectly hard fulcrum – which is never the case.† The data are almost wholly deficient for the complete solution of any one problem in natural science. Had physicists waited until their data were perfectly precise before they brought in the aid of mathematics, we should have still been in the age of science which terminated at the time of Galileo.

When we examine the less precise physical sciences, we find that physicists are, of all men, most bold in developing their mathematical theories in advance of their data. Let anyone who doubts this examine Airy's 'Theory of the Tides', as given in the *Encyclopaedia Metropolitana*;[20] he will there find a wonderfully complex mathematical theory which is confessed by its author to be incapable of exact or even approximate application, because the results of the various and often unknown contours of the seas do not admit of numerical verification. In this and many other cases we have mathematical theory without the data requisite for precise calculation.

The greater or less accuracy attainable in a mathematical science is a matter of accident, and does not affect the fundamental character of the science. There can be but two classes of sciences – those which are *simply logical*, and *those which, besides being logical, are also mathematical*. If there be any science which

---

*This subject of the approximate character of quantitative science is pursued, at some length, in my *Principles of Science*, ch. XXI, on 'The Theory of Approximation', and elsewhere in the same work.

†Thomson and Tait's *Treatise on Natural Philosophy*, vol. I, p. 337.

determines merely whether a thing be or be not – whether an event will happen, or will not happen – it must be a purely logical science; but if the thing may be greater or less, or the event may happen sooner or later, nearer or farther, then quantitative notions enter, and the science must be mathematical in nature, by whatever name we call it.

Capability of Exact Measurement

Many will object, no doubt, that the notions which we treat in this science are incapable of any measurement. We cannot weigh, nor gauge, nor test the feelings of the mind; there is no unit of labour, or suffering, or enjoyment. It might thus seem as if a mathematical theory of economics would be necessarily deprived for ever of numerical data.

I answer, in the first place, that nothing is less warranted in science than an uninquiring and unhoping spirit. In matters of this kind, those who despair are almost invariably those who have never tried to succeed. A man might be despondent had he spent a lifetime on a difficult task without a gleam of encouragement; but the popular opinions on the extension of mathematical theory tend to deter any man from attempting tasks which, however difficult, ought, some day, to be achieved.

If we trace the history of other sciences, we gather no lessons of discouragement. In the case of almost everything which is now exactly measured, we can go back to the age when the vaguest notions prevailed. Previous to the time of Pascal, who would have thought of measuring *doubt* and *belief*? Who could have conceived that the investigation of petty games of chance would have led to the creation of perhaps the most sublime branch of mathematical science – the theory of probabilities? There are sciences which, even within the memory of men now living, have become exactly quantitative. While Quesnay and Baudeau and Le Trosne and Condillac were founding political economy in France, and Adam Smith in England, electricity was a vague phenomenon, which was known, indeed, to be capable of becoming greater or less, but was not measured nor calculated: it is within the last forty or fifty years that a mathematical theory of electricity, founded on exact data, has been established. We now enjoy precise quantitative notions concerning heat, and can measure the temperature of a body to less than $\frac{1}{5000}$ part of a degree Centigrade. Compare this precision with that of the earliest makers of thermometers, the Academicians del Cimento, who used to graduate their instruments by placing them in the sun's rays to obtain a point of fixed temperature.*

De Morgan excellently said†

As to some magnitudes, the clear idea of measurement comes soon: in the case of length, for example. But let us take a more difficult one, and trace the steps by which we acquire and fix the idea: say *weight*. What weight is, we need not know. ... We know it as a magnitude before we give it a name: any child can discover the *more* that there is in a bullet, and the less that there is in a cork of twice its size. Had it not been for the simple contrivance of the balance, which we are well assured (how, it matters not here) enables us to poise equal weights against one another, that is, to detect equality and inequality, and thence to ascertain how many times the greater contains the less, we might not to this day have had much clearer ideas on the subject of weight, as a magnitude, than we have on those of talent, prudence, or self-denial, looked at in the same light.

All who are ever so little of geometers will remember the time when their notions of an angle, as a magnitude, were as vague as, perhaps more so than, those of a moral quality; and they will also remember the steps by which this vagueness became clearness and precision.

Now there can be no doubt that pleasure, pain, labour, utility, value, wealth, money, capital, etc., are all notions admitting of quantity; nay, the whole of our actions in industry and trade certainly depend upon comparing quantities of advantage or disadvantage. Even the theories of moralists have recognized the quantitative character of the subject. Bentham's *Introduction to the Principles of Morals and Legislation* is thoroughly mathematical in the character of the method. He tells us‡ to estimate

* See *Principles of Science*, ch. XIII, on 'The Exact Measurement of Phenomena', 3rd ed., p. 270.
† *Formal Logic*, p. 175.
‡ Chapter IV, on the 'Value of a Lot of Pleasure or Pain, How to be Measured', sec. v, 5.

the tendency of an action thus: 'Sum up all the values of all the pleasures on the one side, and those of all the pains on the other. The balance, if it be on the side of pleasure, will give the good tendency of the act upon the whole, with respect to the interests of that individual person; if on the side of pain, the bad tendency of it upon the whole.' The mathematical character of Bentham's treatment of moral science is also well exemplified in his remarkable tract entitled, 'A Table of the Springs of Action', printed in 1817, as in p. 3, and elsewhere.

'But where', the reader will perhaps ask, 'are your numerical data for estimating pleasures and pains in political economy?' I answer, that my numerical data are more abundant and precise than those possessed by any other science, but that we have not yet known how to employ them. The very abundance of our data is perplexing. There is not a clerk nor book-keeper in the country who is not engaged in recording numerical facts for the economist. The private-account books, the great ledgers of merchants and bankers and public offices, the share lists, price lists, bank returns, monetary intelligence, custom-house and other government returns, are all full of the kind of numerical data required to render economics an exact mathematical science. Thousands of folio volumes of statistical, parliamentary, or other publications await the labour of the investigator. It is partly the very extent and complexity of the information which deters us from its proper use. But it is chiefly a want of method and completeness in this vast mass of information which prevents our employing it in the scientific investigation of the natural laws of economics.

I hesitate to say that men will ever have the means of measuring directly the feelings of the human heart. A unit of pleasure or of pain is difficult even to conceive; but it is the amount of these feelings which is continually prompting us to buying and selling, borrowing and lending, labouring and resting, producing and consuming; and *it is from the quantitative effects of the feelings that we must estimate their comparative amounts.*[21] We can no more know nor measure gravity in its own nature than we can measure a feeling; but, just as we measure gravity by its effects in the motion of a pendulum, so we may estimate the equality or inequality of feelings by the decisions of the human mind. The will is our pendulum, and its oscillations are minutely registered in the price lists of the markets. I know not when we shall have a perfect system of statistics, but the want of it is the only insuperable obstacle in the way of making economics an exact science. In the absence of complete statistics, the science will not be less mathematical, though it will be immensely less useful than if it were, comparatively speaking, exact. A correct theory is the first step towards improvement, by showing what we need and what we might accomplish.

Measurement of Feeling and Motives

Many readers may, even after reading the preceding remarks, consider it quite impossible to create such a calculus as is here contemplated, because we have no means of defining and measuring quantities of feeling, like we can measure a mile, or a right angle, or any other physical quantity. I have granted that we can hardly form the conception of a unit of pleasure or pain, so that the numerical expression of quantities of feeling seems to be out of the question. But we only employ units of measurement in other things to facilitate the comparison of quantities; and if we can compare the quantities directly, we do not need the units. Now the mind of an individual is the balance which makes its own comparisons, and is the final judge of quantities of feeling. As Mr Bain says,* 'It is only an identical proposition to affirm that the greatest of two pleasures, or what appears such, sways the resulting action; for it is this resulting action that alone determines which is the greater.'

Pleasures, in short, are, for the time being, as the mind estimates them; so that we cannot make a choice, or manifest the will in any way, without indicating thereby an excess of pleasure in some direction. It is true that the mind often hesitates and is perplexed in making a choice of great importance: this indicates either varying estimates of the motives, or a feeling of incapacity to grasp the quantities concerned. I should not think of claiming for the mind any accurate power of measuring and adding and

* *The Emotions and the Will*, 1st ed., London, 1859, p. 447.

subtracting feelings, so as to get an exact balance. We can seldom or never affirm that one pleasure is an exact multiple of another; but the reader who carefully criticizes the following theory will find that it seldom involves the comparison of quantities of feeling differing much in amount. The theory turns upon those critical points where pleasures are nearly, if not quite, equal. I never attempt to estimate the whole pleasure gained by purchasing a commodity; the theory merely expresses that, when a man has purchased enough, he would derive equal pleasure from the possession of a small quantity more as he would from the money price of it. Similarly, the whole amount of pleasure that a man gains by a day's labour hardly enters into the question; it is when a man is doubtful whether to increase his hours of labour or not, that we discover an equality between the pain of that extension and the pleasure of the increase of possessions derived from it.

The reader will find, again, that there is never, in any single instance, an attempt made to compare the amount of feeling in one mind with that in another. I see no means by which such comparison can be accomplished. The susceptibility of one mind may, for what we know, be a thousand times greater than that of another. But, provided that the susceptibility was different in a like ratio in all directions, we should never be able to discover the difference. Every mind is thus inscrutable to every other mind, and no common denominator of feeling seems to be possible.[22] But even if we could compare the feelings of different minds, we should not need to do so; for one mind only affects another indirectly. Every event in the outward world is represented in the mind by a corresponding motive, and it is by the balance of these that the will is swayed. But the motive in one mind is weighed only against other motives in the same mind, never against the motives in other minds. Each person is to other persons a portion of the outward world – the *non-ego* as the metaphysicians call it. Thus motives in the mind of A may give rise to phenomena which may be represented by motives in the mind of B; but between A and B there is a gulf. Hence the weighing of motives must always be confined to the bosom of the individual.

I must here point out that, though the theory presumes to investigate the condition of a mind, and bases upon this investigation the whole of economics, practically it is an aggregate of individuals which will be treated. The general forms of the laws of economics are the same in the case of individuals and nations; and, in reality, it is a law operating in the case of multitudes of individuals which gives rise to the aggregate represented in the transactions of a nation.[23] Practically, however, it is quite impossible to detect the operation of general laws of this kind in the actions of one or a few individuals. The motives and conditions are so numerous and complicated that the resulting actions have the appearance of caprice, and are beyond the analytic powers of science. With every increase in the price of such a commodity as sugar, we ought, theoretically speaking, to find every person reducing his consumption by a small amount, and according to some regular law. In reality, many persons would make no change at all; a few, probably, would go to the extent of dispensing with the use of sugar altogether so long as its cost continued to be excessive. It would be by examining the average consumption of sugar in a large population that we might detect a continuous variation, connected with the variation of price by a constant law. It would not, of necessity, happen that the law would be exactly the same in the case of aggregates and individuals, unless all those individuals were of the same character and position as regards wealth and habits; but there would be a more or less regular law to which the same kind of formulae would apply. The use of an average, or, what is the same, an aggregate result, depends upon the high probability that accidental and disturbing causes will operate, in the long run, as often in one direction as the other, so as to neutralize each other. Provided that we have a sufficient number of independent cases, we may then detect the effect of any *tendency*, however slight. Accordingly, questions which appear, and perhaps are, quite indeterminate as regards individuals, may be capable of exact investigation and solution in regard to great masses and wide averages.*

* Concerning the meaning and employment of averages, see *Principles of Science*, ch. XVI, on 'The Method of Means'.

Logical Method of Economics

The logical method of economics as a branch of the social sciences is a subject on which much might be written, and on which very diverse opinions are held at the present day (1879). In this place I can only make a few brief remarks. I think that John Stuart Mill is substantially correct in considering our science to be a case of what he calls* the 'physical or concrete deductive method'; he considers that we may start from some obvious psychological law, as for instance, that a greater gain is preferred to a smaller one, and we may then reason downwards, and predict the phenomena which will be produced in society by such a law. The causes in action in any community are, indeed, so complicated that we shall seldom be able to discover the undisturbed effects of any one law, but, so far as we can analyse the statistical phenomena observed, we obtain a verification of our reasoning. This view of the matter is almost identical with that adopted by the late Professor Cairnes in his lectures on 'The Character and Logical Method of Political Economy'.†

The principal objection to be urged against this treatment of the subject is that Mill has described the concrete deductive method as if it were one of many inductive methods. In my Elementary Lessons in Logic (p. 258), I proposed to call the method the *complete method*, as implying that it combines observation, deduction and induction in the most complete and perfect way. But I subsequently arrived at the conclusion that this so-called inductive method is no special method at all, but simply induction itself in its essential form. As I have fully explained,‡ induction is an *inverse operation*, the inverse of deduction, and can only be performed by the use of deduction. Possessing certain facts of observation, we frame a hypothesis as to the laws governing those facts; we reason from the hypothesis deductively to the results to be expected; and we then examine these results in connexion with the facts in question; coincidence confirms the whole reasoning; conflict obliges us either to seek for disturbing causes, or else to abandon our hypothesis. In this

---

* *System of Logic*, Book VI, ch. IX, sec. iii. † 2nd ed., (Macmillan), 1875.
‡ *Principles of Science*, chs. VII, IX, XII, etc.

procedure there is nothing peculiar; when properly understood it is found to be the method of all the inductive sciences.

The science of economics, however, is in some degree peculiar, owing to the fact, pointed out by J. S. Mill and Cairnes, that its ultimate laws are known to us immediately by intuition, or, at any rate, they are furnished to us ready-made by other mental or physical sciences. That every person will choose the greater apparent good; that human wants are more or less quickly satiated; that prolonged labour becomes more and more painful, are a few of the simple inductions on which we can proceed to reason deductively with great confidence. From these axioms we can deduce the laws of supply and demand, the laws of that difficult conception, value, and all the intricate results of commerce, so far as data are available. The final agreement of our inferences with *a posteriori* observations ratifies our method. But unfortunately this verification is often the least satisfactory part of the process, because, as J. S. Mill has fully explained, the circumstances of a nation are infinitely complicated, and we seldom get two or more instances which are comparable. To fulfil the conditions of inductive inquiry, we ought to be able to observe the effects of a cause coming singly into action, while all other causes remain unaltered. Entirely to prove the good effects of Free Trade in England, for example, we ought to have the nation unaltered in every circumstance except the abolition of burdens and restrictions on trade.* But it is obvious that while Free Trade was being introduced into England, many other causes of prosperity were also coming into action – the progress of invention, the construction of railways, the profuse consumption of coal, the extension of the colonies, etc., etc. Although, then, the beneficent results of Free Trade are great and unquestionable, they could hardly be proved to exist *a posteriori*; they are to be believed because deductive reasoning from premises of almost certain truth leads us confidently to expect such results, and there is nothing in experience which in the least conflicts with our expectations. In spite of occasional revulsions, due to periodical fluctuations depending on physical causes, the immense prosperity of the country since the adoption of Free Trade confirms

* *Principles of Science*, ch. XIX, on 'Experiment'.

our anticipations as far as, under complex circumstances, facts are capable of doing so. It will thus be seen that political economy tends to be more deductive than many of the physical sciences, in which closely approximate verification is often possible; but, even so far as the science is inductive, it involves the use of deductive reasoning, as already explained.

Within the last year or two, much discussion has been raised concerning the philosophical method of political economy, by Mr T. E. Cliffe Leslie's interesting essay on that subject,* as also by the recent address of Dr Ingram at the Dublin meeting of the British Association.† I quite concur with these able and eminent economists so far as to allow that historical investigation is of great importance in social science. But, instead of converting our present science of economics into an historical science, utterly destroying it in the process, I would perfect and develop what we already possess, and at the same time erect a new branch of social science on an historical foundation. This new branch of science, on which many learned men, such as Richard Jones, De Laveleye, Lavergne, Cliffe Leslie, Sir Henry Maine, Thorold Rogers,[24] have already laboured, is doubtless a portion of what Herbert Spencer calls sociology, the science of the evolution of social relations. Political economy is in a chaotic state at present, because there is need of subdividing a too extensive sphere of knowledge. Quesnay, Sir James Steuart, Baudeau, Le Trosne and Condillac first differentiated economics sufficiently to lead it to be regarded as a distinct science; it has since been loaded with great accretions due to the progress of investigation. It is only by subdivision, by recognizing a branch of economic sociology, together possibly with two or three other branches of statistical, jural or social science, that we can rescue our science from its confused state. I have already endeavoured to show the need of this step in a lecture delivered at the University College, in October 1876,‡ and I shall perhaps have a future opportunity of enlarging more upon the subject.

* *Hermathena,* no. iv, Dublin, 1876, p. 1.

† *Statistical Journal,* January 1879, vol. XLI, p. 602. Also reprint by Longmans, 1878.

‡ *Fortnightly Review,* Dec. 1876, 'The Future of Political Economy'. (Reprinted in the author's *Principles of Economics,* 1905.)

To return, however, to the topic of the present work, the theory here given may be described as *the mechanics of utility and self-interest*. Oversights may have been committed in tracing out its details, but in its main features this theory must be the true one. Its method is as sure and demonstrative as that of kinematics or statics, nay, almost as self-evident as are the elements of Euclid, when the real meaning of the formulae is fully seized.

I do not hesitate to say, too, that economics might be gradually erected into an exact science, if only commercial statistics were far more complete and accurate than they are at present, so that the formulae could be endowed with exact meaning by the aid of numerical data. These data would consist chiefly in accurate accounts of the quantities of goods possessed and consumed by the community, and the prices at which they are exchanged. There is no reason whatever why we should not have those statistics, except the cost and trouble of collecting them, and the unwillingness of persons to afford information. The quantities themselves to be measured and registered are most concrete and precise. In a few cases we already have information approximating to completeness, as when a commodity like tea, sugar, coffee or tobacco is wholly imported. But when articles are un-taxed, and partly produced within the country, we have yet the vaguest notions of the quantities consumed. Some slight success is now, at last, attending the efforts to gather agricultural statistics; and the great need felt by men engaged in the cotton and other trades to obtain accurate accounts of stocks, imports and consumption, will probably lead to the publication of far more complete information than we have hitherto enjoyed.

The deductive science of economics must be verified and rendered useful by the purely empirical science of statistics. Theory must be invested with the reality and life of fact. But the difficulties of this union are immensely great, and I appreciate them quite as much as does Cairnes in his admirable lectures 'On the Character and Logical Method of Political Economy'. I make hardly any attempt to employ statistics in this work, and thus I do not pretend to any numerical precision. But, before we attempt any investigation of facts, we must have correct theoretical notions; and of what are here presented, I would say, in the words of Hume, in his *Essay on Commerce*, 'If false, let them be rejected: but no one has a right to entertain a prejudice against them merely because they are out of the common road.'[25]

Relation of Economics to Ethics

I wish to say a few words, in this place, on the relation of economics to moral science. The theory which follows is entirely based on a calculus of pleasure and pain; and the object of economics is to maximize happiness by purchasing pleasure, as it were, at the lowest cost of pain. The language employed may be open to misapprehension, and it may seem as if pleasures and pains of a gross kind were treated as the all-sufficient motives to guide the mind of man. I have no hesitation in accepting the utilitarian theory of morals which does uphold the effect upon the happiness of mankind as the criterion of what is right and wrong. But I have never felt that there is anything in that theory to prevent our putting the widest and highest interpretation upon the terms used.

Jeremy Bentham put forward the utilitarian theory in the most uncompromising manner. According to him, whatever is of interest or importance to us must be the cause of pleasure or of pain; and when the terms are used with a sufficiently wide meaning, pleasure and pain include all the forces which drive us to action. They are explicitly or implicitly the matter of all our calculations, and form the ultimate quantities to be treated in all the moral sciences. The words of Bentham on this subject may require some explanation and qualification, but they are too grand and too full of truth to be omitted.

Nature, [he says] has placed mankind under the governance of two sovereign masters – *pain* and *pleasure*. It is for them alone to point out what we ought to do, as well as to determine what we shall do. On the one hand the standard of right and wrong, on the other the chain of causes and effects, are fastened to their throne. They govern us in all we do, in all we say, in all we think: every effort we can make to throw off our subjection will serve but to demonstrate and confirm it. In words a man may pretend to abjure their empire; but, in reality, he will remain subject to it all the while. The *principle of utility* recognizes this subjection, and assumes it for the foundation of that system, the object of which is to rear the fabric of felicity by the hands of reason and of law. Systems which attempt to question it deal in sounds instead of sense, in caprice instead of reason, in darkness instead of light.*

In connexion with this passage we may take that of Paley, who says, with his usual clear brevity,† 'I hold that pleasures differ in nothing but in continuance and intensity.'

The acceptance or non-acceptance of the basis of the utilitarian doctrine depends, in my mind, on the exact interpretation of the language used. As it seems to me, the feelings of which a man is capable are of various grades. He is always subject to mere physical pleasure or pain, necessarily arising from his bodily wants and susceptibilities. He is capable also of mental and moral feelings of several degrees of elevation. A higher motive may rightly overbalance all considerations belonging even to the next lower range of feelings; but so long as the higher motive does not intervene, it is surely both desirable and right that the lower motives should be balanced against each other. Starting with the lowest stage – it is a man's duty, as it is his natural inclination, to earn sufficient food and whatever else may best satisfy his proper and moderate desires. If the claims of a family or of friends fall upon him, it may become desirable that he should deny his own desires and even his physical needs their full customary gratification. But the claims of a family are only a step to a higher grade of duties.

The safety of a nation, the welfare of great populations, may happen to depend upon his exertions, if he be a soldier or a statesman; claims of a very strong kind may now be overbalanced by claims of a still stronger kind. Nor should I venture to say that, at any point, we have reached the highest rank – the supreme motives which should guide the mind. The statesman may discover a conflict between motives; a measure may promise, as it would seem, the greatest good to great numbers, and yet there may be motives of uprightness and honour that may hinder his promoting the measure. How such difficult questions may be rightly determined it is not my purpose to inquire here.

* *An Introduction to the Principles of Morals and Legislation*, by Jeremy Bentham. Edition of 1823, vol. I, p. 1.

† *Principles of Moral and Political Philosophy*, Book I, ch. VI.

The utilitarian theory holds that all forces influencing the mind of man are pleasures and pains; and Paley went so far as to say that all pleasures and pains are of one kind only. Mr Bain has carried out this view to its complete extent, saying,* 'No amount of complication is ever able to disguise the general fact, that our voluntary activity is moved by only two great classes of stimulants; either a pleasure or a pain, present or remote, must lurk in every situation that drives us into action.' The question certainly appears to turn upon the language used. Call any motive which attracts us to a certain course of conduct, pleasure; and call any motive which deters us from that conduct, pain; and it becomes impossible to deny that all actions are governed by pleasure and pain. But it then becomes indispensable to admit that a single higher pleasure will sometimes neutralize a vast extent and continuance of lower pains. It seems hardly possible to admit Paley's statement, except with an interpretation that would probably reverse his intended meaning. Motives and feelings are certainly of the same kind to the extent that we are able to weight them against each other; but they are, nevertheless, almost incomparable in power and authority.

My present purpose is accomplished in pointing out this hierarchy of feeling, and assigning a proper place to the pleasures and pains with which the economist deals. It is the lowest rank of feelings which we here treat. The calculus of utility aims at supplying the ordinary wants of man at the least cost of labour. Each labourer, in the absence of other motives, is supposed to devote his energy to the accumulation of wealth. A higher calculus of moral right and wrong would be needed to show how he may best employ that wealth for the good of others as well as himself. But when that higher calculus gives no prohibition, we need the lower calculus to gain us the utmost good in matters of moral indifference. There is no rule of morals to forbid our making two blades of grass grow instead of one, if, by the wise expenditure of labour, we can do so. And we may certainly say, with Francis Bacon, 'while philosophers are disputing whether virtue or pleasure be the proper aim of life, do you provide yourself with the instruments of either'.

*The Emotions and the Will, 1st ed., p. 460.

CHAPTER II

Theory of Pleasure and Pain

===

Pleasure and Pain as Quantities

PROCEEDING to consider how pleasure and pain can be estimated as magnitudes, we must undoubtedly accept what Bentham has laid down upon this subject.

> To a person, [he says] considered *by himself*, the value of a pleasure or pain, considered *by itself*, will be greater or less according to the four following circumstances:
> (1) Its *intensity*.
> (2) Its *duration*.
> (3) Its *certainty* or *uncertainty*.
> (4) Its *propinquity* or *remoteness*.
> These are the circumstances which are to be considered in estimating a pleasure or a pain considered each of them by itself.*

Bentham† goes on to consider three other circumstances which relate to the ultimate and complete result of any act or feeling; these are:

> (5) *Fecundity*, or the chance a feeling has of being followed by feelings of the same kind; that is, pleasures, if it be a pleasure; pains, if it be a pain.
> (6) *Purity*, or the chance it has of not being followed by feelings of an opposite kind. And
> (7) *Extent*, or the number of persons to whom it extends, and who are affected by it.

These three last circumstances are of high importance as regards the theory of morals; but they will not enter into the more

* An Introduction to the Principles of Morals and Legislation, 2nd ed., 1823, vol. I, p. 49. The earliest writer who, so far as I know, has treated pleasure and pain in a definitely quantitative manner, is Francis Hutcheson, in his *Essay on the Nature and Conduct of the Passions and Affections*, 1728, pp. 34–43, 126, etc.
  † Introduction, p. 50.

simple and restricted problem which we attempt to solve in economics.

A feeling, whether of pleasure or of pain, must be regarded as having two dimensions, or modes of varying in regard to quantity. Every feeling must last some time, and it may last a longer or shorter time; while it lasts, it may be more or less acute and intense. If in two cases the duration of feeling is the same, that case will produce the greater quantity which is the more intense; or we may say that, with the same duration, the quantity will be proportional to the intensity. On the other hand, if the intensity of a feeling were to remain constant, the quantity of feeling would increase with its duration. Two days of the same degree of happiness are to be twice as much desired as one day; two days of suffering are to be twice as much feared. If the intensity ever continued fixed, the whole quantity would be found by multiplying the number of units of intensity into the number of units of duration. Pleasure and pain, then, are quantities possessing two dimensions, just as superficies possesses the two dimensions of length and breadth.

In almost every case, however, the intensity of feeling will change from moment to moment. Incessant variation characterizes our states of mind, and this is the source of the main difficulties of the subject. Nevertheless, if these variations can be traced out at all, or any approach to method and law can be detected, it will be possible to form a conception of the resulting quantity of feeling. We may imagine that the intensity changes at the end of every minute, but remains constant in the intervals. The quantity during each minute may be represented, as in figure 1, by a rectangle whose base is supposed to correspond to the duration of a minute, and whose height is proportional to the intensity of the feeling during the minute in question. Along the line ox we measure *time*, and along parallels to the perpendicular line oy we measure *intensity*. Each of the rectangles between pm and qn represents the feeling of one minute. The aggregate quantity of feeling generated during the time mn will then be represented by the aggregate area of the rectangles between pm and qn. In this case the intensity of the feeling is supposed to be gradually declining.

But it is an artificial assumption that the intensity would vary by sudden steps and at regular intervals. The error thus introduced will not be great if the intervals of time are very short, and will

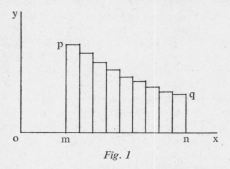

Fig. 1

be less the shorter the intervals are made. To avoid all error, we must imagine the intervals of time to be infinitely short; that is, we must treat the intensity as varying continuously. Thus the proper representation of the variation of feeling is found in a

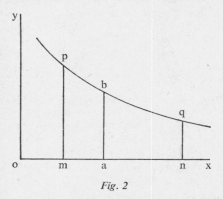

Fig. 2

curve of more or less complex character. In figure 2 the height of each point of the curve *pq*, above the horizontal line *ox*, indicates the intensity of feeling in a moment of time; and the whole quantity of feeling generated in the time *mn* is measured by the area bounded by the lines *pm*, *qn*, *mn* and *pq*. The feeling belonging to any other time, *ma*, will be measured by the space *mabp* cut off by the perpendicular line *ab*.

Pain the Negative of Pleasure

It will be readily conceded that pain is the opposite of pleasure; so that to decrease pain is to increase pleasure; to add pain is to decrease pleasure. Thus we may treat pleasure and pain as positive and negative quantities are treated in algebra. The algebraic sum of a series of pleasures and pains will be obtained by adding the pleasures together and the pains together, and then striking the balance by subtracting the smaller amount from the greater. Our object will always be to maximize the resulting sum in the direction of pleasure, which we may fairly call the positive direction. This object we shall accomplish by accepting everything, and undertaking every action of which the resulting pleasure exceeds the pain which is undergone; we must avoid every object or action which leaves a balance in the other direction.

The most important parts of the theory will turn upon the exact equality, without regard to sign, of the pleasure derived from the possession of an object, and the pain encountered in its acquisition. I am glad, therefore, to quote the following passage from Mr Bain's treatise on *The Emotions and the Will*,* in which he exactly expresses the opposition of pleasure and pain:

When pain is followed by pleasure, there is a tendency in the one, more or less, to neutralize the other. When the pleasure exactly assuages the pain, we say that the two are equivalent, or equal in amount, although of opposite nature, like hot and cold, positive and negative; and when two different kinds of pleasure have the power of satiating the same amount of pain, there is fair ground for pronouncing them of equal emotional power. Just as acids are pronounced equivalent when in amount sufficient to neutralize the same portion of alkali, and as heat is estimated by the quantity of snow melted by it, so pleasures are fairly compared as to their total efficacy on the mind, by the amount of pain that they are capable of submerging. In this sense there may be an effective estimate of degree.

* 1st ed., p. 30.

Anticipated Feeling

Bentham has stated* that one of the main elements in estimating the force of a pleasure or pain is its *propinquity* or *remoteness*. It is certain that a very large part of what we experience in life depends not on the actual circumstances of the moment so much as on the anticipation of future events. As Mr Bain says,† 'The foretaste of pleasure is pleasure begun: every actual delight casts before it a corresponding ideal.' Every one must have felt that the enjoyment actually experienced at any moment is but limited in amount, and usually fails to answer to the anticipations which have been formed. 'Man never is but always to be blest' is a correct description of our ordinary state of mind; and there is little doubt that, in minds of much intelligence and foresight, the greatest force of feeling and motive arises from the anticipation of a long-continued future.

Now, between the actual amount of feeling anticipated and that which is felt there must be some natural relation, very variable no doubt according to circumstances, the intellectual standing of the race, or the character of the individual; and yet subject to some general laws of variation. The intensity of present anticipated feeling must, to use a mathematical expression, be *some function of the future actual feeling and of the intervening time*, and it must increase as we approach the moment of realization. The change, again, must be less rapid the farther we are from the moment, and more rapid as we come nearer to it. An event which is to happen a year hence affects us on the average about as much one day as another; but an event of importance, which is to take place three days hence, will probably affect us on each of the intervening days more acutely than the last.‡

This power of anticipation must have a large influence in economics; for upon it is based all accumulation of stocks of commodity to be consumed at a future time. That class or race

* See above, p. 94.
† *The Emotions and the Will*, 1st ed., p. 74.
‡ Meaning presumably: '. . . more acutely than on the previous day'. – H.S.J.

of men who have the most foresight will work most for the future. The untutored savage, like the child, is wholly occupied with the pleasures and the troubles of the moment; the morrow is dimly felt; the limit of his horizon is but a few days off. The wants of a future year, or of a lifetime, are wholly unforeseen. But, in a state of civilization, a vague though powerful feeling of the future is the main incentive to industry and saving. The cares of the moment are but ripples on the tide of achievement and hope. We may safely call that man happy who, however lowly his position and limited his possessions, can always hope for more than he has, and can feel that every moment of exertion tends to realize his aspirations. He, on the contrary, who seizes the enjoyment of the passing moment without regard to coming times, must discover sooner or later that his stock of pleasure is on the wane, and that even hope begins to fail.

Uncertainty of Future Events

In admitting the force of anticipated feeling, we are compelled to take account of the uncertainty of all future events. We ought never to estimate the value of that which may or may not happen as if it would certainly happen. When it is as likely as not that I shall receive £100, the chance is worth but £50, because if, for a great many times in succession, I purchase the chance at this rate, I shall almost certainly neither lose nor gain. The test of correct estimation of probabilities is that the calculations agree with fact on the average. If we apply this rule to all future interests, we must reduce our estimate of any feeling in the ratio of the numbers expressing the probability of its occurrence. If the probability is only one in ten that I shall have a certain day of pleasure, I ought to anticipate the pleasure with one-tenth of the force which would belong to it if certain. In selecting a course of action which depends on uncertain events, as, in fact, does everything in life, I should multiply the quantity of feeling attaching to every future event by the fraction denoting its probability. A great casualty, which is very unlikely to happen, may not be so important as a slight casualty which is nearly sure to happen.

Almost unconsciously we make calculations of this kind more or less accurately in all the ordinary affairs of life; and in systems of life, fire, marine, or other insurance, we carry out the calculations to great perfection. In all industry directed to future purposes, we must take similar account of our want of knowledge of what is to be.

CHAPTER III

Theory of Utility

Definition of Terms

PLEASURE and pain are undoubtedly the ultimate objects of the calculus of economics. To satisfy our wants to the utmost with the least effort – to procure the greatest amount of what is desirable at the expense of the least that is undesirable – in other words, *to maximize pleasure*, is the problem of economics. But it is convenient to transfer our attention as soon as possible to the physical objects or actions which are the source to us of pleasures and pains. A very large part of the labour of any community is spent upon the production of the ordinary necessaries and conveniences of life, such as food, clothing, buildings, utensils, furniture, ornaments, etc.; and the aggregate of these things, therefore, is the immediate object of our attention.

It is desirable to introduce at once, and to define, some terms which facilitate the expression of the principles of economics. By a *commodity* we shall understand any object, substance, action or service, which can afford pleasure or ward off pain. The name was originally abstract, and denoted the quality of anything by which it was capable of serving man. Having acquired, by a common process of confusion, a concrete signification, it will be well to retain the word entirely for that signification, and employ the term *utility* to denote the abstract quality whereby an object serves our purposes, and becomes entitled to rank as a commodity. Whatever can produce pleasure or prevent pain *may* possess utility. J.-B. Say has correctly and briefly defined utility as '*la faculté qu'ont les choses de pouvoir servir à l'homme, de quelque manière que ce soit*'. The food which prevents the pangs of hunger, the clothes which fend off the cold of winter, possess incontestable utility; but we must beware of restricting the meaning of the word by any moral considerations. Anything

101

which an individual is found to desire and to labour for must be assumed to possess for him utility. In the science of economics we treat men not as they ought to be, but as they are. Bentham, in establishing the foundations of moral science in his great *Introduction to the Principles of Morals and Legislation* (p. 3), thus comprehensively defines the term in question: 'By utility is meant that property in any object, whereby it tends to produce benefit, advantage, pleasure, good, or happiness (all this, in the present case, comes to the same thing), or (what comes again to the same thing) to prevent the happening of mischief, pain, evil, or unhappiness to the party whose interest is considered.'

This perfectly expresses the meaning of the word in economics, provided that the will or inclination of the person immediately concerned is taken as the sole criterion, for the time, of what is or is not useful.

The Laws of Human Want

Economics must be founded upon a full and accurate investigation of the conditions of utility; and, to understand this element, we must necessarily examine the wants and desires of man. We, first of all, need a theory of the consumption of wealth. J. S. Mill, indeed, has given an opinion inconsistent with this. 'Political economy', he says,* 'has nothing to do with the consumption of wealth, further than as the consideration of it is inseparable from that of production, or from that of distribution. We know not of any laws of the consumption of wealth, as the subject of a distinct science; they can be no other than the laws of human enjoyment.'

But it is surely obvious that economics does rest upon the laws of human enjoyment; and that, if those laws are developed by no other science, they must be developed by economists. We labour to produce with the sole object of consuming, and the kinds and amounts of goods produced must be determined with regard to what we want to consume. Every manufacturer knows and feels how closely he must anticipate the tastes and needs of

* *Essays on some Unsettled Questions of Political Economy*, London, 1844, p. 132.

his customers: his whole success depends upon it; and, in like manner, the theory of economics must begin with a correct theory of consumption. Many economists have had a clear perception of this truth. Lord Lauderdale distinctly states * that 'the great and important step towards ascertaining the causes of the direction which industry takes in nations . . . seems to be the discovery of what dictates the proportion of demand for the various articles which are produced'. Senior, in his admirable treatise, has also recognized this truth, and pointed out what he calls the *law of variety* in human requirements. The necessaries of life are so few and simple that a man is soon satisfied in regard to these, and desires to extend his range of enjoyment. His first object is to vary his food; but there soon arises the desire of variety and elegance in dress; and to this succeeds the desire to build, to ornament and to furnish – tastes which, where they exist, are absolutely insatiable, and seem to increase with every improvement in civilization.†

Many French economists also have observed that human wants are the ultimate subject-matter of economics; Bastiat, for instance, in his *Harmonies of Political Economy*, says,‡ '*Wants, Efforts, Satisfaction* – this is the circle of Political Economy.'

In still later years, Courcelle-Seneuil actually commenced his treatise with a definition of *want* – '*Le besoin économique est un désir qui a pour but la possession et la jouissance d'un objet matériel.*' § And I conceive that he has given the best possible statement of the problem of economics when he expresses its object as '*à satisfaire nos besoins avec la moindre somme de travail possible*'.¶

Professor Hearn also begins his excellent treatise, entitled *Plutology, or the Theory of Efforts to supply Human Wants*, with a

* *Inquiry into the Nature and Origin of Public Wealth*, 2nd ed., 1819, p. 306; 1st ed., 1804.

† *Encyclopaedia Metropolitana*, article 'Political Economy', p. 133; 5th ed. of reprint, p. 11.[26]

‡ *Harmonies of Political Economy*, translated by P. J. Stirling, 1860, p. 65.

§ *Traité Théorique et Pratique d'Économie Politique*, par J. G. Courcelle-Seneuil, 2me ed., Paris, 1867, tome I, p. 25.

¶ Ibid., p. 33.

chapter in which he considers the nature of the wants impelling man to exertion.

The writer, however, who seems to me to have reached the deepest comprehension of the foundations of economics is T. E. Banfield. His course of lectures delivered in the University of Cambridge in 1844, and published under the title of *The Organization of Labour*, is highly interesting, though not always correct. In the following passage* he profoundly points out that the scientific basis of economics is in a theory of consumption; I need make no excuse for quoting this passage at full length.

The lower wants man experiences in common with brutes. The cravings of hunger and thirst, the effects of heat and cold, of drought and damp, he feels with more acuteness than the rest of the animal world. His sufferings are doubtless sharpened by the consciousness that he has no right to be subject to such inflictions. Experience, however, shows that privations of various kinds affect men differently in degree according to the circumstances in which they are placed. For some men the privation of certain enjoyments is intolerable, whose loss is not even felt by others. Some, again, sacrifice all that others hold dear for the gratification of longings and aspirations that are incomprehensible to their neighbours. Upon this complex foundation of low wants and high aspirations the Political Economist has to build the theory of production and consumption.

An examination of the nature and intensity of man's wants shows that this connection between them gives to Political Economy its scientific basis. The first proposition of the theory of consumption is, that *the satisfaction of every lower want in the scale creates a desire of a higher character*. If the higher desire existed previous to the satisfaction of the primary want, it becomes more intense when the latter is removed. The removal of a primary want commonly awakens the sense of more than one secondary privation: thus a full supply of ordinary food not only excites to delicacy in eating, but awakens attention to clothing. The highest grade in the scale of wants, that of pleasure derived from the beauties of nature and art, is usually confined to men who are exempted from all the lower privations. Thus the demand for, and the consumption of, objects of refined enjoyment has its lever in the facility with which the primary wants are satisfied. This,

*2nd ed., p. 11.

therefore, is the key to the true theory of value. Without relative value in the objects to the acquirement of which we direct our power, there would be no foundation for Political Economy as a science.

Utility is not an Intrinsic Quality

My principal work now lies in tracing out the exact nature and conditions of utility. It seems strange indeed that economists have not bestowed more minute attention on a subject which doubtless furnishes the true key to the problem of economics.

In the first place, utility, though a quality of things, is *no inherent quality*. It is better described as *a circumstance of things* arising from their relation to man's requirements. As Senior most accurately says, 'Utility denotes no intrinsic quality in the things which we call useful; it merely expresses their relations to the pains and pleasures of mankind.' We can never, therefore, say absolutely that some objects have utility and others have not. The ore lying in the mine, the diamond escaping the eye of the searcher, the wheat lying unreaped, the fruit ungathered for want of consumers, have no utility at all. The most wholesome and necessary kinds of food are useless unless there are hands to collect and mouths to eat them sooner or later. Nor, when we consider the matter closely, can we say that all portions of the same commodity possess equal utility. Water, for instance, may be roughly described as the most useful of all substances. A quart of water per day has the high utility of saving a person from dying in a most distressing manner. Several gallons a day may possess much utility for such purposes as cooking and washing; but after an adequate supply is secured for these uses, any additional quantity is a matter of comparative indifference. All that we can say, then, is, that water, up to a certain quantity, is indispensable; that further quantities will have various degrees of utility; but that beyond a certain quantity the utility sinks gradually to zero; it may even become negative, that is to say, further supplies of the same substance may become inconvenient and hurtful.

Exactly the same considerations apply more or less clearly to every other article. A pound of bread per day supplied to a person saves him from starvation, and has the highest conceivable utility.

A second pound per day has also no slight utility: it keeps him in a state of comparative plenty, though it be not altogether indispensable. A third pound would begin to be superfluous. It is clear, then, that *utility is not proportional to commodity*: the very same articles vary in utility according as we already possess more or less of the same article. The like may be said of other things. One suit of clothes per annum is necessary, a second convenient, a third desirable, a fourth not unacceptable; but we, sooner or later, reach a point at which further supplies are not desired with any perceptible force, unless it be for subsequent use.

Law of the Variation of Utility

Let us now investigate this subject a little more closely. Utility must be considered as measured by, or even as actually identical with, the addition made to a person's happiness. It is a convenient name for the aggregate of the favourable balance of feeling produced – the sum of the pleasure created and the pain prevented. We must now carefully discriminate between the *total utility* arising from any commodity and the utility attaching to any particular portion of it. Thus the total utility of the food we eat consists in maintaining life, and may be considered as infinitely great; but if we were to subtract a tenth part from what we eat daily, our loss would be but slight. We should certainly not lose a tenth part of the whole utility of food to us. It might be doubtful whether we should suffer any harm at all.

Let us imagine the whole quantity of food which a person consumes on an average during twenty-four hours to be divided into ten equal parts. If his food be reduced by the last part, he will suffer but little; if a second tenth part be deficient, he will feel the want distinctly; the subtraction of the third tenth part will be decidedly injurious; with every subsequent subtraction of a tenth part his sufferings will be more and more serious, until at length he will be on the verge of starvation. Now, if we call each of the tenth parts *an increment*, the meaning of these facts is that each increment of food is less necessary, or possesses less utility, than the previous one. To explain this variation of utility we may make use of space-representations, which I have found convenient in illustrating the laws of economics in my college lectures during fifteen years past.

Let the line *ox* be used as a measure of the quantity of food, and let it be divided into ten equal parts to correspond to the ten portions of food mentioned above. On these equal lines are constructed rectangles, and the area of each rectangle may be assumed to represent the utility of the increment of food corre-

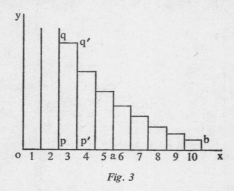

Fig. 3

sponding to its base. Thus the utility of the last increment is small, being proportional to the small rectangle on x. As we approach towards *o*, each increment bears a larger rectangle, that standing upon 3 being the largest complete rectangle. The utility of the next increment, 2, is undefined, as also that of 1, since these portions of food would be indispensable to life, and their utility, therefore, infinitely great.

We can now form a clear notion of the utility of the whole food, or of any part of it, for we have only to add together the proper rectangles. The utility of the first half of the food will be the sum of the rectangles standing on the line *oa*; that of the second half will be represented by the sum of the smaller rectangles between *a* and *b*. The total utility of the food will be the whole sum of the rectangles, and will be infinitely great.

The comparative utility of the several portions is, however, the most important point. <u>Utility may be treated</u> * as *a quantity*

* The theory of dimensions of utility is fully stated in a subsequent section.

107

of two dimensions, one dimension consisting in the quantity of the commodity, and another in the intensity of the effect produced upon the consumer. Now, the quantity of the commodity is measured on the horizontal line *ox*, and the intensity of utility will be measured by the length of the upright lines, or *ordinates*. The intensity of utility of the third increment is measured either by *pq*, or *p'q'*, and its utility is the product of the units in *pp'* multiplied by those in *pq*.

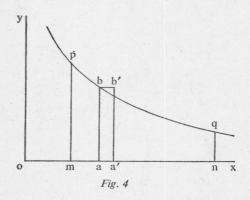

Fig. 4

But the division of the food into ten equal parts is an arbitrary supposition. If we had taken twenty or a hundred or more equal parts, the same general principle would hold true, namely, that each small portion would be less useful and necessary than the last. The law may be considered to hold true theoretically, however small the increments are made; and in this way we shall at last reach a figure which is undistinguishable from a continuous curve. The notion of infinitely small quantities of food may seem absurd as regards the consumption of one individual; but, when we consider the consumption of a nation as a whole, the consumption may well be conceived to increase or diminish by quantities which are, practically speaking, infinitely small compared with the whole consumption. The laws which we are about to trace out are to be conceived as theoretically true of the individual; they can only be practically verified as regards the aggregate transactions, productions, and consumptions of a large body of people. But the laws of the aggregate depend of course upon the laws applying to individual cases.

The law of the variation of the degree of utility of food may thus be represented by a continuous curve pbq (figure 4), and the perpendicular height of each point of the curve above the line ox, represents the degree of utility of the commodity when a certain amount has been consumed.

Thus, when the quantity oa has been consumed, the degree of utility corresponds to the length of the line ab; for if we take a very little more food, aa', its utility will be the product of aa' and ab very nearly, and more nearly the less is the magnitude of aa'. The degree of utility is thus properly measured by the height of a very narrow rectangle corresponding to a very small quantity of food, which theoretically ought to be infinitely small.

Total Utility and Degree of Utility

We are now in a position to appreciate perfectly the difference between the *total utility* of any commodity and *the degree of utility* of the commodity at any point. These are, in fact, quantities of altogether different kinds, the first being represented by an area, and the second by a line. We must consider how we may express these notions in appropriate mathematical language.

Let x signify, as is usual in mathematical books, the quantity which varies independently – in this case the quantity of commodity. Let u denote the *whole utility* proceeding from the consumption of x. Then u will be, as mathematicians say, *a function of x*; that is, it will vary in some continuous and regular, but probably unknown, manner, when x is made to vary. Our great object at present, however, is to express the *degree of utility*.

Mathematicians employ the sign Δ prefixed to a sign of quantity, such as x, to signify that a quantity of the same nature as x, but small in proportion to x, is taken into consideration. Thus Δx means a small portion of x, and $x + \Delta x$ is therefore a quantity a little greater than x. Now, when x is a quantity of commodity, the utility of $x + \Delta x$ will be more than that of x as a general rule. Let the whole utility of $x + \Delta x$ be denoted by

$u + \Delta u$; then it is obvious that the increment of utility Δu belongs to the increment of commodity Δx; and if, for the sake of argument, we suppose the degree of utility uniform over the whole of Δx, which is nearly true owing to its smallness, we shall find the corresponding degree of utility by dividing Δu by Δx.

We find these considerations fully illustrated by figure 4, in which oa represents x, and ab is the degree of utility at the point a. Now, if we increase x by the small quantity aa', or Δx, the utility is increased by the small rectangle $abb'a'$, or Δu; and, since a rectangle is the product of its sides, we find that the length of the line ab, the degree of utility, is represented by the fraction $\dfrac{\Delta u}{\Delta x}$.

As already explained, however, the utility of a commodity may be considered to vary with perfect continuity, so that we commit a small error in assuming it to be uniform over the whole increment Δx. To avoid this we must imagine Δx to be reduced to an infinitely small size, Δu decreasing with it. The smaller the quantities are, the more nearly we shall have a correct expression for ab, the degree of utility at the point a. Thus the *limit* of this fraction $\dfrac{\Delta u}{\Delta x}$, or, as it is commonly expressed, $\dfrac{du}{dx}$, is the degree of utility corresponding to the quantity of commodity x. *The degree of utility is*, in mathematical language, *the differential coefficient of u considered as a function of x*, and will itself be another function of x.

We shall seldom need to consider the degree of utility except as regards the last increment which has been consumed, or, which comes to the same thing, the next increment which is about to be consumed. I shall therefore commonly use the expression *final degree of utility*, as meaning the degree of utility of the last addition, or the next possible addition of a very small, or infinitely small, quantity to the existing stock. In ordinary circumstances, too, the final degree of utility will not be great compared with what it might be. Only in famine or other extreme circumstances do we approach the higher degrees of utility. Accordingly, we can often treat the lower portions of the curves of variation bq, figure 4) which concern ordinary commercial transactions, we leave out of sight the portions beyond p or q. It is also evident that we may know the degree of utility at any point while ignorant of the total utility, that is, the area of the whole curve. To be able to estimate the total enjoyment of a person would be an interesting thing, but it would not be really so important as to be able to estimate the additions and subtractions to his enjoyment, which circumstances occasion. In the same way a very wealthy person may be quite unable to form any accurate statement of his aggregate wealth; but he may nevertheless have exact accounts of income and expenditure, that is, of additions and subtractions.

Variation of the Final Degree of Utility

The final degree of utility is that function upon which the theory of economics will be found to turn. Economists, generally speaking, have failed to discriminate between this function and the total utility, and from this confusion has arisen much perplexity. Many commodities which are most useful to us are esteemed and desired but little. We cannot live without water, and yet in ordinary circumstances we set no value on it. Why is this? Simply because we usually have so much of it that its final degree of utility is reduced nearly to zero. We enjoy, every day, the almost infinite utility of water, but then we do not need to consume more than we have. Let the supply run short by drought, and we begin to feel the higher degrees of utility, of which we think but little at other times.

The variation of the function expressing the final degree of utility is the all-important point in economic problems. We may state as a general law, that *the degree of utility varies with the quantity of commodity, and ultimately decreases as that quantity increases*. No commodity can be named which we continue to desire with the same force, whatever be the quantity already in use or possession. All our appetites are capable of *satisfaction* or *satiety* sooner or later, in fact, both these words mean, etymologically, that we have had *enough*, so that more is of no use to us. It does not follow, indeed, that the degree of utility will always sink to zero. This may be the case with some things, especially the simple animal requirements, such as food, water, air, etc.

111

But the more refined and intellectual our needs become, the less are they capable of satiety. To the desire for articles of taste, science or curiosity, when once excited, there is hardly a limit.

This great principle of the ultimate decrease of the final degree of utility of any commodity is implied in the writings of many economists, though seldom distinctly stated. It is the real law which lies at the basis of Senior's so-called 'law of variety'. Indeed, Senior incidentally states the law itself. He says,

It is obvious that our desires do not aim so much at quantity as at diversity. Not only are there limits to the pleasure which commodities of any given class can afford, but the pleasure diminishes in a rapidly increasing ratio long before these limits are reached. Two articles of the same kind will seldom afford twice the pleasure of one, and still less will ten give five times the pleasure of two. In proportion, therefore, as any article is abundant, the number of those who are provided with it, and do not wish, or wish but little, to increase their provision, is likely to be great; and, so far as they are concerned, the additional supply loses all, or nearly all, its utility. And, in proportion to its scarcity, the number of those who are in want of it, and the degree in which they want it, are likely to be increased; and its utility, or, in other words, the pleasure which the possession of a given quantity of it will afford, increases proportionally.*

Banfield's 'law of the subordination of wants' also rests upon the same basis. It cannot be said, with accuracy, that the satisfaction of a lower want *creates* a higher want; it merely permits the higher want to manifest itself.[27] We distribute our labour and possessions in such a way as to satisfy the more pressing wants first. If food runs short, the all-absorbing question is how to obtain more, because, at the moment, more pleasure or pain depends upon food than upon any other commodity. But, when food is moderately abundant, its final degree of utility falls very low, and wants of a more complex and less satiable nature become comparatively prominent.

The writer, however, who appears to me to have most clearly appreciated the nature and importance of the law of utility, is Richard Jennings, who, in 1855, published a small book called

* *Encyclopaedia Metropolitana*, p. 133. Reprint, p. 12.

the *Natural Elements of Political Economy*.* This work treats of the physical groundwork of economics, showing its dependence on physiological laws. It displays great insight into the real basis of economics; yet I am not aware that economists have bestowed the slightest attention on Jennings's views.† I give, therefore, a full extract from his remarks on the nature of utility. It will be seen that the law, as I state it, is no novelty, and that careful deduction from principles in our possession is alone needed to give us a correct theory of economics.

To turn from the relative effect of commodities, in producing sensations, to those which are absolute, or dependent only on the quantity of each commodity, it is but too well known to every condition of men, that the degree of each sensation which is produced, is by no means commensurate with the quantity of the commodity applied to the senses. . . . These effects require to be closely observed, because they are the foundation of the changes of money price, which valuable objects command in times of varied scarcity and abundance; we shall therefore here direct our attention to them for the purpose of ascertaining the nature of the law according to which the sensations that attend on consumption vary in degree with changes in the quantity of the commodity consumed.

We may gaze upon an object until we can no longer discern it, listen until we can no longer hear, smell until the sense of odour is exhausted, taste until the object becomes nauseous, and touch until it becomes painful; we may consume food until we are fully satisfied, and use stimulants until more would cause pain. On the other hand, the same object offered to the special senses for a moderate duration of time, and the same food or stimulants consumed when we are exhausted or weary, may convey much gratification. If the whole quantity of the commodity consumed during the interval of these two states of sensation, the state of satiety and the state of inanition, be conceived to be divided into a number of equal parts, each marked with its proper degrees of sensation, the question to be determined will be, what relation does the difference in the degrees of the sensation bear to the difference in the quantities of the commodity?

First, with respect to all commodities, our feelings show that the

* London, Longmans.

† Cairnes is, however, an exception. See his work on *The Character and Logical Method of Political Economy*, London, 1857, p. 81; 2nd ed., Macmillan, 1875, pp. 56, 110, 224, App. B.

degrees of satisfaction do not proceed *pari passu* with the quantities consumed; they do not advance equally with each instalment of the commodity offered to the senses, and then suddenly stop; but diminish gradually, until they ultimately disappear, and further instalments can produce no further satisfaction. In this progressive scale the increments of sensation resulting from equal increments of the commodity are obviously less and less at each step – each degree of sensation is less than the preceding degree. Placing ourselves at that middle point of sensation, the *juste milieu*, the *aurea mediocritas*, the ἀριστον μετρον of sages, which is the most usual status of the mass of mankind, and which, therefore, is the best position that can be chosen for measuring deviations from the usual amount, we may say that the law which expresses the relation of degrees of sensation to quantities of commodities is of this character: if the average or temperate quantity of commodities be increased, the satisfaction derived is increased in a less degree, and ultimately ceases to be increased at all; if the average or temperate quantity be diminished, the loss of more and more satisfaction will continually ensue, and the detriment thence arising will ultimately become exceedingly great.*

Disutility and Discommodity

A few words will suffice to suggest that as utility corresponds to the production of pleasure, or, at least, a favourable alteration in the balance of pleasure and pain, so negative utility will consist in the production of pain, or the unfavourable alteration of the balance. In reality we must be almost as often concerned with the one as with the other; nevertheless, economists have not employed any distinct technical terms to express that production of pain, which accompanies so many actions of life. They have fixed their attention on the more agreeable aspect of the matter. It will be allowable, however, to appropriate the good English word *discommodity*, to signify any substance or action which is the opposite of *commodity*, that is to say, *anything which we desire to get rid of*, like ashes or sewage. Discommodity is, indeed, properly an abstract form signifying inconvenience, or disadvantage; but, as the noun *commodities* has been used in the English language for four hundred years at least as a concrete term,† so we may now

*Pp. 96–9.

†It is used precisely in its present economic sense in the remarkable 'Processe of the Libelle of English Policie', probably written in the fifteenth

convert discommodity into a concrete term, and speak of *discommodities* as substances or things which possess the quality of causing inconvenience or harm. For the abstract notion, the opposite or negative of utility, we may invent the term *disutility*, which will mean something different from inutility, or the absence of utility. It is obvious that utility passes through inutility before changing into disutility, these notions being related as $+$, 0 and $-$.

Distribution of Commodity in Different Uses

The principles of utility may be illustrated by considering the mode in which we distribute a commodity when it is capable of several uses. There are articles which may be employed for many distinct purposes: thus, barley may be used either to make beer, spirits, bread, or to feed cattle; sugar may be used to eat, or for producing alcohol; timber may be used in construction, or as fuel; iron and other metals may be applied to many different purposes. Imagine, then, a community in the possession of a certain stock of barley; what principles will regulate their mode of consuming it? Or, as we have not yet reached the subject of exchange, imagine an isolated family, or even an individual, possessing an adequate stock, and using some in one way and some in another. The theory of utility gives, theoretically speaking, a complete solution of the question.

Let s be the whole stock of some commodity, and let it be capable of two distinct uses. Then we may represent the two quantities appropriated to these uses by x_1 and y_1, it being a condition that $x_1 + y_1 = s$. The person may be conceived as successively expending small quantities of the commodity. Now it is the inevitable tendency of human nature to choose that course which appears to offer the greatest advantage at the moment. Hence, when the person remains satisfied with the distribution he has made, it follows that no alteration would yield him more

century, and printed in Hakluyt's *Voyages*. (Richard Hakluyt, *The Principal Navigations, Voyages, Traffiques and Discoveries of the English Nation*, London 1598; reprinted Glasgow, 1902, vol. II, pp. 144–7.)

pleasure; which amounts to saying that an increment of commodity would yield exactly as much utility in one use as in another. Let Δu_1, Δu_2, be the increments of utility, which might arise respectively from consuming an increment of commodity in the two different ways. When the distribution is completed, we ought to have $\Delta u_1 = \Delta u_2$; or at the limit we have the equation

$$\frac{du_1}{dx} = \frac{du_2}{dy}$$

which is true when x, y are respectively equal to x_1, y_1. We must, in other words, have the *final degrees of utility* in the two uses equal.[28]

The same reasoning which applies to uses of the same commodity will evidently apply to any two uses, and hence to all uses simultaneously, so that we obtain a series of equations less numerous by a unit than the number of ways of using the commodity. The general result is that commodity, if consumed by a perfectly wise being, must be consumed with a maximum production of utility.

We should often find these equations to fail. Even when x is equal to $\frac{99}{100}$ of the stock, its degree of utility might still exceed the utility attaching to the remaining $\frac{1}{100}$ part in either of the other uses. This would mean that it was preferable to give the whole commodity to the first use. Such a case might perhaps be said to be not the exception but the rule; for, whenever a commodity is capable of only one use, the circumstance is theoretically represented by saying, that the final degree of utility in this employment always exceeds that in any other employment.

Under peculiar circumstances great changes may take place in the consumption of a commodity. In a time of scarcity the utility of barley as food might rise so high as to exceed altogether its utility, even as regards the smallest quantity, in producing alcoholic liquors; its consumption in the latter way would then cease. In a besieged town the employment of articles becomes revolutionized. Things of great utility in other respects are ruthlessly applied to strange purposes. In Paris a vast stock of horses were eaten, not so much because they were useless in other ways, as because they were needed more strongly as food. A certain stock of horses had, indeed, to be retained as a necessary aid to locomotion, so that the equation of the degrees of utility never wholly failed.

Theory of Dimensions of Economic Quantities

In the recent progress of physical science, it has been found requisite to use notation for the purpose of displaying clearly the natures and relations of its various kinds of quantities concerned. Each different sort of quantity is, of course, expressed in terms of its own appropriate unit – length in terms of yards, or metres; surface, or area, in terms of square yards or square metres; time in terms of seconds, days or years; and so forth. But the more complicated quantities are evidently related to the simpler ones. Surface is measured by the *square yard* – that is to say, the unit of length is involved twice over, and if by L we denote one dimension of length, then the dimensions of surface are LL, or L^2. The dimensions of cubic capacity are in like manner LLL, or L^3.

In these cases the dimensions all enter *positively*, because the number of units in the cubical body, for instance, is found by *multiplying* the numbers of units in its length, breadth and depth. In other cases a dimension enters *negatively*. Thus denoting time by T, it is easy to see that the dimensions of velocity will be L *divided by* T, or LT^{-1}, because the number of units in the velocity of a body is found by *dividing* the units of length passed over by the units of time occupied in passing. In expressing the dimensions of thermal and electric quantities, fractional exponents often become necessary, and the subject assumes the form of a theory of considerable complexity. The reader to whom this branch of science is new will find a section briefly describing it in my *Principles of Science*, 3rd ed., p. 325, or he may refer to the works there mentioned.*

Now, if such a theory of dimensions is requisite in dealing with

---

*J. D. Everett's *Illustrations of the Centimetre-gramme-second System of Units*, 1875, 5th ed., 1902; Fleeming Jenkin's *Text-Book of Electricity and Magnetism*, 1873; Clerk-Maxwell's *Theory of Heat*, or the commencement of his great *Treatise on Electricity*, vol. I, p. 2.

the precise ideas of physical magnitudes, it seems to be still more desirable as regards the quantities with which we are concerned in economics. One of the first and most difficult steps in a science is to conceive clearly the nature of the magnitudes about which we are arguing. Heat was long the subject of discussion and experiment before physicists formed any definite idea how its quantity could be measured and connected with other physical quantities. Yet, until that was done, it could not be considered the subject of an exact science. For one or two centuries economists have been wrangling about wealth, demand and supply, value, production, capital, interest and the like; but hardly any-one could say exactly what were the natures of the quantities in question. Believing that it is in forming these primary ideas that we require to exercise the greatest care, I have thought it well worth the trouble and space to enter fully into a discussion of the dimensions of economic quantities.

Beginning with the easiest and simplest ideas, the *dimensions of commodity*, regarded merely as a physical quantity, will be *the dimensions of mass*. It is true that commodities are measured in various ways – thread by length, carpet by length, corn and liquids by cubic measure, eggs by number, metals and most other goods by weight. But it is obvious that, though the carpet be sold by length, the breadth and the weight of the cloth are equally taken into account in fixing the terms of sale. There will generally be a tacit reference to weight, and through weight to mass of materials in all measurement of commodity. Even if this be not always the case, we may, for the sake of simplifying our symbols in the first treatment of the subject, assume that it is so. We need hardly recede to any ultimate analysis of the physi-cal conditions of the commodity, but may take it to be measured by *mass*, symbolized by M, the sign usually employed in physical science to denote this dimension.

A little consideration will show, however, that we have really little to do with absolute quantities of commodity. One hundred sacks of corn regarded merely by themselves can have no import-ant meaning for the economist. Whether the quantity is large or small, enough or too much, depends in the first place upon the number of consumers for whom it is intended, and, in the second place, upon the time for which it is to last them. We may perhaps throw out of view the number of consumers in this theory, by supposing that we are always dealing with the single average individual, the unit of which population is made up. Still, we cannot similarly get rid of the element of time. Quantity of supply must necessarily be estimated by the number of units of commodity divided by the number of units in the time over which it is to be expended. Thus it will involve M positively and T negatively, and its dimensions will be presented by MT^{-1}. Thus in reality *supply should be taken to mean not supply absolutely, but rate of supply*.

Consumption of commodity must have the same dimensions. For goods must be consumed in time; any action or effect endures a greater or less time, and commodity which will be abundant for a less time may be scanty for a greater time. To say that a town consumes fifty million gallons of water is unmeaning *per se*. Before we can form any judgement about the statement, we must know whether it is consumed in a day, or a week, or a month.

Following out this course of thought we shall arrive at the conclusion that time enters into all economic questions. We live in time, and think and act in time; we are in fact altogether the creatures of time. Accordingly it is rate of supply, rate of production, rate of consumption, per unit of time that we shall be really treating; but it does not follow that T^{-1} enters into all the dimensions with which we deal.

As was fully explained in chapter II, the ultimate quantities which we treat in economics are pleasures and pains, and our most difficult task will be to express their dimensions correctly. In the first place, pleasure and pain must be regarded as measured upon the same scale, and as having, therefore, the same dimensions, being quantities of the same kind, which can be added and subtracted; they differ only in sign or direction. Now, the only dimension belonging properly to feeling seems to be *intensity*, and this intensity must be independent both of time and of the quantity of commodity enjoyed. *The intensity of feeling must mean, then, the instantaneous state produced by an elementary or infinitesimal quantity of commodity consumed.*

Intensity of feeling, however, is only another name for degree of utility, which represents the favourable effect produced upon the human frame by the consumption of commodity, that is by an elementary or infinitesimal quantity of commodity. Putting U to indicate this dimension, we must remember that U will not represent even the full dimensions of the instantaneous state of pleasure or pain, much less the continued state which extends over a certain duration of time. The instantaneous state depends upon the sufficiency or insufficiency of supply of commodity. To enjoy a highly pleasurable condition, a person must want a good deal of commodity, and must be well supplied with it. Now, this supply is, as already explained, rate of supply, so that we must multiply U by MT^{-1} in order to arrive at the real instantaneous state of feeling. The kind of quantity thus symbolized by MUT^{-1} must be interpreted as meaning *so much commodity producing a certain amount of pleasurable effect per unit of time*. But this quantity will not be *quantity of utility* itself. It will only be that quantity which, when multiplied by time, will produce quantity of utility. Pleasure, as was stated at the outset, has the dimensions of intensity and duration. It is then this *intensity* which is symbolized by MUT^{-1}, and we must multiply this last symbol by T in order to obtain the dimensions of utility or quantity of pleasure produced. But in making this multiplication, $MUT^{-1}T$ reduces to MU, which must therefore be taken to denote the dimensions of *quantity of utility*.

We here meet with an explanation of the fact, so long perplexing to me, that the element of time does not appear throughout the diagrams and problems of this theory relating to utility and exchange. All goes on in time, and time is a necessary element of the question; yet it does not explicitly appear. Recurring to our diagrams, that for instance on p. 107, it is obvious that the dimension U, or degree of utility, is measured upon the perpendicular axis oy. The horizontal axis must, therefore, be that upon which rate of supply of commodity or MT^{-1} is measured, strictly speaking. If now we introduce the duration of the utility, we should apparently need a third axis, perpendicular to the plane of the page, upon which to denote it. But were we to introduce this third dimension, we should obtain a solid figure, representing a quantity truly of three dimensions. This would be erroneous, because the third dimension T enters negatively into the quantity represented by the horizontal axis. Thus time eliminates itself, and we arrive at a quantity of two dimensions correctly represented by a curvilinear area, one dimension of which corresponds to each of the factors in MU.

This result is at first sight paradoxical; but the difficulty is exactly analogous to that which occurs in the question of interest, and which led so profound a mathematician as Dean Peacock into a blunder, as will be shown in the chapter on capital. Interest of money is proportional to the length of time for which the principal is lent, and also to the amount of money lent and the rate of interest. But this rate of interest involves time negatively, so that time is ultimately eliminated, and interest emerges with the same dimensions as the principal sum. In the case of utility we begin with a certain absolute stock of commodity, M. In expending it we must spread it over more or less time, so that it is really rate of supply which is to be considered; but it is this rate MT^{-1}, not simply M, which influences the final degree of utility, U, at which it is consumed. If the same commodity be made to last a longer time, the degree of utility will be higher, because the necessity of the consumer will be less satisfied. Thus the absolute amount of utility produced will, as a general rule, be greater as the time of expenditure is greater; but this will also be the case with the quantity symbolized by MU, because the quantity U will under those circumstances be greater, while M remains constant.

To clear up the matter still further if possible, I will recapitulate the results we have arrived at.

M means absolute amount of commodity.

MT^{-1} means amount of commodity applied, so much per unit of time.

U means the resulting pleasurable effect of any increment of that supply, an infinitesimal quantity supplied per unit of time.

MUT^{-1} means therefore so much pleasurable effect produced per unit of commodity per unit of time.[29]

$MUT^{-1}T$, or MU, means therefore so much absolute pleasurable effect produced by commodity in an unspecified duration of time.

Actual, Prospective and Potential Utility

The difficulties of economics are mainly the difficulties of conceiving clearly and fully the conditions of utility. Even at the risk of being tiresome, I will therefore point out more minutely how various are the senses in which a thing may be said to have utility.

It is quite usual, and perhaps correct, to call iron or water or timber a useful substance; but we may mean by these words at least three distinct facts. We may mean that a particular piece of iron is at the present moment actually useful to some person; or that, although not actually useful, it is expected to be useful at a future time; or we may only mean that it would be useful if it were in the possession of some person needing it. The iron rails of a railway, the iron which composes the Britannia Bridge,[30] or an ocean steamer, is actually useful; the iron lying in a merchant's store is not useful at present, though it is expected soon to be so; but there is a vast quantity of iron existing in the bowels of the earth, which has all the physical properties of iron, and might be useful if extracted, though it never will be. These are instances of *actual, prospective and potential utility*.

It will be apparent that *potential utility* does not really enter into the science of economics, and when I speak of *utility* simply, I do not mean to include potential utility. It is a question of physical science whether a substance possesses qualities which might make it suitable to our needs if it were within our reach. Only when there arises some degree of probability, however slight, that a particular object will be needed, does it acquire *prospective utility*, capable or rendering it a desirable possession. As Condillac correctly remarks,* '*On diroit que les choses ne commencement à exister pour eux, qu'au moment où ils ont un intérêt à savoir qu'elles existent.*' But a very large part in industry, and the science of industry, belongs to *prospective utility*. We can at any one moment use only a very small fraction of what we possess. By far the greater part of what we hold might be allowed to perish at any moment, without harm, if we could have it

* Condillac, *Le Commerce et le gouvernement*, seconde partie, Introduction. *Oeuvres complètes*, Paris, 1803, tome VII, p. 2.

re-created with equal ease at a future moment, when need of it arises.

We might also distinguish, as is customary with French economists, between *direct* and *indirect utility*. Direct utility attaches to a thing like food, which we can actually supply to satisfy our wants. But things which have no direct utility may be the means of procuring us such by exchange, and they may therefore be said to have indirect utility.* To the latter form of utility I have elsewhere applied the name *acquired utility*.† This distinction is not the same as that which is made in the theory of capital between *mediate and immediate utility*, the former being that of any implement, machine or other means of procuring commodities possessing *immediate* and *direct utility* – that is, the power of satisfying want.[31]

Distribution of a Commodity in Time

We have seen that when a commodity is capable of being used for different purposes, definite principles regulate its application to those purposes. A similar question arises when a stock of commodity is in hand, and must be expended over a certain interval of time more or less definite. The science of economics must point out the mode of consuming it to the greatest advantage – that is, with a maximum result of utility. If we reckon all future pleasures and pains as if they were present, the solution will be the same as in the case of different uses. If a commodity has to be distributed over n days' use, and v_1, v_2, etc., be the final degrees of utility on each day's consumption, then we ought clearly to have

$$v_1 = v_2 = v_3 = \ldots = v_n.$$

It may, however, be uncertain during how many days we may require the stock to last. The commodity might be of a perishable nature, so that if we were to keep some of it for ten days, it might become unserviceable, and its utility be sacrificed. Assuming that we can estimate more or less exactly the probability of its remaining

* Garnier, *Traité d'économie politique*, 5me ed., p. 11.
† See ch. IV, p. 168.

good, let p_1, p_2, $p_3 \ldots p_{10}$ be these probabilities. Then, on the principle (p. 99) that a future pleasure or pain must be reduced in proportion to its want of certainty, we have the equations

$$v_1 p_1 = v_2 p_2 = \ldots = v_{10} p_{10}.$$

The general result is that as the probability is less, the commodity assigned to each day is less, so that v, its final degree of utility, will be greater.

So far we have taken no account of the varying influence of an event according to its propinquity or remoteness. The distribution of commodity described is that which should be made, and would be made by a being of perfect good sense and foresight. To secure a maximum of benefit in life, all future events, all future pleasures or pains, should act upon us with the same force as if they were present, allowance being made for their uncertainty. The factor expressing the effect of remoteness should, in short, always be unity, so that time should have no influence. But no human mind is constituted in this perfect way: a future feeling is always less influential than a present one. To take this fact into account, let q_1, q_2, q_3, etc., be the undetermined fractions which express the ratios of the present pleasures or pains to those future ones from whose anticipation they arise. Having a stock of commodity in hand, our tendency will be to distribute it so that the following equations will hold true –

$$v_1 p_1 q_1 = v_2 p_2 q_2 = v_3 p_3 q_3 = \ldots = v_n p_n q_n.$$

It will be an obvious consequence of these equations that less commodity will be assigned to future days in some proportion to the intervening time.

An illustrative problem, involving questions of prospective utility and probability, is found in the case of a vessel at sea, which is insufficiently victualled for the probable length of the voyage to the nearest port. The actual length of the voyage depends on the winds, and must be uncertain; but we may suppose that it will almost certainly last ten days or more, but not more than thirty days. It is apparent that if the food were divided into thirty equal parts, partial famine and suffering would be certainly endured for the first ten days, to ward off later evils which may not be encountered. To consume one-tenth part of the food on each of the first ten days would be still worse, as almost certainly entailing starvation on the following days. To determine the most beneficial distribution of the food, we should require to know the probability of each day between the tenth and thirtieth days forming part of the voyage, and also the law of variation of the degree of utility of food. The whole stock ought then to be divided into thirty portions, allotted to each of the thirty days, and of such magnitudes that the final degrees of utility multiplied by the probabilities may be equal. Thus, let v_1, v_2, v_3, etc., be the final degrees of utility of the first, second, third and other days supplied, and p_1, p_2, p_3, etc., the probabilities that the days in question will form part of the voyage; then we ought to

have $$p_1 v_1 = p_2 v_2 = p_3 v_3 = \ldots = p_{29} v_{29} = p_{30} v_{30}.$$

If these equations did not hold true, it would be beneficial to transfer a small portion from one lot to some other lot. As the voyage is supposed certainly to last the first ten days, we have

$$p_1 = p_2 = \ldots = p_{10} = 1;$$

hence we must have

$$v_1 = v_2 = \ldots = v_{10};$$

that is to say, the allotments to the first ten days should be equal. They should afterwards decrease according to some regular law; for, as the probability decreases, the final degree of utility should increase in inverse proportion.

CHAPTER IV

Theory of Exchange

Importance of Exchange in Economics

EXCHANGE is so important a process in the maximizing of utility and the saving of labour, that some economists have regarded their science as treating of this operation alone. Utility arises from commodities being brought in suitable quantities and at the proper times into the possession of persons needing them; and it is by exchange, more than any other means, that this is effected. Trade is not indeed the only method of economizing: a single individual may gain in utility by a proper consumption of the stock in his possession. The best employment of labour and capital by a single person is also a question disconnected from that of exchange, and which must yet be treated in the science. But, with these exceptions, I am perfectly willing to agree with the high importance attributed to exchange.

It is impossible to have a correct idea of the science of economics without a perfect comprehension of the theory of exchange; and I find it both possible and desirable to consider this subject before introducing any notions concerning labour or the production of commodities. In these words of J. S. Mill I thoroughly concur: 'Almost every speculation respecting the economical interests of a society thus constituted, implies some theory of Value: the smallest error on that subject infects with corresponding error all our other conclusions; and anything vague or misty in our conception of it creates confusion and uncertainty in everything else.' But when he proceeds to say 'Happily, there is nothing in the laws of Value which remains for the present or any future writer to clear up; the theory of the subject is complete',* – he utters that which it would be rash to say of any of the sciences.

* *Principles of Political Economy*, Book III, ch. I, sec. 1.

Ambiguity of the Term Value

I must, in the first place, point out the thoroughly ambiguous and unscientific character of the term *value*. Adam Smith noticed the extreme difference of meaning between *value in use* and *value in exchange*; and it is usual for writers on economics to caution their readers against the confusion of thought to which they are liable. But I do not believe that either writers or readers can avoid the confusion so long as they use the word. In spite of the most acute feeling of the danger, I often detect myself using the word improperly; nor do I think that the best authors escape the danger.

Let us turn to Mill's definition of exchange value,* and we see at once the misleading power of the term. He tells us 'Value is a relative term. The value of a thing means the quantity of some other thing, or of things in general, which it exchanges for.' Now, if there is any fact certain about exchange value, it is that it means not an object at all, but a circumstance of an object. Value implies, in fact, a relation; but if so, it cannot possibly be *some other thing*. A student of economics has no hope of ever being clear and correct in his ideas of the science if he thinks of value as at all a *thing* or an *object*, or even as anything which lies in a thing or object. Persons are thus led to speak of such a nonentity as *intrinsic value*. There are, doubtless, qualities inherent in such a substance as gold or iron which influence its value; but the word value, so far as it can be correctly used, merely expresses *the circumstance of its exchanging in a certain ratio for some other substance*.

Value Expresses Ratio of Exchange

If a ton of pig-iron exchanges in a market for an ounce of standard gold, neither the iron is value nor the gold; nor is there value in the iron nor in the gold. The notion of value is concerned only in the fact or circumstance of one exchanging for the other. Thus it is scientifically incorrect to say that the value of the ton of iron *is* the ounce of gold: we thus convert value into a

* *Principles of Political Economy*, Book III, ch. VI.

concrete thing; and it is, of course, equally incorrect to say that the value of the ounce of gold is the ton of iron. The more correct and safe expression is, that *the value of the ton of iron is equal to the value of the ounce of gold*, or that their values are as one to one.

Value in exchange expresses nothing but a ratio, and the term should not be used in any other sense. To speak simply of the value of an ounce of gold is as absurd as to speak of *the ratio of the number seventeen*. What is the ratio of the number seventeen? The question admits no answer, for there must be another number named in order to make a ratio; and the ratio will differ according to the number suggested. What is the value of iron compared with that of gold? – is an intelligible question. The answer consists in stating the ratio of the quantities exchanged.

Popular Use of the Term Value

In the popular use of the word value no less than three distinct though connected meanings seem to be confused together. These may be described as

    (1) value in use;
    (2) esteem, or urgency of desire;
    (3) ratio of exchange.

Adam Smith, in the familiar passage already referred to, distinguished between the first and the third meanings. He said,*

The word value, it is to be observed, has two different meanings, and sometimes expresses the utility of some particular object and sometimes the power of purchasing other goods which the possession of that object conveys. The one may be called 'value in use'; the other 'value in exchange'. The things which have the greatest value in use have frequently little or no value in exchange; and, on the contrary, those which have the greatest value in exchange have frequently little or no value in use. Nothing is more useful than water: but it will purchase scarce anything; scarce anything can be had in exchange for it. A diamond, on the contrary, has scarce any value in use; but a very great quantity of other goods may frequently be had in exchange for it.

    * *Wealth of Nations*, Book I, ch. IV, near the end. [in Cannan's ed., vol. I, p. 30.]

It is sufficiently plain that, when Smith speaks of water as being highly useful and yet devoid of purchasing power, he means *water in abundance*, that is to say, water so abundantly supplied that it has exerted its full useful effect, or its *total utility*. Water, when it becomes very scarce, as in a dry desert, acquires exceedingly great purchasing power. Thus Smith evidently means by value in use, *the total utility of a substance of which the degree of utility has sunk very low, because the want of such substance has been well-nigh satisfied.* By purchasing power he clearly means the ratio of exchange for other commodities. But here he fails to point out that the quantity of goods received in exchange depends just as much upon the nature of the goods received, as on the nature of those given for them. In exchange for a diamond we can get a great quantity of iron, or corn, or paving-stones, or other commodity of which there is abundance; but we can get very few rubies, sapphires or other precious stones. Silver is of high purchasing power compared with zinc, or lead, or iron, but of small purchasing power compared with gold, platinum or iridium. Yet we might well say in any case that diamond and silver are things of high value. Thus I am led to think that the word value is often used in reality to mean *intensity of desire or esteem for a thing*. A silver ornament is a beautiful object apart from all ideas of traffic; it may thus be valued or esteemed simply because it suits the taste and fancy of its owner, and is the only one possessed. Even Robinson Crusoe must have looked upon each of his possessions with varying esteem and desire for more, although he was incapable of exchanging with any other person. Now, in this sense value seems to be identical with the final degree of utility of a commodity, as defined in a previous page (p. 110); it is measured by the intensity of the pleasure or benefit which would be obtained from a new increment of the same commodity. No doubt there is a close connexion between value in this meaning, and value as ratio of exchange. Nothing can have a high purchasing power unless it be highly esteemed in itself; but it may be highly esteemed apart from all comparison with other things; and, though highly esteemed, it may have a low purchasing power, because those things against which it is measured are still more esteemed.

Thus I come to the conclusion that, in the use of the word value, three distinct meanings are habitually confused together, and require to be thus distinguished:

(1) value in use = total utility;
(2) esteem = final degree of utility;
(3) purchasing power = ratio of exchange.

It is not to be expected that we could profitably discuss such matters as economic doctrines, while the fundamental ideas of the subject are thus jumbled up together in one ambiguous word. The only thorough remedy consists in substituting for the dangerous name *value* that one of the three stated meanings which is intended in each case. In this work, therefore, I shall discontinue the use of the word value altogether, and when, as will be most often the case in the remainder of the book, I need to refer to the third meaning, often called by economists *exchange or exchangeable value*, I shall substitute the wholly unequivocal expression *ratio of exchange*, specifying at the same time what are the *two articles* exchanged. When we speak of the ratio of exchange of pig-iron and gold, there can be no possible doubt that we intend to refer to the ratio of the number of units of the one commodity to the number of units of the other commodity for which it exchanges, the units being arbitrary concrete magnitudes, but the ratio an abstract number.

When I proposed, in the first edition of this book, to use ratio of exchange instead of the word value, the expression had been so little, if at all, employed by English economists, that it amounted to an innovation. J. S. Mill, indeed, in his chapters on value, speaks once and again of things exchanging for each other 'in the ratio of their cost of production', but he always omits to say distinctly that exchange value is itself a matter of ratio. As to Ricardo, Malthus, Adam Smith and other great English economists, although they usually discourse at some length upon the meanings of the word value, I am not aware that they ever explicitly apply the name *ratio* to exchange or exchangeable value. Yet ratio is unquestionably the correct scientific term, and the only term which is strictly and entirely correct.

It is interesting, therefore, to find that, although overlooked by English economists, the expression had been used by two or more of the truly scientific French economists, namely, Le Trosne and Condillac. Le Trosne carefully defines value in the following terms,* '*La valeur consiste dans le rapport d'échange qui se trouve entre telle chose et telle autre, entre telle mesure d'une production et telle mesure des autres.*' Condillac apparently adopts the words of Le Trosne, saying† of value, '*Qu'elle consiste dans le rapport d'échange entre telle chose et telle autre.*' Such economical works as those of Baudeau, Le Trosne and Condillac were almost wholly unknown to English readers until attention was drawn to them by Mr H. D. Macleod and Professor Adamson[32]; but I shall endeavour for the future to make proper use of them.

Dimension of Value

There is no difficulty in seeing that, when we use the word value in the sense of ratio of exchange, its dimension will be simply zero. Value will be expressed, like angular magnitude and other ratios in general, by abstract number. Angular magnitude is measured by the ratio of a line to a line, the ratio of the arc subtended by the angle to the radius of the circle. So value in this sense is a ratio of the quantity of one commodity to the quantity of some other commodity exchanged for it. If we compare the commodities simply as physical quantities, we have the dimensions M divided by M, or MM^{-1}, or M^0. Exactly the same result would be obtained if, instead of taking the mere physical quantities, we were to compare their utilities, for we should then have MU divided by MU or M^0U^0, which, as it really means *unity*,[33] is identical in meaning with M^0.

When we use the word value in the sense of esteem, or urgency of desire, the feeling with which Oliver Twist must have regarded a few more mouthfuls when he 'asked for more', the meaning of the word, as already explained, is identical with *degree of utility*, of which the dimension is U. Lastly, the *value in use* of Adam Smith, or the *total utility*, is the integral of $U.dM$, and has the

* *De l'Intérêt social*, 1777, ch. I, sec. iv.

† *Le Commerce et le gouvernement*, 1776; *Oeuvres complètes de Condillac*, 1803, tome VI, p. 20.

dimensions MU. We may thus tabulate our results concerning the ambiguous uses of the word *value*:

Popular Expression of Meaning	Scientific Expression	Dimensions
(1) Value in use	Total Utility	MU
(2) Esteem, or Urgency of Desire for more	Final Degree of Utility	U
(3) Purchasing Power	Ratio of Exchange	M^0

Definition of Market

Before proceeding to the theory of exchange, it will be desirable to place beyond doubt the meanings of two other terms which I shall frequently employ.

By a *market* I shall mean much what commercial men use it to express. Originally a market was a public place in a town where provisions and other objects were exposed for sale, but the word has been generalized, so as to mean any body of persons who are in intimate business relations and carry on extensive transactions in any commodity. A great city may contain as many markets as there are important branches of trade, and these markets may or may not be localized. The central point of a market is the public exchange – mart or auction rooms – where the traders agree to meet and transact business. In London, the Stock Market, the Corn Market, the Coal Market, the Sugar Market and many others, are distinctly localized; in Manchester, the Cotton Market, the Cotton Waste Market and others. But this distinction of locality is not necessary. The traders may be spread over a whole town, or region of country, and yet make a market, if they are, by means of fairs, meetings, published price lists, the post office or otherwise, in close communication with each other. Thus, the common expression *Money Market* denotes no locality: it is applied to the aggregate of those bankers, capitalists and other traders who lend or borrow money, and who constantly exchange information concerning the course of business.*

* I find that Cournot has long since defined the economic use of the word *market*, with admirable brevity and precision, but exactly to the same effect

In economics we may usefully adopt this term with a clear and well-defined meaning. <u>By a market I shall mean two or more persons dealing in two or more commodities, whose stocks of those commodities and intentions of exchanging are known to all.</u> It is also essential that the ratio of exchange between any two persons should be known to all the others. It is only so far as this community of knowledge extends that the market extends. Any persons who are not acquainted at the moment with the prevailing ratio of exchange, or whose stocks are not available for want of communication, must not be considered part of the market. Secret or unknown stocks of a commodity must also be considered beyond reach of a market so long as they remain secret and unknown. Every individual must be considered as exchanging from a pure regard to his own requirements or private interests, and there must be perfectly free competition, so that anyone will exchange with anyone else for the slightest apparent advantage. There must be no conspiracies for absorbing and holding supplies to produce unnatural ratios of exchange. Were a conspiracy of farmers to withhold all corn from market, the consumers might be driven, by starvation, to pay prices bearing no proper relation to the existing supplies, and the ordinary conditions of the market would be thus overthrown.

The theoretical conception of a perfect market is more or less completely carried out in practice. It is the work of brokers in any extensive market to organize exchange, so that every purchase shall be made with the most thorough acquaintance with the conditions of the trade. Each broker strives to gain the best knowledge of the conditions of supply and demand, and the earliest intimation of any change. He is in communication with as many other traders as possible, in order to have the widest range of information, and the greatest chance of making

---

as the text above. He incidentally says in a footnote (*Recherches sur les principes mathématiques de la théorie des richesses*, Paris, 1838, p. 55), '*On sait que les économistes entendent par* marché, *non pas un lieu déterminé ou se consomment les achats et les ventes, mais tout un territoire dont les parties sont unies par des rapports de libre commerce, en sorte que les prix s'y nivellent avec facilité et promptitude.*' [Translation by Bacon, Macmillan, 1897, p. 51, note.]

suitable exchanges. It is only thus that a definite market price can be ascertained at every moment, and varied according to the frequent news capable of affecting buyers and sellers. By the mediation of a body of brokers a complete *consensus* is established, and the stock of every seller or the demand of every buyer brought into the market. It is the very essence of trade to have wide and constant information. A market, then, is theoretically perfect only when all traders have perfect knowledge of the conditions of supply and demand, and the consequent ratio of exchange; and in such a market, as we shall now see, there can only be one ratio of exchange of one uniform commodity at any moment.[34]

So essential is a knowledge of the real state of supply and demand to the smooth procedure of trade and the real good of the community, that I conceive it would be quite legitimate to compel the publication of any requisite statistics. Secrecy can only conduce to the profit of speculators who gain from great fluctuations of prices. Speculation is advantageous to the public only so far as it tends to equalize prices; and it is, therefore, against the public good to allow speculators to foster artificially the inequalities of prices by which they profit. The welfare of millions, both of consumers and producers, depends upon an accurate knowledge of the stocks of cotton and corn; and it would, therefore, be no unwarrantable interference with the liberty of the subject to require any information as to the stocks in hand. In Billingsgate fish market there was long ago a regulation to the effect that salesmen shall fix up in a conspicuous place every morning a statement of the kind and amount of their stock.* The same principle has long been recognized in the Acts of Parliament concerning the collection of statistics of the quantities and prices of corn sold in English market towns. More recently similar legislation has taken place as regards the cotton trade, in the Cotton Statistics Act of 1868. Publicity, whenever it can thus be enforced on markets by public authority, tends almost always to the advantage of everybody except perhaps a few speculators and financiers.

* Waterston's *Cyclopaedia of Commerce*, ed. 1846, p. 466.

Definition of Trading Body[35]

I find it necessary to adopt some expression for any number of people whose aggregate influence in a market, either in the way of supply or demand, we have to consider. By a *trading body* I mean, in the most general manner, any body either of buyers or sellers. The trading body may be a single individual in one case; it may be the whole inhabitants of a continent in another; it may be the individuals of a trade diffused through a country in a third. England and North America will be trading bodies if we are considering the corn we receive from America in exchange for iron and other goods. The continent of Europe is a trading body as purchasing coal from England. The farmers of England are a trading body when they sell corn to the millers, and the millers both when they buy corn from the farmers and sell flour to the bakers.

We must use the expression with this wide meaning, because the principles of exchange are the same in nature, however wide or narrow may be the market considered. Every trading body is either an individual or an aggregate of individuals, and the law, in the case of the aggregate, must depend upon the fulfilment of law in the individuals. We cannot usually observe any precise and continuous variation in the wants and deeds of an individual, because the action of extraneous motives, or what would seem to be caprice, overwhelms minute tendencies. As I have already remarked (p. 86), a single individual does not vary his consumption of sugar, butter or eggs from week to week by infinitesimal amounts, according to each small change in the price. He probably continues his ordinary consumption until accident directs his attention to a rise in price, and he then, perhaps, discontinues the use of the articles altogether for a time. But the aggregate, or what is the same, the average consumption, of a large community will be found to vary continuously or nearly so. The most minute tendencies make themselves apparent in a wide average. Thus, our laws of economics will be theoretically true in the case of individuals, and practically true in the case of large aggregates; but the general principles will be the same, whatever the extent of the trading body considered. We shall be justified, then, in using the expression with the utmost generality.

It should be remarked, however, that the economic laws representing the conduct of large aggregates of individuals will never represent exactly the conduct of any one individual. If we could imagine that there were a thousand individuals all exactly alike in regard to their demand for commodities, and their capabilities of supplying them, then the average laws of supply and demand deduced from the conduct of such individuals would agree with the conduct of any one individual. But a community is composed of persons differing widely in their powers, wants, habits and possessions. In such circumstances the average laws applying to them will come under what I have elsewhere * called the 'Fictitious Mean', that is to say, they are numerical results which do not pretend to represent the character of any existing thing. But average laws would not on this account be less useful, if we could obtain them, for the movements of trade and industry depend on averages and aggregates, not on the whims of individuals.

The Law of Indifference

When a commodity is perfectly uniform or homogeneous in quality, any portion may be indifferently used in place of an equal portion: hence, in the same market, and at the same moment, all portions must be exchanged at the same ratio. There can be no reason why a person should treat exactly similar things differently, and the slightest excess in what is demanded for one over the other will cause him to take the latter instead of the former. In nicely balanced exchanges it is a very minute scruple which turns the scale and governs the choice. A minute difference of quality in a commodity may thus give rise to preference, and cause the ratio of exchange to differ. But where no difference exists at all, or where no difference is known to exist, there can be no ground for preference whatever. If, in selling a quantity of perfectly equal and uniform barrels of flour, a merchant arbitrarily fixed different prices on them, a purchaser would of course select the cheaper ones; and where there was absolutely no

* *Principles of Science*, 1st ed., vol. I, p. 422; 3rd ed., p. 363.

difference in the thing purchased, even an excess of a penny in the price of a thing worth a thousand pounds would be a valid ground of choice. Hence follows what is undoubtedly true, with proper explanations, that *in the same open market, at any one moment, there cannot be two prices for the same kind of article.* Such differences as may practically occur arise from extraneous circumstances, such as the defective credit of the purchasers, their imperfect knowledge of the market, and so on.

The principle above expressed is a general law of the utmost importance in economics, and I propose to call it the *law of indifference*, meaning that, when two objects or commodities are subject to no important difference as regards the purpose in view, they will either of them be taken instead of the other with perfect indifference by a purchaser. Every such act of indifferent choice gives rise to an equation of degrees of utility, so that in this principle of indifference we have one of the central pivots of the theory.

Though the price of the same commodity must be uniform at any one moment, it may vary from moment to moment, and must be conceived as in a state of continual change. Theoretically speaking, it would not usually be possible to buy two portions of the same commodity *successively* at the same ratio of exchange, because no sooner would the first portion have been bought than the conditions of utility would be altered. When exchanges are made on a large scale, this result will be verified in practice.* If a wealthy person invested £100,000 in the funds in the morning, it is hardly likely that the operation could be repeated in the afternoon at the same price. In any market, if a person goes on buying largely, he will ultimately raise the price against himself. Thus it is apparent that extensive purchases would best be made gradually, so as to secure the advantage of a lower price upon the earlier portions.

---

*It is, I believe, verified in the New York stock markets, where it is the practice to sell stocks by auction in successive lots, without disclosing the total amount to be put up. When the amount offered begins to exceed what was expected, then each successive lot brings a less price, and those who bought the earlier lots suffer. But if the amount offered is small, the early buyers have the advantage. Such an auction sale only exhibits in miniature what is constantly going on in the markets generally on a large scale.

In theory this effect of exchange upon the ratio of exchange must be conceived to exist in some degree, however small may be the purchases made. Strictly speaking, the ratio of exchange at any moment is that of dy to dx, of an infinitely small quantity of one commodity to the infinitely small quantity of another which is given for it. The ratio of exchange is really a differential coefficient. The quantity of any article purchased is a function of the price at which it is purchased, and the ratio of exchange expresses the rate at which the quantity of the article increases compared with what is given for it.

We must carefully distinguish, at the same time, between the statics and dynamics of this subject. The real condition of industry is one of perpetual motion and change. Commodities are being continually manufactured and exchanged and consumed. If we wished to have a complete solution of the problem in all its natural complexity, we should have to treat it as a problem of motion – a problem of dynamics. But it would surely be absurd to attempt the more difficult question when the more easy one is yet so imperfectly within our power. It is only as a purely statical problem that I can venture to treat the action of exchange. Holders of commodities will be regarded not as continuously passing on these commodities in streams of trade, but as possessing certain fixed amounts which they exchange until they come to equilibrium.

It is much more easy to determine the point at which a pendulum will come to rest than to calculate the velocity at which it will move when displaced from that point of rest. Just so, it is a far more easy task to lay down the conditions under which trade is completed and interchange ceases, than to attempt to ascertain at what rate trade will go on when equilibrium is not attained.

The difference will present itself in this form: dynamically we could not treat the ratio of exchange otherwise than as the ratio of dy and dx, infinitesimal quantities of commodity. Our equations would then be regarded as differential equations, which would have to be integrated. But in the statical view of the question we can substitute the ratio of the finite quantities y and x. Thus, from the self-evident principle, stated on p. 137, that there cannot, in the same market, at the same moment, be two different prices for the same uniform commodity, it follows that *the last increments in an act of exchange must be exchanged in the same ratio as the whole quantities exchanged*. Suppose that two commodities are bartered in the ratio of x for y; then every mth part of x is given for the mth part of y, and it does not matter for which of the mth parts. No part of the commodity can be treated differently from any other part. We may carry this division to an indefinite extent by imagining m to be constantly increased, so that, at the limit, even an infinitely small part of x must be exchanged for an infinitely small part of y, in the same ratio as the whole quantities. This result we may express by stating that the increments concerned in the process of exchange must obey the equation

$$\frac{dy}{dx} = \frac{y}{x}.$$

The use which we shall make of this equation will be seen in the next section.

The Theory of Exchange

The keystone of the whole theory of exchange, and of the principal problems of economics, lies in this proposition – *The ratio of exchange of any two commodities will be the reciprocal of the ratio of the final degrees of utility of the quantities of commodity available for consumption after the exchange is completed.* When the reader has reflected a little upon the meaning of this proposition, he will see, I think, that it is necessarily true, if the principles of human nature have been correctly represented in previous pages.

Imagine that there is one trading body possessing only corn, and another possessing only beef. It is certain that, under these circumstances, a portion of the corn may be given in exchange for a portion of the beef with a considerable increase of utility. How are we to determine at what point the exchange will cease to be beneficial? This question must involve both the ratio of exchange and the degrees of utility. Suppose, for a moment, that the ratio of exchange is approximately that of ten pounds of corn for one pound of beef: then if, to the trading body which possesses

139

corn, ten pounds of corn are less useful than one of beef, that body will desire to carry the exchange further. Should the other body possessing beef find one pound less useful than ten pounds of corn, this body will also be desirous to continue the exchange. Exchange will thus go on until each party has obtained all the benefit that is possible, and loss of utility would result if more were exchanged. Both parties, then, rest in satisfaction and equilibrium, and the degrees of utility have come to their level, as it were.

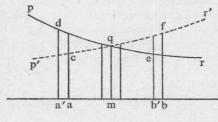

Fig. 5

This point of equilibrium will be known by the criterion that an infinitely small amount of commodity exchanged in addition, at the same rate, will bring neither gain nor loss of utility. In other words, if increments of commodities be exchanged at the established ratio, their utilities will be equal for both parties. Thus, if ten pounds of corn were of exactly the same utility as one pound of beef, there would be neither harm nor good in further exchange at this ratio.

It is hardly possible to represent this theory completely by means of a diagram, but the accompanying figure may, perhaps, render it clearer. Suppose the line *pqr* to be a small portion of the curve of utility of one commodity, while the broken line *p'qr'* is the like curve of another commodity which has been reversed and superposed on the other. Owing to this reversal, the quantities of the first commodity are measured along the base line from *a* towards *b*, whereas those of the second must be measured in the opposite direction. Let units of both commodities be represented by equal lengths; then the little line *a'a* indicates an increase of the first commodity, and a decrease of the second. Assume the ratio of exchange to be that of unit for unit, or 1 to 1; then, by receiving the commodity $a'a$ the person will gain the utility ad, and lose the utility $a'c$; or he will make a net gain of the utility corresponding to the mixtilinear figure cd. He will, therefore, wish to extend the exchange. If he were to go up to the point b', and were still proceeding, he would, by the next small exchange, receive the utility be, and part with $b'f$; or he would have a net loss of ef. He would, therefore, have gone too far; and it is pretty obvious that the point of intersection, q, defines the place where he would stop with the greatest advantage. It is there that a net gain is converted into a net loss, or rather where, for an infinitely small quantity, there is neither gain nor loss. To represent an infinitely small quantity, or even an exceedingly small quantity, on a diagram is, of course, impossible; but on either side of the line mq I have represented the utilities of a small quantity of commodity more or less, and it is apparent that the net gain or loss upon the exchange of these quantities would be trifling.

Symbolic Statement of the Theory

To represent this process of reasoning in symbols, let Δx denote a small increment of corn, and Δy a small increment of beef exchanged for it. Now our law of indifference comes into play. As both the corn and the beef are homogeneous commodities, no parts can be exchanged at a different ratio from other parts in the same market; hence, if x be the whole quantity of corn given for y the whole quantity of beef received, Δy must have the same ratio to Δx as y to x; we have then,

$$\frac{\Delta y}{\Delta x} = \frac{y}{x}, \text{ or } \Delta y = \frac{y}{x}\Delta x.$$

In a state of equilibrium, the utilities of these increments must be equal in the case of each party, in order that neither more nor less exchange would be desirable. Now the increment of beef, Δy, is $\frac{y}{x}$ times as great as the increment of corn, Δx, so that, in order that their utilities shall be equal, the degree of utility of beef must be $\dfrac{x}{y}$ times as great as the degree of utility of corn. Thus we arrive at the principle that *the degrees of utility of commodities exchanged will be in the inverse proportion of the magnitudes of the increments exchanged.*

Let us now suppose that the first body, A, originally possessed the quantity a of corn, and that the second body, B, possessed the quantity b of beef. As the exchange consists in giving x of corn for y of beef, the state of things after exchange will be as follows:

A holds $a - x$ of corn, and y of beef,
B holds x of corn, and $b - y$ of beef.

Let $\varphi_1(a - x)$ denote the final degree of utility of corn to A, and $\varphi_2 x$ the corresponding function for B. Also let $\psi_1 y$ denote A's final degree of utility for beef, and $\psi_2(b - y)$ B's similar function. Then, as explained on p. 140, A will not be satisfied unless the following equation holds true:

$$\varphi_1(a - x) \,.\, dx = \psi_1 y \,.\, dy;$$
$$\text{or } \frac{\varphi_1(a - x)}{\psi_1 y} = \frac{dy}{dx}.$$

Hence, substituting for the second member by the equation given on p. 139, we have

$$\frac{\varphi_1(a - x)}{\psi_1 y} = \frac{y}{x}.$$

What holds true of A will also hold true of B, *mutatis mutandis*. He must also derive exactly equal utility from the final increments, otherwise it will be for his interest to exchange either more or less, and he will disturb the conditions of exchange. Accordingly the following equation must hold true:

$$\psi_2(b - y) \,.\, dy = \varphi_2 x \,.\, dx;$$

or, substituting as before,

$$\frac{\varphi_2 x}{\psi_2(b - y)} = \frac{y}{x}.$$

142

We arrive, then, at the conclusion that whenever two commodities are exchanged for each other, and *more or less can be given or received in infinitely small quantities*, the quantities exchanged satisfy two equations, which may be thus stated in a concise form –

$$\frac{\varphi_1(a-x)}{\psi_1 y} = \frac{y}{x} = \frac{\varphi_2 x}{\psi_2(b-y)}.$$

The two equations are sufficient to determine the results of exchange; for there are only two unknown quantities concerned, namely, x, and y, the quantities given and received.

A vague notion has existed in the minds of economical writers, that the conditions of exchange may be expressed in the form of an equation. Thus, J. S. Mill has said: * 'The idea of a *ratio*, as between demand and supply, is out of place, and has no concern in the matter: the proper mathematical analogy is that of an *equation*. Demand and supply, the quantity demanded and the quantity supplied, will be made equal.' Mill here speaks of an equation as only a proper mathematical *analogy*. But if economics is to be a real science at all, it must not deal merely with analogies; it must reason by real equations, like all the other sciences which have reached at all a systematic character. Mill's equation, indeed, is not explicitly the same as any at which we have arrived above. His equation states that the quantity of a commodity given by A is equal to the quantity received by B. This seems at first sight to be a mere truism, for this equality must necessarily exist if any exchange takes place at all. The theory of value, as expounded by Mill, fails to reach the root of the matter, and shows how the amount of demand or supply is caused to vary. And Mill does not perceive that, as there must be two parties and two quantities to every exchange, there must be two equations.

Nevertheless, our theory is perfectly consistent with the laws of supply and demand; and if we had the functions of utility determined, it would be possible to throw them into a form clearly expressing the equivalence of supply and demand. We may regard x as the quantity demanded on one side and supplied

* *Principles of Political Economy*, Book III, ch. II, sec. iv.

on the other; similarly, y is the quantity supplied on the one side and demanded on the other. Now, when we hold the two equations to be simultaneously true, we assume that the x and y of one equation equal those of the other. The laws of supply and demand are thus a result of what seems to me the true theory of value or exchange.

Analogy to the Theory of the Lever

I have heard objections made to the general character of the equations employed in this book. It is remarked that the equations in question continually involve infinitesimal quantities, and yet they are not treated as differential equations usually are, that is integrated.[36] There is, indeed, no reason why the process of integration should not be applied when it is required, and I will here show that the equations employed do not differ in general character from those which are really treated in many branches of physical science. Whenever, in fact, we deal with continuously varying quantities, the ultimate equations must lie between infinitesimals. The process of integration, if I understand the matter aright, only ascertains other equations, the truth of which follows from the fundamental differential equation.

The mode in which mechanics is usually treated in elementary work tends to disguise the real foundation of the science which is to be found in the so-called *theory of virtual velocities*. Let us take the description of the lever of the first order as it is given in some of the best modern elementary works, as, for instance, in Mr Magnus's *Lessons in Elementary Mechanics*,[37] p. 128. We here read as follows:

Let AB be a lever turning freely about C, the fulcrum, and let P be the force applied at A, and W the force exerted, or resistance overcome, or weight raised at B. Suppose the lever turned through the angle ACA', then the work done by P equals $P \times$ arc AA', and work done by W equals $W \times$ arc BB', if P and W act perpendicularly to the arm. Therefore, by the law of energy,

$$P \times AA' = W \times BB', \text{ and since } \frac{AA'}{BB'} = \frac{AC}{BC} \text{ we have}$$
$$P \times AC = W \times BC,$$
$$\text{or, } P \times \text{ its arm} = W \times \text{ its arm.}$$

Now, in such a statement as this, we seem to be dealing with plain finite quantities, and there is no apparent difficulty in the matter. In reality the difficulty is only disguised by assuming that P and W act perpendicularly to the arm through finite arcs. This condition is, indeed, carried out with approximate exactness in the problem of the wheel and axle,* which may be regarded as combining together an infinite series of straight levers, coming successively into operation. In this machine, therefore, the weights, roughly speaking, always act perpendicularly to arms of invariable length. But, in the generality of cases of the lever, the theory is only true for infinitely small displacements, and no sooner has the lever begun to move through any finite arc AA', than it ceases to be exactly true that the work done by P equals $P \times$ arc AA'. Nevertheless, the theory is quite correct as applied to the lever considered statically, that is, as in a state of rest and equilibrium, because the finite arcs of displacement, when it really is displaced, are exactly proportional to the infinitely small arcs, known as virtual velocities, through which it would be displaced, if instead of being at rest, it suffered an infinitely small displacement.

It is curious, moreover, that, when we take the theory of the lever treated according to the principle of virtual velocities, we get equations exactly similar in form to those of the theory of value as established above. The general principle of virtual velocities is to the effect that, if any number of forces be in equilibrium at one or more points of a rigid body, and if this body receive an infinitely small displacement, the algebraic sum of the products of each force into its displacement is equal to zero. In the case of a lever of the first order, this amounts to saying that one force multiplied into its displacement will be neutralized by the other force multiplied into its *negative* displacement. But inasmuch as the displacements are exactly proportional to the lengths of the arms of the lever, we obtain as a derivative equation that the forces multiplied each by its own arm are equal to each other. No doubt in the quotation given above, $P \times AC = W \times BC$ is an equation between finite quantities; but the real equation derived immediately from the principle of virtual velocities, is $P \times AA' = W \times BB'$, in which P and W are finite, but AA'

*See Magnus's *Lessons*, sec. xci.

and BB' are in strictness infinitely small displacements. Let us write this equation in the form $\frac{W}{P} = \frac{AA'}{BB'}$; then as we also have $\frac{AA'}{BB'} = \frac{AC}{BB}$ we can substitute; hence $\frac{W}{P} = \frac{AC}{BC}$.

I dwell upon this matter at some length because we here have exactly the forms of the equations of exchange. As we have seen, the original equation is of the general form $\frac{\varphi x}{\psi y} = \frac{dy}{dx}$, where ψy and φx represent finite expressions for the degrees of utility of the commodities Y and X, as regards some individual, and dy and dx are infinitesimal quantities of these commodities exchanged. But these infinitesimals may in this case at least be eliminated, because, in virtue of the law of indifference, they are exactly proportional to the whole finite quantities exchanged. Hence for $\frac{dy}{dx}$ we substitute $\frac{y}{x}$. We may write the equations one below the other, so as to make the analogy visible – thus

$$\frac{W}{P} = \frac{AA'}{BB'} = \frac{AC}{BC}$$

$$\frac{\varphi x}{\psi y} = \frac{dy}{dx} = \frac{y}{x}.$$

To put this analogy of the theories of exchange and of the lever in the clearest possible light, I give below a diagram, in which the several economic qualities are represented by the parts of the diagram to which they correspond or are proportional.

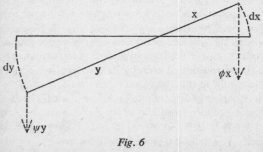

Fig. 6

Now in statical problems no such process as integration is applicable. The equation lies actually between imaginary infinitesimal quantities, and there is no effect to be summed up. Yet there is no statical problem which is not subject to the principle of virtual velocities, and Poisson, in his *Traité de Mécanique*, which commences with statical theorems, asserts explicitly,[*] '*Dans cet ouvrage, j'emploierai exclusivement la méthode* des infiniment petits.'

Impediments to Exchange

We have hitherto treated the theory of exchange as if the action of exchange could be carried on without trouble or cost. In reality, the cost of conveyance is almost always of importance, and it is sometimes the principal element in the question. To the cost of mere transport must be added a variety of charges of brokers, agents, packers, dock, harbour, light dues, etc., together with any customs duties imposed either on the importation or exportation of commodities. All these charges, whether necessary or arbitrary, are so many impediments to commerce, and tend to reduce its advantages. The effect of any one such charge, or of the aggregate of the costs of exchange, can be represented in our formulae in a very simple manner.

In whatever modes the charges are payable, they may be conceived as paid by the surrender on importation of a certain fraction of the commodity received; for the amount of the charges will usually be proportional to the quantity of goods, and, if expressed in money, can be considered as turned into commodity.

Thus, if A gives x in exchange, this is not the quantity received by B; a part of x is previously subtracted, so that B receives say mx, which is less than x, and the terms of exchange must be adjusted on his part so as to agree with this condition. Hence the second equation will be

$$\frac{y}{mx} = \frac{\varphi_2(mx)}{\psi_2(b - y)}.$$

[*] Seconde édition, Paris, 1833, sec. xii, vol. I, p. 14.

Again, A, though giving x, will not receive the whole of y; but say ny, so that his equation similarly will be

$$\frac{\varphi_1(a - x)}{\psi_1(ny)} = \frac{ny}{x}.$$

The result is that there is not one ratio of exchange, but two ratios; and the more these differ, the less advantage will there be in exchange. It is obvious that A has either to remain satisfied with less of the second commodity than before, or has to give more of his own in purchasing it. By an obvious transfer of the factors m and n we may state the equations of impeded exchange in the concise form:

$$\frac{\varphi_1(a - x)}{n \cdot \psi_1(ny)} = \frac{y}{x} = \frac{m \cdot \varphi_2(mx)}{\psi_2(b - y)}.$$

Illustrations of the Theory of Exchange

As stated above, the theory of exchange may seem to be of a somewhat abstract and perplexing character; but it is not difficult to find practical illustrations which will show how it is verified in the actual working of a great market. The ordinary laws of supply and demand, when properly stated, are the practical manifestation of the theory. Considerable discussion has taken place concerning these laws, in consequence of Mr W. T. Thornton's writings upon the subject in the *Fortnightly Review*, and in his work on the *Claims of Labour*. Mill, although he had previously declared the theory of value to be complete and perfect (see p. 126), was led by Mr Thornton's arguments to allow that modification was required.[38]

For my own part, I think that most of Mr Thornton's arguments are beside the question. He suggests that there are no regular laws of supply and demand, because he adduces certain cases in which no regular variation can take place. Those cases might be indefinitely multiplied, and yet the laws in question would not be touched. Of course, laws which assume a continuity of variation are inapplicable where continuous variation is impossible. Economists can never be free from difficulties unless they will distinguish between a theory and the *application of a*

148

theory. Because, in retail trade, in English or Dutch auction, or other particular modes of traffic, we cannot at once observe the operation of the laws of supply and demand, it is not in the least to be supposed that those laws are false. In fact, Mr Thornton seems to allow that, if prospective demand and supply are taken into account, they become substantially true. But, in the actual working of any market, the influence of future events should never be neglected, neither by a merchant nor an economist.

Though Mr Thornton's objections are mostly beside the question, his remarks have served to show that the action of the laws of supply and demand was inadequately explained by previous economists. What constitutes the demand and the supply was not carefully enough investigated. As Mr Thornton points out, there may be a number of persons willing to buy; but if their highest offer is ever so little short of the lowest price which the seller is willing to take, their influence is nil. If in an auction there are ten people willing to buy a horse at £20, but not higher, their demand instantly ceases when any one person offers £21. I am inclined not only to accept such a view, but to carry it further. Any change in the price of an article will be determined not with regard to the large numbers who might or might not buy it at other prices, but by the few who will or will not buy it according as a change is made close to the existing price.

The theory consists in carrying out this view to the point of asserting that it is only comparatively insignificant quantities of supply and demand which are at any moment operative on the ratio of exchange. This is practically verified by what takes place in any very large market – say that of the Consolidated Three Per Cent Annuities. As the whole amount of the English funds is nearly eight hundred millions sterling, the quantity bought or sold by any ordinary purchaser is inconsiderably small in comparison. Even £1,000 worth of stock may be taken as an infinitesimally small increment, because it does not appreciably affect the total existing supply. Now the theory consists in asserting that the market price of the funds is affected from hour to hour not by the enormous amounts which *might* be bought or sold at extreme prices, but by the comparatively insignificant amounts which *are* being sold or bought at the existing prices. A change of price is always occasioned by the overbalancing of the inclinations of those who will or will not sell just about the point at which prices stand. When Consols are at $93\frac{1}{2}$, and business is in a tranquil state, it matters not how many buyers there are at 93, or sellers at 94. They are really off the market. Those only are operative who may be made to buy or sell by a rise or fall of an eighth. The question is, whether the price shall remain at $93\frac{1}{2}$, or rise to $93\frac{5}{8}$, or fall to $93\frac{3}{8}$. This is determined by the sale or purchase of comparatively very small amounts. It is the purchasers who find a little stock more profitable to them than the corresponding sum of money who make the price rise by $\frac{1}{8}$. When the price of the funds is very steady and the market quiescent, it means that the stocks are distributed among holders in such a way that the exchange of more or less at the prevailing price is a matter of indifference.

In practice, no market ever long fulfils the theoretical conditions of equilibrium, because, from the various accidents of life and business, there are sure to be people every day compelled to sell, or having sudden inducements to buy. There is nearly always, again, the influence of prospective supply or demand, depending upon the political intelligence of the moment. Speculation complicates the action of the laws of supply and demand in a high degree, but does not in the least degree arrest their action or alter their nature. We shall never have a science of economics unless we learn to discern the operation of law even among the most perplexing complications and apparent interruptions.

Problems in the Theory of Exchange

We have hitherto considered only one simple case of the theory of exchange. In all other cases where the commodities are capable of indefinite subdivision, the principles will be exactly the same, but the particular conditions may be subject to variation.

We may, firstly, express the conditions of a great market where vast quantities of some stock are available, so that any one small trader will not appreciably affect the ratio of exchange. This ratio is, then, approximately a fixed number, and each trader exchanges at that ratio just so much as suits him. These circumstances may be represented by supposing A to be a trading body possessing two very large stocks of commodities, a and b. Let C be a person who possesses a comparatively small quantity c of the second commodity, and gives a portion of it, y, which is very small compared with b, in exchange for a portion of x of a, which is very small compared with a. Then, after exchange, we shall find A in possession of the quantities $a - x$ and $b + y$, and C in possession of x and $c - y$. The equations will become

$$\frac{\varphi_1(a - x)}{\psi_1(b + y)} = \frac{y}{x} = \frac{\varphi_2 x}{\psi_2(c - y)}.$$

Since $a - x$ and $b + y$, by supposition, do not appreciably differ from a and b, we may substitute the latter quantities, and we have, for the first equation, approximately,

$$\frac{\varphi_1 a}{\psi_1 b} = \frac{y}{x} = m.$$

The ratio of exchange being an approximately fixed ratio determined by the conditions of the trading body A, there is, in reality, only one undetermined quantity, x, the quantity of commodity which C finds it advantageous to purchase by expending part of c. This will now be determined by the equation

$$\frac{\varphi_1 a}{\psi_1 b} = \frac{\varphi_2 x}{\psi_2(c - mx)}.$$

This equation will represent the condition in regard to any one distinct commodity of a very small country trading with a much larger one. It might represent, to some extent, the circumstances of trade between the Channel Islands and the great markets of England, though, of course, it is never absolutely verified, because the smallest purchasers do affect the market in some degree. The equation still more accurately represents the position of an individual consumer with regard to the aggregate trade of a large community, since he must buy at the current prices, which he cannot in an appreciable degree affect.

A still simpler formula, however, is needed to represent the conditions of a large part of our purchases. In many cases we want so little of a commodity, that an individual need not give more than a very small fraction of his possessions to obtain it. We may suppose, then, that y in the last problem is a very small part of c, so that $\psi_2(c - y)$ does not differ appreciably from $\psi_2 c$. Taking m as before to be the existing ratio of exchange, we have only one equation –

$$\frac{\varphi_2 x}{\psi_2 c} = m,$$

or $\qquad \varphi_2 x = m \cdot \psi_2 c.$

This means that C will buy of the commodity until its degree of utility falls below that of the commodity he gives. A person's expenditure on salt is in this country an inconsiderable item of expense; what he thus spends does not make him appreciably poorer; yet, if the established price or ratio is one penny for each pound of salt, he buys in any time, say one year, so many pounds of salt that an additional pound would not have so much utility to him as a penny. In the above equation $m \cdot \psi_2 c$ represents the utility to him of a penny, which being an inconsiderable fraction of his possessions, is approximately invariable in utility, and he buys salt until $\varphi_2 x$, which is approximately the utility of the next pound, is equal to, or it may be somewhat less than that of the penny. But this case must not be confused with that of purchases which appreciably affect the possessions of the purchaser. Thus, if a poor family purchase much butchers'-meat, they will probably have to go without something else. The more they buy, the lower the final degree of utility of the meat, and *the higher the final degree of utility of something else*; and thus these purchases will be the more narrowly limited.

Complex Cases of the Theory

We have hitherto considered the theory of exchange as applying only to two trading bodies possessing and dealing in two commodities. Exactly the same principles hold true, however numerous and complicated may be the conditions. The main point to be remembered in tracing out the results of the theory is that the same pair of commodities in the same market can have only one ratio of exchange, which must therefore prevail between each body and each other, the costs of conveyance being considered as nil. The equations become rapidly more numerous as additional bodies or commodities are considered; but we may exhibit them as they apply to the case of three trading bodies and three commodities.

Thus, suppose that

> A possesses the stock a of cotton, and gives
> x_1 of it to B, x_2 to C.
> B possesses the stock b of silk, and gives
> y_1 to A, y_2 to C.
> C possesses the stock c of wool, and gives
> z_1 to A, z_2 to B.

We have here altogether six unknown quantities – x_1, x_2, y_1, y_2, z_1, z_2; but we have also sufficient means of determining them. They are exchanged as follows:

> A gives x_1 for y_1, and x_2 for z_1.
> B ,, y_1 for x_1, and y_2 for z_2.
> C ,, z_1 for x_2, and z_2 for y_2.

These may be treated as independent exchanges; each body must be satisfied in regard to each of its exchanges, and we must therefore take into account the functions of utility or the final degrees of utility of each commodity in respect of each body. Let us express these functions as follows:

φ_1, ψ_1, χ_1 are the respective functions of utility for A.
φ_2, ψ_2, χ_2 . . . . B.
φ_3, ψ_3, χ_3 . . . . C.

Now A, after the exchange, will hold $a - x_1 - x_2$ of cotton and y_1 of silk; and B will hold x_1 of cotton and $b - y_1 - y_2$ of silk: their ratio of exchange, y_1 for x_1, will therefore be governed by the following pair of equations:

$$\frac{\varphi_1 (a - x_1 - x_2)}{\psi_1 y_1} = \frac{y_1}{x_1} = \frac{\varphi_2 x_1}{\psi_2 (b - y_1 - y_2)}.$$

The exchange of A with C will be similarly determined by the ratio of the degrees of utility of wool and cotton on each side subsequent to the exchange; hence we have

$$\frac{\varphi_1(a - x_1 - x_2)}{\chi_1 z_1} = \frac{z_1}{x_2} = \frac{\varphi_3 x_2}{\chi_3(c - z_1 - z_2)}.$$

There will also be interchange between B and C which will be independently regulated on similar principles, so that we have another pair of equations to complete the conditions, namely –

$$\frac{\psi_2(b - y_1 - y_2)}{\chi_2 z_2} = \frac{z_2}{y_2} = \frac{\psi_3 y_2}{\chi_3(c - z_1 - z_2)}.$$

We might proceed in the same way to lay down the conditions of exchange between more numerous bodies, but the principles would be exactly the same. For every quantity of commodity which is given in exchange something must be received; and if portions of the same kind of commodity be received from several distinct parties, then we may conceive the quantity which is given for that commodity to be broken up into as many distinct portions. The exchanges in the most complicated case may thus always be decomposed into simple exchanges, and every exchange will give rise to two equations sufficient to determine the quantities involved. The same can also be done when there are two or more commodities in the possession of each trading body.

Competition in Exchange

One case of the theory of exchange is of considerable importance, and arises when two parties compete together in supplying a third party with a certain commodity. Thus, suppose that A, with the quantity of one commodity denoted by a, purchases another kind of commodity both from B and from C, who respectively possess b and c of it. All the quantities concerned are as follows:

A gives x_1 of a to B and x_2 to C,
B „ y_1 of b to A,
C „ y_2 of c to A.

As each commodity may be supposed to be perfectly homogeneous, the ratio of exchange must be the same in one case as in the other, so that we have one equation thus furnished –

$$\frac{y_1}{x_1} = \frac{y_2}{x_2}. \tag{1}$$

Now, provided that A gets the right commodity in the proper quantity, he does not care whence it comes, so that we need not, in his equation, distinguish the source or destination of the quantities; he simply gives $x_1 + x_2$, and receives in exchange $y_1 + y_2$. Observing, then, that by (1)

$$\frac{y_1 + y_2}{x_1 + x_2} = \frac{y_1}{x_1}$$

we have the usual equation of exchange –

$$\frac{\varphi_1 (a - x_1 - x_2)}{\psi_1 (y_1 + y_2)} = \frac{y_1}{x_1}. \tag{2}$$

But B and C must both be separately satisfied with their shares in the transaction. Thus

$$\frac{\varphi_2 x_1}{\psi_2 (b - y_1)} = \frac{y_1}{x_1}; \tag{3}$$

$$\frac{\varphi_3 x_2}{\psi_3 (c - y_2)} = \frac{y_2}{x_2}. \tag{4}$$

There are altogether four unknown quantities – x_1, x_2, y_1, y_2; and we have four equations by which to determine them. Various suppositions might be made as to the comparative magnitudes of the quantities b and c, or the character of the functions concerned; and conclusions could then be drawn as to the effect upon the trade. The general result would be, that the smaller holder must more or less conform to the prices of the larger holder.

Failure of the Equations of Exchange

Cases constantly occur in which equations of the kind set forth in the preceding pages fail to hold true, or lead to impossible results. Such failure may indicate that no exchange at all takes place, but it may also have a different meaning.

In the first case, it may happen that the commodity possessed by A has a high degree of utility to A, and a low degree to B, and that vice versa B's commodity has a high degree of utility to B and less to A. This difference of utility might exist to such an extent, that though B were to receive very little of A's commodity, yet the final degree of utility to him would be less than that of his own commodity, of which he enjoys much more. In such a case no benefit can arise from exchange, and no exchange will consequently take place. This failure of exchange will be indicated by a failure of the equations.

It may also happen that the whole quantities of commodity possessed are exchanged, and yet the equations fail. A may have so low a desire for consuming his own commodity, that the very last increment of it has less degree of utility to him than a small addition to the commodity received in exchange. The same state of things might happen to exist with B as regards his commodity; under these circumstances the whole possessions of one might be exchanged for the whole of the other, and the ratio of exchange would of course be defined by the ratio of these quantities. Yet each party might desire the last increment of the commodity received more than he desires the last increment of that given, so that the equations would fail to be true. This case will hardly occur practically in international trade, since two nations usually trade in many commodities, a fact which would alter the conditions.

Again, the equations of exchange will fail to be possible when the commodity or useful article possessed on one or both sides is indivisible. We have always assumed hitherto that more or less of a commodity may be had, down to infinitely small quantities. This is approximately true of all ordinary trade, especially international trade between great industrial nations. Any one sack of corn or any one bar of iron is practically infinitesimal compared with the quantities exchanged by America and England; and even one cargo or parcel of corn or iron is a small fraction of the whole. But, in exceptional cases, even international trade might involve indivisible articles. We might conceive the British Government giving the Koh-i-noor diamond to the Khedive of Egypt in exchange for Pompey's Pillar, in which case it would certainly not answer the purpose to break up one article or the other.* When an island or portion of territory is transferred from one possessor to another, it is often necessary to take the whole, or none. America, in purchasing Alaska from Russia, would hardly have consented to purchase less than the whole. In every sale of a house, factory or other building, it is usually impracticable to make any division without greatly lessening the utility of the whole. In all such cases our equations must fail to exist, because we cannot contemplate the existence of an increment or a decrement to an indivisible article.

Suppose, for example, that A and B each possess a book; they cannot break up the books, and must therefore exchange them entire, if at all. Under what conditions will they do so? Plainly on the condition that each makes a gain of utility by so doing. Here we deal not with the final degree of utility depending on an infinitesimal quantity, but on the *whole utility of the complete article*. Now let us assign the symbols as follows:

$$u_1 = \text{the utility of A's book to A,}$$
$$u_2 \quad ,, \quad ,, \quad \text{A's} \quad ,, \quad \text{to B,}$$
$$v_1 \quad ,, \quad ,, \quad \text{B's} \quad ,, \quad \text{to A,}$$
$$v_2 \quad ,, \quad ,, \quad \text{B's} \quad ,, \quad \text{to B.}$$

Then the conditions of exchange are simply

$$v_1 > u_1,$$
$$u_2 > v_2.$$

We might indeed theoretically contemplate the case where the utilities were exactly equal on one side; thus

$$v_1 > u_1,$$
$$u_2 = v_2;$$

* Since the above was written the value of Cleopatra's Needle has actually formed the subject of decision in the Admiralty Court, in connexion with the award of salvage. The fact, however, is that in the absence of any act of exchange concerning such an object, the notion of value is not applicable at all. At the best the value assigned, namely £25,000, is a mere fiction arbitrarily invented to represent what might conceivably be given for such an object if there were a purchaser. It is, moreover, curious that since the first edition was printed Russia has actually made an exchange of islands with Japan. [In 1875 Japan ceded the southern portion of Saghalien to Russia in exchange for the northern half of the Kurile islands. – H.S.J.]

B would then be wholly indifferent to the exchange, and I do not see any means of deciding whether he would or would not consent to it. But we need hardly consider the case, as it could seldom practically occur. Were the utilities exactly equal on both sides in respect to both objects, there would obviously be no motive to exchange. Again, the slightest loss of utility on either side would be a complete bar to the transaction, because we are not supposing, at present, that any other commodities are in possession so as to allow of separate inducements, or that any other motives than such as arise out of simple desire of one's own convenience enter into the question.

A much more difficult problem arises when we suppose an indivisible article exchanged for a divisible commodity. When Russia sold Alaska this was a practically indivisible thing; but it was bought with money of which more or less might be given to indefinitely small quantities. A bargain of this kind is exceedingly common; indeed it occurs in the case of every house, mansion, estate, factory, ship, or other complete whole, which is sold for money. Our former equations of exchange certainly fail, for they involve increments of commodity on both sides. The theory seems to give a very unsatisfactory answer, for the problem proves to be, within certain limits, indeterminate.

Let X be the indivisible article; u_1 its utility to its possessor A, and u_2 its utility to B. Let y be the quantity of commodity given for it, a commodity which is supposed to be divisible *ad infinitum*; let v_1 be the total utility of y to A, and v_2 its total utility to B. Then it is quite evident that, in order to give rise to exchange, v_1 must be greater than u_1, and u_2 must be greater than v_2; that is, there must, as before, be a gain of utility on each side. The quantity y must not be so great then as to deprive B of gain, nor so small as to deprive A of gain. The following is an extract from Mr Thornton's work which exactly expresses the problem:

There are two opposite extremes – one above which the price of a commodity cannot rise, the other below which it cannot fall. The upper of these limits is marked by the utility, real or supposed, of the commodity to the customer; the lower, of its utility to the dealer. No one will give for a commodity a quantity of money or money's worth, which, in his opinion, would be of more use to him than the commodity itself. No one will take for a commodity a quantity of money or of anything else which he thinks would be of less use to himself than the commodity. The price eventually given and taken may be either at one of the opposite extremes, or may be anywhere intermediate between them.*

Three distinct cases might occur, which can best be illustrated by a concrete example. Suppose we can read the thoughts of the parties in the sale of a house. If A says £1,200 is the least price which will satisfy him, and B holds that £800 is the highest price which it will be profitable for him to give, no exchange can possibly take place. If A should find £1,000 to be his lowest limit, while B happens to name the same sum for his highest limit, the transaction can be closed, and the price will be exactly defined. But supposing, finally, that A is really willing to sell at £900, and B is prepared to buy at £1,100, in what manner can we theoretically determine the price? I see no mode of solving the question. Any price between £900 and £1,100 will leave a profit on each side, and both parties will lose if they do not come to terms. I conceive that such a transaction must be settled upon other than strictly economic grounds. The result of the bargain will greatly depend upon the comparative amount of knowledge of each other's position and needs which either bargainer may possess or manage to obtain in the course of the transaction. Thus the power of reading another man's thoughts is of high importance in business, and the art of bargaining mainly consists in the buyer ascertaining the lowest price at which the seller is willing to part with his object, without disclosing if possible the highest price which he, the buyer, is willing to give. The disposition and force of character of the parties, their comparative persistency, their adroitness and experience in business, or it may be feelings of justice or of kindliness, will also influence the decision. These are motives more or less extraneous to a theory of economics, and yet they appear necessary considerations in this problem. It may be that indeterminate bargains of this kind are best arranged by an arbitrator or third party.

*Thornton, *On Labour; its Wrongful Claims and Rightful Dues*, 1869, p. 58.

The equations of exchange may fail again when commodities are divisible, but not to infinitely small quantities. There is always, in retail trade, a convenient unit below which we do not descend in purchases. Paper may be bought in quires, or even in packets, which it may not be desirable to break up. Wine cannot be bought from the wine merchant in less than a bottle at a time. In all such cases exchange cannot, theoretically speaking, be perfectly

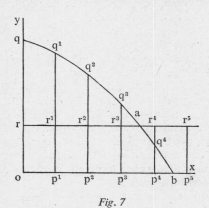

Fig. 7

adjusted, because it will be infinitely improbable that an integral number of units will precisely verify the equations of exchange. In a large proportion of cases, indeed, the unit may be so small compared with the whole quantities exchanged as practically to be infinitely small. But suppose that a person be buying ink which is only to be had, under the circumstances, in one-shilling bottles. If one bottle be not quite enough, how will he decide whether to take a second or not? Clearly by estimating the aggregate utility of the bottle of ink compared with the shilling. If there be an excess, he will certainly purchase it, and proceed to consider whether a third be desirable or not.

This case might be illustrated by figure 7, in which the spaces $o\, q_1$, $p_1\, q_2$, $p_2\, q_3$, etc., represent the total utilities of successive bottles of ink; while the equal spaces $o\, r_1$, $p_1\, r_2$, etc., represent the total utilities of successive shillings, which we may assume to be practically invariable. There is no doubt that three bottles will be purchased, but the fourth will not be purchased unless the mixtilinear figure $p_3 q_3 q_4 p_4$ exceed in area the rectangle $p_3 r_3 r_4 p_4$.

Cases of this kind are similar to those treated in pp. 156–9, where the things exchanged are indivisible, except that the question of exchange or no exchange occurs over and over again with respect to each successive unit, and is decided in respect to each by the excess of the total utility of the unit to be received over the total utility of that to be given. There is indeed perfect harmony between the cases where equations can and where they cannot be established; for we have only to imagine the indivisible units of commodity to be indefinitely lessened in size to enable us to pass gradually down to the case where equality of the increments of utility is ultimately established.

Negative and Zero Value

Only a few economists, notably Mr H. D. Macleod in several of his publications, have noticed the fact that there may be such a thing as negative value. Yet there cannot be the least doubt that people often labour, or pay money to other labourers, in order to get rid of things, and they would not do this unless such things were hurtful, that is, had the opposite quality to utility – disutility. Water, when it gets into a mine, is a costly thing to get out again, and many people have been ruined by wet mines. Quarries and mines usually produce great quantities of valueless rock or earth, variously called duff, spoil, waste, rubbish, and no inconsiderable part of the cost of working arises from the need of raising and carrying this profitless mass of matter and then finding land on which to deposit it. Every furnace yields cinders, dross or slag, which can seldom be sold for any money, and every household is at the expense of getting rid, in one way or another, of sewage, ashes, swill and other *rejectanea*. Reflection soon shows, in short, that no inconsiderable part of the values with which we deal in practical economics must be *negative values*.

It will hardly be needful to show at full length that this negative value may be regarded as varying continuously in the same way as positive value. If after a long drought rain begins to fall heavily, it is at first hailed as a great benefit; the rain-water may be so valuable as to produce a crop, when otherwise successful agriculture would have been impossible. Rain may thus avert famine; but after the rain has fallen for a certain length of time, the farmer begins to think he has had enough of it; more rain will retard his operations, or injure the growing plants. As the rain continues to fall he fears further injury; water begins to flood his land, and there is even danger of the soil and crops being all washed away together. But the rain unfortunately pours down more and more heavily, until at length perhaps the crops, soil, house, stock – nay, the farmer himself, are all swept bodily away. That same water, then, which in moderate quantity would have been of the greatest possible benefit, has only to be supplied in greater and greater quantities to become injurious, until it ends with occasioning the ruin, and even the death, of the individual. Those acquainted with the floods and droughts of Australia know that this is no fancy sketch.*

In many other cases it might be shown similarly that matter. we can hardly call it commodity, acquires a higher and higher degree of *disutility* the greater the quantity which has to be disposed of. Such is the case with the sewage of great towns, the foul or poisoned water from mines, dye-works, etc. Any obstacle however, may be regarded as so much discommodity, whether it be a mountain which has to be bored through to make a railway. or a hollow which has to be filled up with an expensive embankment. If a building site requires a certain expenditure in levelling and draining before it can be made use of, the cost of this work is, of course, subtracted from the value which the land would otherwise possess. As every advantage in property gives rise to value, so every disadvantage must be set against that value.

We now come to the question how negative value is to be represented in our equations. Let us suppose a person possessing a of some commodity to find it insufficient; then it has positive degree of utility for him, that is to say $\varphi(a)$ is positive. Suppose x

* See the author's 'History of the Floods and Droughts of New South Wales', in the *Australian Almanack*, Sydney, 1859, p. 61. Also Mr H. C Russell's *Climate of New South Wales*, Sydney, 1877.

to be added to a and gradually increased; $\varphi(a + x)$ will gradually decrease. Let us assume that for a certain value of x it becomes zero; then, if the further increase of x turns utility into disutility, $\varphi(a + x)$ will become a negative quantity. How will this negative sign affect the validity of the equations which we have been employing in preceding pages, and in which each member has appeared to be both formally and intrinsically positive? It is plain that we cannot equate a positive to a negative quantity; but it will be found that if, at the same time that we introduce negative utility, we also assign to each increment of commodity the positive or negative sign, according as it is added to or subtracted from the exchanger's possessions, that is to say, received or given in exchange, no such difficulty arises.

Suppose A and B respectively to hold a and b, and to exchange dx and dy of the commodities X and Y. Then it will be apparent from the general character of the argument on pp. 141–3, that the fundamental equation there adopted will be included in the more general form –

$$\varphi(a \pm x) . dx + \psi(b \pm y) . dy = 0.$$

In this equation either factor of either term may be intrinsically negative, while the alternative signs before x and y allow for every possible case of giving and receiving in exchange.

Four possible cases will arise. In the first case, both commodities have utility for each person, that is to say, φ and ψ are both positive functions; but A gives some of X in return for some of Y. This means that dx is negative, and dy positive, while the quantities in possession after exchange are $a - x$, and $b + y$. Thus the equation becomes

$$-\varphi(a - x) . dx + \psi(b + y) . dy = 0.$$

We should have merely to transpose the negative term to the other side of the equation, and to assume $b = 0$, to obtain the equation on p. 142.

As the second case, suppose that Y possesses disutility for A, so that the function ψ becomes for him negative; in order to get rid of y, he must also pay x with it, and both these quantities as well as dy and dx receive the negative sign. Then the equation takes the shape

$$\varphi(a - x) \times (-dx) - \psi(b - y) \times (-dy) = 0,$$

or

$$-\varphi(a - x) \cdot dx + \psi(b - y) \cdot dy = 0.$$

The third case is the counterpart of the last, and represents B's position, who receives both x and y, on the ground that one of these quantities is *discommodity* to him. But putting the matter as the case of A, we may assume φ to be positive, ψ negative, and giving the positive sign to all of x, y, dx and dy, we obtain the equation –

$$\varphi(a + x) \cdot dx - \psi(b + y) \cdot dy = 0.$$

It is possible to conceive yet a fourth case in which people should be exchanging two discommodities; that is to say, getting rid of one hurtful substance by accepting in place of it what is felt to be less hurtful, though still possessing disutility. In this case we have both φ and ψ negative, as well as one of the quantities exchanged; taking x and dx as positive, and y and dy as negative, the equation assumes the form

$$-\varphi(a + x) \cdot dx - \psi(b - y) \cdot (-dy) = 0,$$

or

$$-\varphi(a + x) \cdot dx + \psi(b - y) \cdot dy = 0.$$

It might be difficult to discover any distinct cases of this last kind of exchange. Generally speaking, when a person receives assistance in getting rid of some inconvenient possession, he pays in money or other commodity for the service of him who helps to remove the burden. It must naturally be a very rare case that the remover has some burden which it would suit the other party to receive in exchange. Yet the contingency may, and no doubt does, sometimes occur. Two adjacent landowners, for instance, might reasonably agree that, if A allows B to throw the spoil of his mine on A's land, then A shall be allowed to drain his mine into B's mine. It might happen that B was comparatively more embarrassed by the great quantity of his spoil than by water, and that A had room for the spoil, but could not get rid of the water in other ways without great difficulty. An exchange of inconveniences would then be plainly beneficial.

Looking at the equations obtained in the four cases as stated above, it is apparent that the general equation of exchange consists in equating to zero the sum of one positive and one negative term, so that the signs, both of the utility functions and of the increments, may be disregarded. Thus the fundamental equation may be written in the general form

$$\frac{\varphi(a \pm x)}{\psi(b \pm y)} = \frac{dy}{dx}.$$

We may express the result of this theory in general terms by saying that the algebraic sum of the utility or disutility received or parted with, as regards the last increments concerned in an act of traffic, will always be zero. It also follows that, without regard to sign, the increments are in magnitude inversely as their degrees of utility or disutility. The reader will not fail to notice the remarkable analogy between this theory and that of the equilibrium of two forces regarded according to the principle of virtual velocities. A rigid lever will remain in equilibrium under the action of two forces, provided that the algebraic sum of the forces, each multiplied by its infinitely small displacement, be zero. Substitute for force degree of utility, positive or negative, and for infinitely small displacements infinitely small quantities of commodity exchanged, and the principles are identical.

It still remains to consider the imaginary case in which substances possess or are supposed to possess neither utility nor disutility, and are yet exchanged in finite quantities. Substituting the ratio of y and x for that of dy and dx, the general equation

$$\frac{\varphi(a \pm x)}{\psi(b \pm y)} = \frac{y}{x}$$

will give the value $\frac{y}{x} = \frac{0}{0}$, both the functions of utility being zero. This means that the quantities exchanged will be indeterminate so far as the theory of utility goes. If one substance possesses utility, and the other does not, the ratio of exchange becomes either $\frac{y}{0}$ or $\frac{0}{y}$, infinity or zero, indicating that there can be no comparison in our theory between things which do and those which do not possess utility. Practically speaking, such cases do not occur except in an approximate manner. Such things as cinders, shavings, nightsoil, etc., have either low degrees of utility or disutility. If the dustman takes them away for nothing, they must have utility for him sufficient to pay the cost of removal. When the dust is riddled, one part is usually found to have utility just sufficient to balance the disutility of the remainder, giving us an instance of the second or third form of the equation of exchange according as we regard the matter from the householder's or the dustman's point of view.

Equivalence of Commodities

Much confusion is thrown into the statistical investigation of questions of supply and demand by the circumstance that one commodity can often replace another, and serve the same purposes more or less perfectly. The same, or nearly the same, substance is often obtained from two or three sources. The constituents of wheat, barley, oats and rye are closely similar, if not identical. Vegetable structures are composed mainly of the same chemical compound in nearly all cases. Animal meat, again, is of nearly the same composition from whatever animal derived. There are endless differences of flavour and quality, but these are often insufficient to prevent one kind from serving in place of another.

Whenever different commodities are thus applicable to the same purposes, their conditions of demand and exchange are not independent. Their mutual ratio of exchange cannot vary much, for it will be closely defined by the ratio of their utilities. Beef and mutton, for instance, differ so slightly, that people eat them almost indifferently. But the wholesale price of mutton, on an average, exceeds that of beef in the ratio of 9 to 8, and we must therefore conclude that people generally esteem mutton more than beef in this proportion, otherwise they would not buy the dearer meat. It follows that the final degrees of utility of these meats are in this ratio, or that if φx be the degree of utility of mutton, and ψy that of beef, we have

$$8\varphi x = 9\psi y.$$

This equation would doubtless not hold true in extreme circumstances; if mutton became comparatively scarce, there would probably be some persons willing to pay a higher price, merely because it would then be considered a delicacy. But this is certain, that, so long as the equation of utilities holds true, the ratio of exchange between mutton and beef will not diverge from that of 8 to 9. If the supply of beef falls off to a small extent, people will not pay a higher price for it, but will eat more mutton; and if the supply of mutton falls off, they will eat more beef. The conditions of supply will have no effect upon the ratio of exchange; we must, in fact, treat beef and mutton as one commodity of two different strengths, just as gold at eighteen and gold at twenty carats are hardly considered as two but rather as one commodity, of which twenty parts of one are equivalent to eighteen of the other.

It is upon this principle that we must explain, in harmony with Cairnes's views, the extraordinary permanence of the ratio of exchange of gold and silver, which from the commencement of the eighteenth century up to recent years never diverged much from 15 to 1. That this fixedness of ratio did not depend entirely upon the amount or cost of production is proved by the very slight effect of the Australian and Californian gold discoveries, which never raised the gold price of silver more than about $4\frac{2}{3}$ per cent, and failed to have a permanent effect of more than $1\frac{1}{2}$ per cent. This permanence of relative values may have been partially due to the fact that gold and silver can be employed for exactly the same purposes, but that the superior brilliancy of gold occasions it to be preferred, unless it be about 15 or $15\frac{1}{2}$ times as costly as silver. Much more probably, however, the explanation of the fact is to be found in the fixed ratio of $15\frac{1}{2}$ to 1, according to which these metals are exchanged in the currency of France and some other continental countries. The French Currency Law of the Year XI established an artificial equation:

$$\text{Utility of gold} = 15\frac{1}{2} \times \text{Utility of silver};$$

and it is probably not without some reason that Wolowski and other recent French economists attributed to this law of replacement an important effect in preventing disturbance in the relations of gold and silver.

Since the first edition of this work was published, the views of Wolowski have received striking verification in the unprecedented fall in the value of silver which has occurred in the last three or four years. The ratio of equivalent weights of silver and gold, which had never before risen much above 16 to 1, commenced to rise in 1874, and was at one time (July 1876) as high as 22·5 to 1 in the London market. Though it has since fallen, the ratio continues to be subject to frequent considerable oscillations. The great production of silver in Nevada may contribute somewhat to this extraordinary result, but the principal cause must be the suspension of the French Law of the double standard, and the demonetization of silver in Germany, Scandinavia and elsewhere. As I have treated the subject of the value of silver and the double standard elsewhere,* I need not pursue it here.

Acquired Utility of Commodities

The theory of exchange, as explained above, rests entirely on the consideration of quantities of utility, and no reference to labour or cost of production has been made. The *value* of a divisible commodity, if I may for a moment use the dangerous term, is measured, not, indeed, by its total utility, but by its final degree of utility, that is by the intensity of the need we have for *more* of it. But the power of exchanging one commodity for another greatly extends the range of utility. We are no longer limited to considering the degree of utility of a commodity as

---

* *Serious Fall in the Value of Gold*, 1863, p. 33 (reprinted in *Investigations in Currency and Finance*, 1884). *Money and the Mechanism of Exchange* (International Scientific Series; also translated into French, German and Italian), ch. XII. This chapter has been translated by M. H. Gravez, and reprinted in the *Bibliothèque Utile*, vol. XLIV, Germer Baillière, Paris, 1878. See also Papers on the Silver Question read before the American Social Science Association at Saratoga, 5 September 1877, Boston, 1877, and *Bankers' Magazine*, December 1877 (reprinted in *Investigations in Currency and Finance*, 1884 and 1908).

regards the wants of its immediate possessor; for it may have a higher usefulness to some other person, and can be transferred to that person in exchange for some commodity of a higher degree of utility to the purchaser. The general result of exchange is that all commodities sink, as it were, to the same level of utility in respect of the last portions consumed.

In the theory of exchange we find that the possessor of any divisible commodity will exchange such a portion of it, that the next increment would have exactly equal utility with the increment of other produce which he would receive for it. This will hold good however various may be the kinds of commodity he requires. Suppose that a person possesses one single kind of commodity, which we may consider to be money, or income, and that p, q, r, s, t, etc., are quantities of other commodities which he purchases with portions of his income. Let x be the uncertain quantity of money which he will desire not to exchange; what relation will exist between these quantities x, p, q, r, etc.? This relation will partly depend upon the ratio of exchange, partly on the final degree of utility[39] of these commodities. Let us assume, for a moment, that all the ratios of exchange are equalities, or that a unit of one is always to be purchased with a unit of another. Then, plainly, we must have the degrees of utility equal, otherwise there would be advantage in acquiring more of that possessing the higher degree of utility. Let the sign φ denote the function of utility, which will be different in each case; then we have simply the equations –

$$\varphi_1 x = \varphi_2 p = \varphi_3 q = \varphi_4 r = \varphi_5 s = \text{etc.}$$

But, as a matter of fact, the ratio of exchange is seldom or never that of unit for unit; and when the quantities exchanged are unequal, the degrees of utility will not be equal. If for one pound of silk I can have three of cotton, then the degree of utility of cotton must be a third that of silk, otherwise I should gain by exchange. Thus the general result of the facility of exchange prevailing in a civilized country is that *a person procures such quantities of commodities that the final degrees of utility of any pair of commodities are inversely as the ratios of exchange of the commodities.*

Let x_1, x_2, x_3, x_4, etc., be the portions of his income given for p, q, r, s, etc., respectively, then we must have

$$\frac{\varphi_2 p}{\varphi_1 x} = \frac{x_1}{p}, \qquad \frac{\varphi_3 q}{\varphi_1 x} = \frac{x_2}{q}, \qquad \frac{\varphi_4 r}{\varphi_1 x} = \frac{x_3}{r},$$

and so on. The theory thus represents the fact that a person distributes his income in such a way as to equalize the utility of the final increments of all commodities consumed. As water runs into hollows until it fills them up to the same level, so wealth runs into all the branches of expenditure. This distribution will vary greatly with different individuals, but it is self-evident that the want which an individual feels most acutely at the moment will be that upon which he will expend the next increment of his income. It obviously follows that *in expending a person's income to the greatest advantage, the algebraic sum of the quantities of commodity received or parted with, each multiplied by its final degree of utility* [after the exchange], *will be zero.*

We can now conceive, in an accurate manner, the utility of money, or of that supply of commodity which forms a person's income. Its final degree of utility is measured by that of any of the other commodities which he consumes. What, for instance, is the utility of one penny to a poor family earning fifty pounds a year? As a penny is an inconsiderable portion of their income, it may represent one of the infinitely small increments, and its utility is equal to the utility of the quantity of bread, tea, sugar, or other articles which they could purchase with it, this utility depending upon the extent to which they were already provided with those articles. To a family possessing one thousand pounds a year, the utility of a penny may be measured in an exactly similar manner; but it will be much less, because their want of any given commodity will be satiated or satisfied to a much greater extent, so that the urgency of need for a pennyworth more of any article is much reduced.

The general result of exchange is thus to produce a certain equality of utility between different commodities, as regards the same individual; but between different individuals no such equality will tend to be produced.[40] In economics we regard only commercial transactions, and no equalization of wealth from charitable motives is considered. The degree of utility of wealth to a very rich man will be governed by its degree of utility in that branch of expenditure in which he continues to feel the most need of further possessions. His primary wants will long since have been fully satisfied; he could find food, if requisite, for a thousand persons, and so, of course, he will have supplied himself with as much as he in the least desires. But so far as is consistent with the inequality of wealth in every community, all commodities are distributed by exchange so as to produce the maximum of benefit. Every person whose wish for a certain thing exceeds his wish for other things, acquires what he wants provided he can make a sufficient sacrifice in other respects. No one is ever required to give what he more desires for what he less desires, so that perfect freedom of exchange must be to the advantage of all.

The Gain by Exchange

It is a most important result of this theory that the ratio of exchange gives no indication of the real benefit derived from the action of exchange. So many trades are occupied in buying and selling, and make their profits by buying low and selling high, that there arises a fallacious tendency to believe that the whole benefit of trade depends upon the differences of prices. It is implied that to pay a high price is worse than doing without the article, and the whole financial system of a great nation may be distorted in the effort to carry out a false theory.

This is the result to which some of J. S. Mill's remarks, in his *Theory of International Trade*, would lead. That theory is always ingenious, and as it seems to me, nearly always true; but he draws from it the following conclusion: *

The countries which carry on their foreign trade on the most advantageous terms are those whose commodities are most in demand by foreign countries, and which have themselves the least demand for foreign commodities. From which, among other consequences, it follows that the richest countries, *cæteris paribus*, gain the least by a

* *Principles of Political Economy*, Book III, ch. XVIII, end of the 8th section.

given amount of foreign commerce: since, having a greater demand for commodities generally, they are likely to have a greater demand for foreign commodities, and thus modify the terms of interchange to their own disadvantage. Their aggregate gains by foreign trade, doubtless, are generally greater than those of poorer countries, since they carry on a greater amount of such trade, and gain the benefit of cheapness on a larger consumption: but their gain is less on each individual article consumed.

In the absence of any explanation to the contrary, this passage must be taken to mean that the advantage of foreign trade depends upon the terms of exchange, and that international trade is less advantageous to a rich than to a poor country. But such a conclusion involves confusion between two distinct things – the price of a commodity and its total utility. A country is not merely like a great mercantile firm buying and selling goods, and making a profit out of the difference of price; it buys goods in order to consume them. But, in estimating the benefit which a consumer derives from a commodity, it is the total utility which must be taken as the measure, not the final degree of utility on which the terms of exchange depend.

To illustrate this truth we may employ the curves in figure 8 to represent the functions of utility of two commodities. Let the wool of Australia be represented by the line *ob*, and its total utility to Australia by the area of the curvilinear figure *obrp*. Let the utility of a second commodity, say cotton goods, to Australia be similarly represented in the lower curve, so that the quantity of commodity measured by *o'b'* gives a total utility represented by the figure *o'p'r'b'*. Then, if Australia gives half its wool, *ab*, for the quantity of cotton goods represented by *o'a'*, it loses the utility *aqrb*, but gains that represented by the larger area *o'p'q'a'*. There is accordingly a considerable net gain of utility, which is the real object of exchange. Even had Australia sold its wool at a lower price, obtaining cotton goods only to the amount of *o'c*, the utility of this amount, *o'p'sc*, would have exceeded that of the wool given for it.

So far is Mill's statement from being fundamentally correct that I believe the truth lies in the opposite direction. As a general rule, the greatness of the price which a country is willing and able to pay for the productions of other countries, measures, or at least manifests, the greatness of the benefit which it derives from such imports. He who pays a high price must either have a very great need of that which he buys, or very little need of that which he pays for it; on either supposition there is gain by

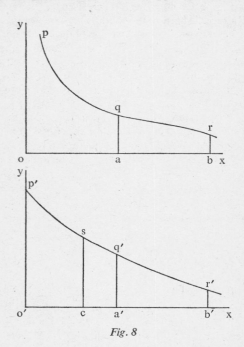

Fig. 8

exchange. In questions of this sort there is but one rule which can be safely laid down, namely that no one will buy a thing unless he expects advantage from the purchase; and perfect freedom of exchange, therefore, tends to the maximizing of utility.

One advantage of the theory of economics, carefully studied, will be to make us very careful in our conclusions when the matter is not of the simplest possible nature. The fact that we can most imperfectly estimate the total utility of any one commodity should prevent us, for instance, from attempting to measure the benefit of any trade. Accordingly, when Mill proceeds from his theory of international trade to that of taxation, and arrives at the conclusion that one nation may, by means of taxes on commodities imported, 'appropriate to itself, at the expense of foreigners, a larger share than would otherwise belong to it of the increase in the general productiveness of the labour and capital of the world',* I venture to question the truth of his results. I conceive that his arguments involve a confusion between the ratio of exchange and the total utility of a commodity, and a far more accurate knowledge of economic laws than anyone yet possesses would be required to estimate the true effect of a tax. Customs duties may be requisite as a means of raising revenue, but the time is past when any economist should give the slightest countenance to their employment for manipulating trade, or for interfering with the natural tendency of exchange to increase utility.

Numerical Determination of the Laws of Utility[41]

The future progress of economics as a strict science must greatly depend upon our acquiring more accurate notions of the variable quantities concerned in the theory. We cannot really tell the effect of any change in trade or manufacture until we can with some approach to truth express the laws of the variation of utility numerically. To do this we need accurate statistics of the quantities of commodities purchased by the whole population at various prices. The price of a commodity is the only test we have of the utility of the commodity to the purchaser; and if we could tell exactly how much people reduce their consumption of each important article when the price rises, we could determine, at least approximately, the variation of the final degree of utility – the all important element in economics.

In such calculations we may at first make use of the simpler equation on p. 152. For the first approximation we may assume

---

* *Principles of Political Economy*, Book V, ch. IV, sec. vi.

that the general utility of a person's income is not affected by the changes of price of the commodity; so that, if in the equation

$$\varphi x = m \cdot \psi c$$

we may have many different corresponding values for x and m, we may treat ψc, the utility of money, as a constant, and determine the general character of the function φx, the final degree of utility. This function would doubtless be a purely empirical one – a mere aggregate of terms devised so that their sum shall vary in accordance with statistical facts. The subject is too complex to allow of our expecting any simple precise law like that of gravity. Nor, when we have got the laws, shall we be able to give any exact explanation of them. They will be of the same character as the empirical formulae used in many of the physical sciences – mere aggregates of mathematical symbols intended to replace a tabular statement.* Nevertheless, their determination will render economics a science as exact as many of the physical sciences; as exact, for instance, as meteorology is likely to be for a very long time to come.

The method of determining the function of utility explained above will hardly apply, however, to the main elements of expenditure. The price of bread, for instance, cannot be properly brought under the equation in question, because, when the price of bread rises much, the resources of poor persons are strained, money becomes scarcer with them, and ψc, the utility of money, rises. The natural result is the lessening of expenditure in other directions; that is to say, all the wants of a poor person are supplied to a less degree of satisfaction when food is dear than when it is cheap. When in the long course of scientific progress a sufficient supply of suitable statistics has been at length obtained, it will become a mathematical problem of no great difficulty how to disentangle the functions expressing the degrees of utility of various commodities. One of the first steps, no doubt, will be to ascertain what proportion of the expenditure of poor people goes to provide food, at various prices of that food. But great difficulty is thrown in the way of all such inquiries

---

* See Jevons's *Principles of Science*, ch. XXII, new ed., pp. 487–9, and the references there given.

by the vast differences in the condition of persons; and still greater difficulties are created by the complicated ways in which one commodity replaces or serves instead of another.

Opinions as to the Variation of Price

There is no difficulty in finding in works of economists remarks upon the relation between a change in the supply of a commodity and the consequent rise of price. The general principles of the variation of utility have been familiar to many writers.

As a general rule the variation of price is much more marked in the case of necessaries of life than in the case of luxuries. This result would follow from the fact observed by Adam Smith, that 'The desire for food is limited in every man by the narrow capacity of the human stomach; but the desire of the conveniences and ornaments of building, dress, equipage and household furniture, seems to have no limit or certain boundary.' As I assert that value depends upon desire for more, it follows that any excessive supply of food will lower its price very much more than in the case of articles of luxury. Reciprocally, a deficiency of food will raise its price much more than would happen in the case of less necessary articles. This conclusion is in harmony with facts; for Chalmers says:

The necessaries of life are far more powerfully affected in the price of them by a variation in their quantity than are the luxuries of life. Let the crop of grain be deficient by one-third in its usual amount, or rather, let the supply of grain in the market, whether from the home produce or by importation, be curtailed to the same extent, and this will create a much greater addition than of one-third to the price of it. It is not an unlikely prediction that its cost would be more than doubled by the short-coming of one-third or one-fourth in the supply.*

He goes on to explain, at considerable length, that the same would not happen with such an article as rum. A deficiency in the supply of rum from the West Indies would occasion a rise of price, but not to any great extent, because there would be a substitution of other kinds of spirits, or else a reduction in the

* Chalmers's *Christian and Economic Polity of a Nation*, vol. II, p. 240.

amount consumed. Men can live without luxuries, but not without necessaries.

A failure in the general supply of esculents to the extent of one-half would more than quadruple the price of the first necessaries of life, and would fall with very aggravated pressure on the lower orders. A failure to the same extent in all the vineyards of the world would most assuredly not raise the price of wine to anything near this proportion. Rather than pay four times the wonted price for Burgundy, there would be a general descent to claret, or from that to port, or from that to the home-made wines of our own country, or from that to its spirituous, or from that to its fermented liquors.*

He points to sugar especially as an article which would be extensively thrown out of consumption by any great rise in price,† because it is a luxury, and at the same time forms a considerable element in expenditure. But he thinks that, if an article occasions a total expenditure of very small amount, variations of price will not much affect its consumption.

Speaking of nutmeg, he says:

There is not sixpence a year consumed of it for each family in Great Britain; and perhaps not one family that spends more than a guinea on this article alone. Let the price then be doubled or trebled; this will have no perceptible effect on the demand; and the price will far rather be paid than the wonted indulgence should in any degree be foregone. . . . The same holds true of cloves, and cinnamon, and Cayenne pepper, and all the precious spiceries of the East; and it is thus that while, in the general, the price of necessaries differs so widely from that of luxuries, in regard to the extent of oscillation, there is a remarkable approximation in this matter between the very commonest of these necessaries and the very rarest of these luxuries.‡

In these interesting observations Chalmers correctly distinguishes between the effect of desire for the commodity in question and that for other commodities. The cost of nutmeg does not appreciably affect the general expenditure on other things, and the equation on p. 152 therefore applies. But if sugar becomes scarce, to consume as before would necessitate a

* Chalmers's *Christian and Economic Polity of a Nation*, vol. II, p. 242.
† Ibid, p. 251.
‡ Ibid, p. 252.

reduction of consumption in other directions; and as the degree
of utility of more necessary articles rises much more rapidly
than that of sugar, it is the latter article which is thrown out of
use by preference. This is a far more complex case, which
includes also the case of corn and all large articles of consumption.

Chalmers's remarks on the price of sugar are strongly supported by facts concerning the course of the sugar markets in
1855–6. In the year 1855, as is stated in Tooke's *History of Prices,*[*]
attention was suddenly drawn to a considerable reduction which
had taken place in the stocks of sugar. The price rapidly advanced
but before it had reached the highest point the demand became
almost wholly suspended. Not only did retail dealers avoid
replenishing their stocks, but there was an immediate and sometimes entire cessation of consumption among extensive classes.
There were instances among the retail grocers of their not selling
a single pound of sugar until prices receded to what the public
was satisfied was a reasonable rate.

Variation of the Price of Corn

As to Chalmers's ingenious remarks upon the consumption of
nutmeg, he seems to be at least partially correct. To a certain
extent he brings into view the principle explained above, that
when only a small quantity of income is required to purchase a
certain kind of commodity in sufficient abundance, the degree
of utility of income will not be appreciably affected by the price
paid, that is to say (p. 152) ψc remains approximately constant.
It follows that $\frac{\varphi x}{m}$ is constant, or in other words the final degree
of utility of the small commodity purchased must be directly
proportional to the price. If then the price rises much, either the
consumer must relinquish the use of that commodity almost
entirely, or else he must feel such need of it, that a small decrease
of consumption is irksome to him; that is to say, looking to our
curves of utility, either we must recede to a part of the curve very
close to the axis of y, or else the curve must be one which rises

* Vol. V, p. 324, etc.

rapidly as we move towards the origin. Now Chalmers assumes that with nutmeg the latter is the case. People accustomed to use it in his time were so fond of it that they would pay a much higher price rather than decrease their consumption considerably. This means that it possessed a high degree of utility to them, which could only be overbalanced by some serious increase in the value of ψc, which would ultimately mean the need of the necessaries of life.

It is very curious that in this subject, which reaches to the very foundations of political economy, we owe more to early than later writers. Before our science could be said to exist at all, writers on political arithmetic had got about as far as we have got at present. In a pamphlet of 1737,* it is remarked that

People who understand trade will readily agree with me, that the tenth part of a commodity in a market, more than there is a brisk demand for, is apt to lower the market, perhaps, twenty or thirty per cent, and that a deficiency of a tenth part will cause as exorbitant an advance.

Sir J. Dalrymple,† again, says:

Merchants observe, that if the commodity in market is diminished one-third beneath its mean quantity, it will be nearly doubled in value; and that if it is augmented one-third above its mean quantity, it will sink near one-half in its value; or that, by further diminishing or augmenting the quantity, these disproportions between the quantity and prices vastly increase.

These remarks bear little signs of accuracy, indeed, for the writers have spoken of commodities in general as if they all varied in price in a similar degree. It is probable that they were thinking of corn or other kinds of the more necessary food. In the *Spectator* we find a conjecture‡ that the production of one-tenth part more of grain than is usually consumed would diminish the value of the grain one-half. I know nothing more strange and discreditable to statists and economists than that in so important

*Quoted in Lauderdale's *Inquiry into the Nature and Origin of Public Wealth*, 2nd ed., 1819, pp. 51, 52.

†Sir John Dalrymple, *Considerations upon the Policy of Entails in Great Britain*, Edinburgh, 1764.

‡No. 200, quoted by Lauderdale, p. 50.

a point as the relations of price and supply of the main article of food, we owe our most accurate estimates to writers who lived from one to two centuries ago.

There is a celebrated estimate of the variation of the price of corn which I have found quoted in innumerable works on economics. It is commonly attributed to Gregory King, whose name should be held in honour as one of the fathers of statistical science in England. Born at Lichfield in 1648, King devoted himself much to mathematical studies, and was often occupied in surveying. His principal public appointments were those of Lancaster Herald and Secretary to the Commissioners of Public Accounts; but he is known to fame by the remarkable statistical tables concerning the population and trade of England, which he completed in the year 1696. His treatise was entitled *Natural and Political Observations and Conclusions upon the State and Condition of England*, 1696. It was never printed in the author's lifetime, but the contents were communicated in a most liberal manner to Dr Davenant, who, making suitable acknowledgements as to the source of his information, founded thereupon his *Essay upon the Probable Methods of making a People gainers in the Balance of Trade.** Our knowledge of Gregory King's conclusions was derived from this and other essays of Davenant, until George Chalmers printed the whole treatise at the end of the third edition of his well-known *Estimate of the Comparative Strength of Great Britain*.[42]

The estimate of which I am about to speak is given by Davenant in the following words:†

We take it, that a defect in the harvest may raise the price of corn in the following proportions:

Defect		Above the common rate
1 Tenth	⎫	3 Tenths
2 Tenths	raises	8 Tenths
3 Tenths	the	1·6 Tenths
4 Tenths	price	2·8 Tenths
5 Tenths	⎭	4·5 Tenths

* London, 1699, *The Political and Commercial Works of Charles Davenant*, 1771, vol. II, p. 163.
† Ibid., p. 224.

So that when corn rises to treble the common rate, it may be presumed that we want above ⅓ of the common produce; and if we should want $\frac{5}{10}$, or half the common produce, the price would rise to near five times the common rate.

Though this estimate has always been attributed to Gregory King, I cannot find it in his published treatise; nor does Davenant, who elsewhere makes full acknowledgements of what he owes to King, here attribute it to his friend. It is therefore, perhaps, due to Davenant.

We may restate this estimate in the following manner, taking the average harvest and the average price of corn as unity:

Quantity of Corn	1·0	0·9	0·8	0·7	0·6	0·5
Price . .	1·0	1·3	1·8	2·6	3·8	5·5

Many writers have commented on this estimate. Thornton * observes that it is probably exceedingly inaccurate, and that it is not clear whether the total stock, or only the harvest of a single year, is to be taken as deficient. Tooke,† however, than whom on such a point there is no higher authority, believes that King's estimate

is not very wide of the truth, judging from the repeated occurrence of the fact that the price of corn in this country has risen from one hundred to two hundred per cent and upwards when the utmost computed deficiency of the crops has not been more than between one-sixth and one-third of an average.

I have endeavoured to ascertain the law to which Davenant's figures conform, and the mathematical function obtained does not greatly differ from what we might have expected. It is probable that the price of corn should never sink to zero, as, if abundant, it could be used for feeding horses, poultry and cattle, or for other purposes for which it is too costly at present. It is said that in America corn, no doubt Indian corn, has been occasionally used as fuel. On the other hand, when the quantity is much diminished, the price should rise rapidly, and should

* *An Inquiry into the Nature and Effects of the Paper Credit of Great Britain*, pp. 270, 271.
† *History of Prices*, vol. I, pp. 13–15.

become infinite before the quantity is zero, because famine would then be impending. The substitution of potatoes and other kinds of food renders the famine point very uncertain; but I think that a total deficiency of corn could not be made up by other food. Now a function of the form $\frac{a}{(x-b)^n}$ fulfils these conditions; for it becomes infinite when x is reduced to b, but for greater values of x always decreases as x increases. An inspection of the numerical data shows that n is about equal to 2, and, assuming it to be exactly 2, I find that the most probable values of a and b are $a = 0.824$ and $b = 0.12$. The formula thus becomes

$$\text{price of corn} = \frac{0.824}{(x - 0.12)^2},$$

or approximately, $= \dfrac{5}{6(x - \frac{1}{8})^2}$.

The following numbers show the degree of approximation between the first of these formulae and the data of Davenant:

Harvest	1.0	0.9	0.8	0.7	0.6	0.5
Price (Davenant)	1.0	1.3	1.8	2.6	3.8	5.5
Price calculated	1.06	1.36	1.78	2.45	3.58	5.71

I cannot undertake to say how nearly Davenant's estimate agrees with experience; but, considering the close approximation in the above numbers, we may safely substitute the empirical formula for his numbers; and there are other reasons already stated for supposing that this formula is not far from the truth.[*] Roughly speaking, the price of corn may be said to vary inversely as the square of the supply, provided that this supply be not unusually small. I find that this is nearly the same conclusion as Whewell drew from the same numbers. He says:[†] 'If the above numbers were to be made the basis of a mathematical rule, it would be found that the price varies inversely as the square of the supply, or rather in a higher ratio.'

There is further reason for believing that the price of corn

[*] See preface to fourth edition.
[†] *Six Lectures on Political Economy*, Cambridge, 1862.

varies more rapidly than in the inverse ratio of the quantity. Tooke estimates* that in 1795 and 1796 the farmers of England gained seven millions sterling in each year by a deficiency of one-eighth part of the wheat crop, not including the considerable profit on the rise of price of other agricultural produce. In each of the years 1799 and 1800, again, farmers probably gained eleven millions sterling by deficiency. If the price of wheat varied in the simple inverse proportion of the quantity, they would neither gain nor lose, and the fact that they gained considerably agrees with our formula as given above.

The variation of utility has not been overlooked by mathematicians, who had observed, as long ago as the early part of last century – before, in fact, there was any science of political economy at all – that the theory of probabilities could not be applied to commerce or gaming without taking notice of the very different utility of the same sum of money to different persons. Suppose that an even and fair bet is made between two persons, one of whom has £10,000 a year, the other £100 a year; let it be an equal chance whether they gain or lose £50. The rich person will, in neither case, feel much difference; but the poor person will receive far more harm by losing £50 than he can be benefited by gaining it. The utility of money to a poor person varies rapidly with the amount; to a rich person less so. Daniel Bernoulli, accordingly, distinguished in any question of probabilities between the *moral expectation* and the *mathematical expectation*, the latter being the simple chance of obtaining some possession, the former the chance as measured by its utility to the person. Having no means of ascertaining numerically the variation of utility, Bernoulli had to make assumptions of an arbitrary kind, and was then able to obtain reasonable answers to many important questions. It is almost self-evident that the utility of money decreases as a person's total wealth increases; if this be granted, it follows at once that gaming is, in the long run, a sure way to lose utility; that every person should, when possible, divide risks, that is, prefer two equal chances of £50 to one similar chance of £100; and the advantage of insurance of all kinds is proved from the same theory. Laplace drew a similar distinction between the

* *History of Prices.*

fortune physique, or the actual amount of a person's income, and the *fortune morale*, or its benefit to him.*

In answer to the objections of an ingenious correspondent, it may be remarked that when we say gaming is a sure way to lose utility, we take no account of the utility – that is, the pleasure – attaching to the pursuit of gaming itself; we regard only the commercial loss or gain. If a person with a certain income prefers to run the risk of losing a portion of it at play, rather than spending it in any other way, it must no doubt be conceded that the political economist, as such, can make no conclusive objection. If the gamester is so devoid of other tastes that to spend money over the gaming-table is the best use he can discover for it, economically speaking, there is nothing further to be said. The question then becomes a moral, legislative, or political one. A source of amusement which, like gaming, betting, dram-drinking, or opium-eating, is not in itself always pernicious, may come to be regarded as immoral, if in a considerable proportion of cases it leads to excessive and disastrous results. But this question evidently leads us into a class of subjects which could not be appropriately discussed in this work treating of pure economic theory.

The Origin of Value

The preceding pages contain, if I am not mistaken, an explanation of the nature of value which will, for the most part, harmonize with previous views upon the subject. Ricardo has stated, like most other economists, that utility is absolutely essential to value; but that 'possessing utility, commodities derive their exchangeable value from two sources: from their scarcity, and from the quantity of labour required to obtain them'.† Senior, again, has admirably defined wealth, or objects possessing value, as 'those things, and those things only, which are transferable, are limited in supply, and are directly or indirectly productive of pleasure or preventive of pain'. Speaking only of things which are transferable, or capable of being passed from hand to hand,

* Todhunter's *History of the Theory of Probability*, London, 1865, ch. XI etc.
† *Principles of Political Economy and Taxation*, 3rd ed., p. 2.

we find that two of the clearest definitions of value recognize *utility* and *scarcity* as the essential qualities. But the moment that we distinguish between the total utility of a mass of commodity and the degree of utility of different portions, we may say that it is scarcity which prevents the fall in the final degree of utility. Bread has the almost infinite utility of maintaining life, and when it becomes a question of life or death, a small quantity of food exceeds in value all other things. But when we enjoy our ordinary supplies of food, a loaf of bread has little value, because the utility of an additional loaf is small, our appetites being satiated by our customary meals.

I have pointed out the excessive ambiguity of the word value, and the apparent impossibility of using it safely. When intended to express the mere fact of certain articles exchanging in a particular ratio, I have proposed to substitute the unequivocal expression – *ratio of exchange*. But I am inclined to believe that a ratio is not the meaning which most persons attach to the word value. There is a certain sense of esteem or desirableness, which we may have with regard to a thing apart from any distinct consciousness of the ratio in which it would exchange for other things. I may suggest that this distinct feeling of value is probably identical with the final degree of utility. While Adam Smith's often-quoted *value in use* is the total utility of a commodity to us, the *value in exchange* is defined by the *terminal utility*, the remaining desire which we or others have for possessing more.

There remains the question of labour as an element of value. Economists have not been wanting who put forward labour as the *cause of value*, asserting that all objects derive their value from the fact that labour has been expended on them; and it is thus implied, if not stated, that value will be proportional to labour. This is a doctrine which cannot stand for a moment, being directly opposed to facts. Ricardo disposes of such an opinion when he says: *

There are some commodities, the value of which is determined by their scarcity alone. No labour can increase the quantity of such goods, and therefore their value cannot be lowered by an increased supply. Some rare statues and pictures, scarce books and coins, wines of a

* *On the Principles of Political Economy and Taxation*, 3rd ed., 1821, p. 2.

peculiar quality, which can be made only from grapes grown on a particular soil, of which there is a very limited quantity, are all of this description. Their value is wholly independent of the quantity of labour originally necessary to produce them, and varies with the varying wealth and inclinations of those who are desirous to possess them.

The mere fact that there are many things, such as rare ancient books, coins, antiquities, etc., which have high values, and which are absolutely incapable of production now, disperses the notion that value depends on labour. Even those things which are producible in any quantity by labour seldom exchange exactly at the corresponding values.* The market price of corn, cotton, iron and most other things is, in the prevalent theories of value, allowed to fluctuate above or below its natural or cost value. There may, again, be any discrepancy between the quantity of labour spent upon an object and the value ultimately attaching to it. A great undertaking like the Great Western Railway, or the Thames Tunnel, may embody a vast amount of labour, but its value depends entirely upon the number of persons who find it useful. If no use could be found for the *Great Eastern* steamship, its value would be nil, except for the utility of some of its materials.[43] On the other hand, a successful undertaking, which happens to possess great utility, may have a value, for a time at least, far exceeding what has been spent upon it, as in the case of the [first] Atlantic cable. The fact is, that *labour once spent has no influence on the future value of any article*: it is gone and lost for ever. In commerce bygones are for ever bygones; and we are always starting clear at each moment, judging the values of things with a view to future utility. Industry is essentially prospective, not retrospective; and seldom does the result of any undertaking exactly coincide with the first intentions of its promoters.

But though labour is never the cause of value, it is in a large proportion of cases the determining circumstance, and in the

* Mr W. L. Sargant, in his *Recent Political Economy*, 8vo, London, 1867, p. 99, states that contracts have been made to manufacture the Enfield rifle, of identically the same pattern, at prices ranging from 70s. each down to 20s., or even lower. The wages of the workmen varied from 40s. or 50s. down to 15s. a week. Such an instance renders it obvious that it is scarcity which governs value, and that it is the value of the produce which determines the wages of the producers.

following way: *Value depends solely on the final degree of utility. How can we vary this degree of utility? – By having more or less of the commodity to consume. And how shall we get more or less of it? – By spending more or less labour in obtaining a supply.* According to this view, then, there are two steps between labour and value. Labour affects supply, and supply affects the degree of utility, which governs value, or the ratio of exchange. In order that there may be no possible mistake about this all-important series of relations, I will restate it in a tabular form, as follows:

> *Cost of production determines supply;*
> *Supply determines final degree of utility;*
> *Final degree of utility determines value.*

But it is easy to go too far in considering labour as the regulator of value; it is equally to be remembered that labour is itself of unequal value. Ricardo, by a violent assumption, founded his theory of value on quantities of labour considered as one uniform thing. He was aware that labour differs infinitely in quality and efficiency, so that each kind is more or less scarce, and is consequently paid at a higher or lower rate of wages. He regarded these differences as disturbing circumstances which would have to be allowed for; but his theory rests on the assumed equality of labour. This theory rests on a wholly different ground. I hold labour to be *essentially variable, so that its value must be determined by the value of the produce, not the value of the produce by that of the labour*. I hold it to be impossible to compare *a priori* the productive powers of a navvy, a carpenter, an iron-puddler, a schoolmaster and a barrister. Accordingly, it will be found that not one of my equations represents a comparison between one man's labour and another's. The equation, if there is one at all, is between the same person in two or more different occupations. The subject is one in which complicated action and reaction takes place, and which we must defer until after we have described, in the next chapter, the theory of labour.

CHAPTER V

Theory of Labour

Definition of Labour

ADAM SMITH said, 'The real price of everything, what everything really costs to the man who wants to acquire it, is the toil and trouble of acquiring it. . . . Labour was the first price, the original purchase-money, that was paid for all things.'* If subjected to a very searching analysis, this celebrated passage might not prove to be so entirely true as it would at first sight seem to most readers to be. Yet it is substantially true, and luminously expresses the fact that labour is the beginning of the processes treated by economists, as consumption is the end and purpose. Labour is the painful exertion which we undergo to ward off pains of greater amount, or to procure pleasures which leave a balance in our favour. Courcelle-Seneuil† and Hearn have stated the problem of economics with the utmost truth and brevity in saying that it is *to satisfy our wants with the least possible sum of labour*.

In defining *labour* for the purposes of the economist we have a choice between two courses. In the first place, we may, if we like, include in it *all exertion of body or mind*. A game of cricket would, in this case, be labour, but if it be undertaken solely for the sake of the enjoyment attaching to it, the question arises whether we need take it under our notice. All exertion not directed to a distant and distinct end must be repaid simultaneously. There is no account of good or evil to be balanced at a future time. We are not prevented in any way from including such cases in our theory of economics; in fact, our theory of labour will, of necessity, apply to them. But we need not occupy our attention by cases which demand no calculus. When we exert ourselves for

* *Wealth of Nations*, Book I, ch. V.
† *Traité théorique et pratique d'économie politique*, 2nd ed., vol. I, p. 33.

the sole amusement of the moment, there is but one rule needed, namely, to stop when we feel inclined – when the pleasure no longer equals the pain.

It will probably be better, therefore, to take the second course and concentrate our attention on such exertion as is not completely repaid by the immediate result. This would give us a definition nearly the same as that of Say, who defined labour as '*Action suivée, dirigée vers un but.*' Labour, I should say, is *any painful exertion of mind or body undergone partly or wholly with a view to future good.** It is true that labour may be both agreeable at the time and conducive to future good; but it is only agreeable in a limited amount, and most men are compelled by their wants to exert themselves longer and more severely than they would otherwise do. When a labourer is inclined to stop, he clearly feels something that is irksome, and our theory will only involve the point where the exertion has become so painful as to nearly balance all other considerations. Whatever there is that is wholesome or agreeable about labour before it reaches this point may be taken as a net profit of good to the labourer, but it does not enter into the problem. It is only when labour becomes effort that we take account of it, and, as Hearn truly says,† 'such effort, as the very term seems to imply, is more or less troublesome'. In fact, we must, as will shortly appear, measure labour by the amount of pain which attaches to it.

* I have altered this definition as it stood in the first edition by inserting the words '*partly or wholly*', and I only give it now as provisionally the best I can suggest. The subject presents itself to me as one of great difficulty, and it is possible that the true solution will consist in treating labour as a case of negative utility, or negative mingled with positive utility. We should thus arrive at a higher generalization which appears to be foreshadowed in the remarkable work of Hermann Heinrich Gossen described in the preface to this edition. Every act, whether of production or of consumption, may be regarded as producing what Bentham calls a *lot* both of pleasures and pains, and the distinction between the two processes will consist in the fact that the algebraic value of the lot in the case of consumption yields a balance of positive utility, while that of production yields a negative or painful balance, at least in that part of the labour involving most effort. In a happy life the negative balance involved in production is more than cleared off by the positive balance of pleasure arising from consumption.

† *Plutology*, p. 24.

Quantitative Notions of Labour

Let us endeavour to form a clear notion of what we mean by amount of labour. It is plain that duration will be one element of it; for a person labouring *uniformly* during two months must be allowed to labour twice as much as during one month. But labour may vary also in intensity. In the same time a man may walk a greater or less distance; may saw a greater or less amount of timber; may pump a greater or less quantity of water; in short, may exert more or less muscular and nervous force. Hence amount of labour will be a quantity of two dimensions, the product of intensity and time when the intensity is uniform, or the sum represented by the area of a curve when the intensity is variable.

But intensity of labour may have more than one meaning; it may mean the quantity of work done, or the painfulness of the effort of doing it. These two things must be carefully distinguished, and both are of great importance for the theory. The one is the reward, the other the penalty, of labour. Or rather, as the produce is only of interest to us so far as it possesses utility, we may say that there are three quantities involved in the theory of labour – the amount of painful exertion, the amount of produce and the amount of utility gained. The variation of utility, as depending on the quantity of commodity possessed, has already been considered; the variation of the amount of produce will be treated in the next chapter; we will here give attention to the variation of the painfulness of labour.

Experience shows that as labour is prolonged the effort becomes as a general rule more and more painful. A few hours' work per day may be considered agreeable rather than otherwise; but so soon as the overflowing energy of the body is drained off, it becomes irksome to remain at work. As exhaustion approaches, continued effort becomes more and more intolerable. Jennings has so clearly stated this law of the variation of labour, that I must quote his words.*

Between these two points, the point of incipient effort and the point of painful suffering, it is quite evident that the degree of toilsome

* *Natural Elements of Political Economy*, p. 119.

sensations endured does not vary directly as the quantity of work performed, but increases much more rapidly, like the resistance offered by an opposing medium to the velocity of a moving body.

When this observation comes to be applied to the toilsome sensations endured by the working classes, it will be found convenient to fix on a middle point, the average amount of toilsome sensation attending the average amount of labour, and to measure from this point the degrees of variation. If, for the sake of illustration, this average amount be assumed to be of ten hours' duration, it would follow that, if at any period the amount were to be supposed to be reduced to five hours, the sensations of labour would be found, at least by the majority of mankind, to be almost merged in the pleasures of occupation and exercise, whilst the amount of work performed would only be diminished by one-half; if, on the contrary, the amount were to be supposed to be increased to twenty hours, the quantity of work produced would only be doubled, whilst the amount of toilsome suffering would become insupportable. Thus, if the quantity produced, greater or less than the average quantity, were to be divided into any number of parts of equal magnitude, the amount of toilsome sensation attending each succeeding increment would be found greater than that which would attend the increment preceding; and the amount of toilsome sensation attending each succeeding decrement would be found less than that which would attend the decrement preceding.

There can be no question of the general truth of the above statement, although we may not have the data for assigning the exact law of the variation. We may imagine the painfulness of labour in proportion to produce to be represented by some such curve as *abcd* in figure 9. In this diagram the height of points above the line *ox* denotes pleasure, and depths below it pain. At the moment of commencing labour it is usually more irksome than when the mind and body are well bent to the work. Thus, at first, the pain is measured by *oa*. At *b* there is neither pain nor pleasure. Between *b* and *c* an excess of pleasure is represented as due to the exertion itself. But after *c* the energy begins to be rapidly exhausted, and the resulting pain is shown by the downward tendency of the line *cd*.

We may at the same time represent the degree of utility of the produce by some such curve as *pq*, the amount of produce being measured along the line *ox*. Agreeably to the theory of utility, already given, the curve shows that the larger the wages earned, the less is the pleasure derived from a further increment. There will, of necessity, be some point m such that $qm = dm$, that is to say, such that the pleasure gained is exactly equal to the labour endured. Now, if we pass the least beyond this point, a balance of pain will result: there will be an ever-decreasing

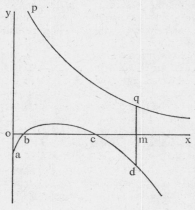

Fig. 9

motive in favour of labour, and an ever-increasing motive against it. The labourer will evidently cease, then, at the point m. It would be inconsistent with human nature for a man to work when the pain of work exceeds the desire of possession, including all the motives for exertion.

We must consider the duration of labour as measured by the number of hours' work per day. The alternation of day and night on the earth has rendered man essentially periodic in his habits and actions. In a natural and wholesome condition a man should return each twenty-four hours to exactly the same state; at any rate, the cycle should be closed within the seven days of the week. Thus the labourer must not be supposed to be either increasing or diminishing his normal strength. But the theory might also be made to apply to cases where special exertion is undergone for many days or weeks in succession, in order to complete work, as in collecting the harvest. Adequate motives may lead to and warrant overwork, but, if long continued, excessive labour reduces the strength and becomes insupportable; and the longer it continues the worse it is, the law being somewhat similar to that of periodic labour.

Symbolic Statement of the Theory

In attempting to represent these conditions of labour with accuracy, we shall find that there are no less than four quantities concerned; let us denote them as follows:

t = time, or duration of labour;
l = amount of labour, as meaning the aggregate balance of pain accompanying it, irrespective of the produce;
x = amount of commodity produced;
u = total utility of that commodity.

The amount of commodity produced will be very different in different cases. In any one case the rate of production will be determined by dividing the whole quantity produced by the time of production, provided that the rate of production has been uniform; it will then be $\frac{x}{t}$. But if the rate of production be variable, it can only be determined at any moment by comparing a small quantity of produce with the small portion of time occupied in its production. More strictly speaking, we must ascertain the ratio of an infinitely small quantity of produce to the corresponding infinitely small portion of time. Thus *the rate of production* is properly denoted by $\frac{\Delta x}{\Delta t}$, or at the limit by $\frac{dx}{dt}$.

Again, the degree of painfulness of labour would be $\frac{l}{t}$ if it remained invariable; but as it is highly variable, we must again compare small increments, and $\frac{\Delta l}{\Delta t}$, or, at the limit, $\frac{dl}{dt}$ correctly represents the *degree of painfulness of labour*. But we must also take into account the fact that the utility of commodity is not constant. If a man works regularly twelve hours a day, he will produce more commodity than in ten hours; therefore the final degree of utility of his commodity, whether he consume it himself or whether he exchange it, will not be quite so high as when he produced less. This degree of utility is denoted, as before, by $\frac{du}{dx}$, the ratio of the increment of utility to the increment of commodity.

The amount of reward of labour can now be expressed; for it is $\frac{dx}{dt} \cdot \frac{du}{dx}$; that is to say, it is the product of the ratio of the commodity produced to the time, multiplied by the ratio of the utility to the amount of produce. Thus, the last two hours of work in the day generally gives less reward, both because less produce is then created in proportion to the time spent, and because that produce is less necessary and useful to one who makes enough to support himself in the other ten hours.

We can now ascertain the length of time which should be selected as the most advantageous term of labour. A free labourer endures the irksomeness of work because the pleasure he expects to receive, or the pain he expects to ward off, by means of the produce, exceeds the pain of exertion. When labour itself is a worse evil than that which it saves him from, there can be no motive for further exertion, and he ceases. Therefore he will cease to labour just at the point when the pain becomes equal to the corresponding pleasure gained; and we thus have t defined by the equation

$$\frac{dl}{dt} = \frac{dx}{dt} \cdot \frac{du}{dx}.$$

In this, as in the other questions of economics, all depends upon the final increments, and we have expressed in the above formula *the final equivalence of labour and utility*. A man must be regarded as earning all through his hours of labour an excess of utility; what he produces must be considered not merely the exact equivalent of the labour he gives for it, for it would be, in that case, a matter of indifference whether he laboured or not. As long as he gains, he labours, and when he ceases to gain, he ceases to labour.

In some cases, as in some kinds of machine labour, the rate of production is uniform, or nearly so, and by choice of suitable units may be made equal to unity; the result may then be put more simply in this way. Labour may be considered as expended in successive small quantities, Δl, each lasting, for instance, for a quarter of an hour; the corresponding benefit derived from the labour will then be denoted by Δu. Now, so long as Δu exceeds in amount of pleasure the negative quantity or pain of Δl, the difference of sign being disregarded, there will be gain inducing to continued labour. Were Δu to fall below Δl, there would be more harm than good in labouring; therefore, the boundary between labour and inactivity will be defined by the equality of Δu and Δl, and at the limit we have the equation

$$\frac{du}{dx} = \frac{dl}{dx}.$$

Dimensions of Labour

If I have correctly laid down, in preceding chapters, the theory of dimensions of utility and value, there ought not to be much difficulty in stating the similar theory as regards labour. We might in fact treat labour as simply one case of *disutility* or negative utility, that is as pain, or at any rate as a generally painful balance of pleasure and pain, endured in the action of acquiring commodity. Thus its dimensions might be described as identical with those of utility; U would then denote intensity of labour, or degree of labour, just as it was used to denote degree of utility. If we measure labour with respect to the quantity of commodity produced, that is, if we make commodity the variable, then total amount of labour will be the integral of UdM, and the dimensions of amount of labour will be MU, identical with those of total utility.

If for any reasons of convenience we prefer to substitute a new symbol, specially appropriated to express the dimensions of labour, and say that *intensity of labour* is represented by E (Endurance), and *total quantity of labour* incurred in the production of certain commodity by ME, it must be remembered that the change is one of convenience only; U and E are essentially quantities of the same nature, and the difference, so far as there is any, arises from the fact that quantities symbolized by E will usually be negative as compared with those symbolized by U. Labour, however, is often measured and bought and sold by *time*, instead of by piecework or commodity produced; in this case, while E continues to express intensity of labour, ET will express the dimensions of amount of labour.

Rate of production will obviously possess the same dimensions as rate of consumption (p. 119), namely, MT^{-1}, and this quantity forms a link between labour as measured by time and by produce; for $ET \times MT^{-1} = ME$. It would be possible to invent various other economic quantities, such as *acceleration of production*, with the dimensions MT^{-2}; but, until it is apparent how such quantities enter into economic theorems, it seems needless to consider them further.

Balance between Need and Labour

In considering this theory of labour an interesting question presents itself. Supposing that circumstances alter the relation of produce to labour, what effect will this have upon the amount of labour which will be exerted? There are two effects to be considered. When labour produces more commodity, there is more reward, and therefore more inducement to labour. If a workman can earn ninepence an hour instead of sixpence, may he not be induced to extend his hours of labour by this increased result? This would doubtless be the case were it not that the very fact of getting half as much more than he did before, lowers the utility to him of any further addition. By the produce of the same number of hours he can satisfy his desires more completely; and if the irksomeness of labour has reached at all a high point, he may gain more pleasure by relaxing that labour than by consuming more products. The question thus depends upon the direction in which the balance between the utility of further commodity and the painfulness of prolonged labour turns.

In our ignorance of the exact form of the functions either of utility or of labour, it will be impossible to decide this question in an *a priori* manner; but there are a few facts which indicate in which direction the balance does usually turn. Statements are given by Porter, in his *Progress of the Nation,** which show that when a sudden rise took place in the prices of provisions in the early part of this century, workmen increased their hours of labour, or, as it is said, worked double time, if they could obtain adequate employment. Now, a rise in the price of food is really the same as a decrease of the produce of labour, since less of the necessaries of life can be acquired in exchange for the same money wages. We may conclude, then, that English labourers enjoying little more than the necessaries of life, will work harder the less the produce; or, which comes to the same thing, will work less hard as the produce increases.

Evidence to the like effect is found in the general tendency to reduce the hours of labour at the present day, owing to the improved real wages now enjoyed by those employed in mills and factories. Artisans, mill-hands, and others, seem generally to prefer greater ease to greater wealth, thus proving that the painfulness of labour varies so rapidly as easily to overbalance the gain of utility. The same rule seems to hold throughout the mercantile employments. The richer a man becomes, the less does he devote himself to business. A successful merchant is generally willing to give a considerable share of his profits to a partner, or to a staff of managers and clerks, rather than bear the constant labour of superintendence himself. There is also a general tendency to reduce the hours of labour in mercantile offices, due to increased comfort and opulence.

It is obvious, however, that there are many intricacies in a matter of this sort. It is not always possible to graduate work to the worker's liking; in some businesses a man who insisted on working only a few hours a day would soon have no work to do. In the professions of law, medicine and the like, it is the reputation of enjoying a large practice which attracts new clients. Thus a successful barrister or physician generally labours more severely as his success increases. This result partly depends upon the fact that the work is not easily capable of being performed by deputy. A successful barrister, too, soon begins to look forward to the extrinsic rewards of a high judicial or parliamentary position. But the case of an eminent solicitor, architect or

* Edition of 1847, pp. 454, 455.

engineer is one where the work is to a great extent done by employees, and done without reference to social or political rewards, and where yet the most successful man endures the most labour, or rather is most constantly at work. This indicates that the irksomeness of the labour does not increase so as to overbalance the utility of the increment of reward. In some characters and in some occupations, in short, success of labour only excites to new exertions, the work itself being of an interesting and stimulating nature. But the general rule is to the contrary effect, namely, that a certain success disinclines a man to increased labour. It may be added that in the highest kinds of labour, such as those of the philosopher, scientific discoverer, artist, etc., it is questionable how far great success is compatible with ease; the mental powers must be kept in perfect training by constant exertion, just as a racehorse or an oarsman needs to be constantly exercised.

It is evident that questions of this kind depend greatly upon the character of the race. Persons of an energetic disposition feel labour less painfully than their fellow-men, and, if they happen to be endowed with various and acute sensibilities, their desire of further acquisition never ceases. A man of lower race, a Negro for instance, enjoys possession less, and loathes labour more; his exertions, therefore, soon stop. A poor savage would be content to gather the almost gratuitous fruits of nature, if they were sufficient to give sustenance; it is only physical want which drives him to exertion. The rich man in modern society is supplied apparently with all he can desire, and yet he often labours unceasingly for more. Bishop Berkeley, in his *Querist*,[44] has very well asked, 'Whether the creating of wants be not the likeliest way to produce industry in a people? And whether, if our [Irish] peasants were accustomed to eat beef and wear shoes, they would not be more industrious?'

Distribution of Labour

We now come to consider the conditions which regulate the comparative amounts of different commodities produced in a country. Theoretically speaking, we might regard each person as capable of producing various commodities, and dividing his labour according to certain rules between the different employments; it would not be impossible, too, to mention cases where such division does take place. But the result of commerce and the division of labour is usually to make a man find his advantage in performing one trade only; and I give the formulae as they would apply to an individual, only because they are identical in general character with those which apply to a whole nation.

Suppose that an individual is capable of producing two kinds of commodity. His sole object, of course, is to produce the greatest amount of utility; but this will depend partly upon the comparative degrees of utility of the commodities, and partly on his comparative facilities for producing them. Let x and y be the respective quantities of the commodities already produced, and suppose that he is about to apply more labour; on which commodity shall he spend the next increment of labour? – Plainly, on that which will yield most utility. Now, if an increment of labour, Δl, will yield either of the increments of commodity Δx and Δy, the ratios of produce to labour, namely,

$$\frac{\Delta x}{\Delta l} \text{ and } \frac{\Delta y}{\Delta l}$$

will form one element in the problem. But to obtain the comparative utilities of these commodities, we must multiply respectively by

$$\frac{\Delta u_1}{\Delta x} \text{ and } \frac{\Delta u_2}{\Delta y}.$$

For instance,

$$\frac{\Delta u_1}{\Delta x} \cdot \frac{\Delta x}{\Delta l_1}$$

expresses the amount of utility which can be obtained by producing a little more of the first commodity; if this be greater than the same expression for the other commodity, it would evidently be best to make more of the first commodity until it ceased to yield any excess of utility. When the labour is finally distributed, we must have the increments of utility from the several employments equal, and at the limit we have the equation –

$$\frac{du_1}{dx} \cdot \frac{dx}{dl_1} = \frac{du_2}{dy} \cdot \frac{dy}{dl_2}.$$

When this equation holds, there can be no motive for altering or regretting the distribution of labour, and the utility produced is at its maximum.

There are in this problem two unknown quantities, namely, the two portions of labour appropriated to the two commodities. To determine them, we require one other equation in addition to the above. If we put

$$l = l_1 + l_2,$$

we have still an unknown quantity to determine, namely, l; but the principles of labour (pp. 190–95) now give us an equation. Labour will be carried on until the increment of utility from any of the employments just balances the increment of pain.[45] This amounts to saying that du_1, the increment of utility derived from the first employment of labour, is equal in amount of feeling to dl_1, the increment of labour by which it is obtained. This gives us then the further equation –

$$\frac{du_1}{dx} \cdot \frac{dx}{dl_1} = 1.$$

If we pay regard to sign, indeed, we must remember that dl is, when measured in the same scale as du, intrinsically negative, but inasmuch as it is given in exchange for du, which is received, it will in this respect be taken negatively, and thus the above equation holds true.*

Relation of the Theories of Labour and Exchange

It may tend to give the reader confidence in the preceding theories when he finds that they lead directly to the well-known law, as stated in the ordinary language of economists, that value is proportional to the cost of production. As I prefer to state the same law, it is to the effect that the ratio of exchange of commodities will conform in the long run to the *ratio of productiveness*,

* While revising this edition it seems to me probable that this, as well as some other parts of the theory, might be more simply and generally stated, but what is given is substantially true and correct, and it must stand for the present. – H.S.J.

which is the reciprocal of the ratio of the costs of production. The somewhat perplexing relations of these quantities will be fully explained in the next section, but we may now proceed to prove the above result symbolically.

To simplify our expressions, let us substitute for the *rate of production** $\frac{dx}{dl}$ the symbol ω. Then ω_1, ω_2, express the relative quantities of two different commodities produced by an increment of labour, and we have the following equation, identical with that on page 199,

$$\varphi x \cdot \omega_1 = \psi y \cdot \omega_2.$$

Let us suppose that the person to whom it applies is in a position to exchange with other persons. The conditions of production will now, in all probability, be modified. For x the quantity of our commodity may perhaps be increased to $x + x_1$, and y diminished to $y - y_1$, by an exchange of the quantities x_1 and y_1. If this be so, we shall, as shown in the theory of exchange, have the equation

$$\frac{\varphi(x + x_1)}{\psi(y - y_1)} = \frac{y_1}{x_1}.$$

Our equation of production will now be modified, and become

$$\varphi(x + x_1)\omega_1 = \psi(y - y_1)\omega_2;$$

$$\text{or} \qquad \frac{\varphi(x + x_1)}{\psi(y - y_1)} = \frac{\omega_2}{\omega_1}.$$

But this equation has its first member identical with the first member of the equation of exchange given above, so that we may at once deduce the all-important equation

$$\frac{\omega_2}{\omega_1} = \frac{y_1}{x_1}.$$

The reader will remember that ω expresses the ratio of produce to labour; thus we have proved that commodities will exchange in any market in the ratio of the quantities produced by the same quantity of labour. But as the increment of labour considered is always the final one, our equation also expresses the truth, that

* That is, the *productiveness* of labour for *one* commodity. – H.S.J

articles will exchange in quantities inversely as the costs of production of the most costly portions, i.e. the last portions added. This result will prove of great importance in the theory of rent.

Let it be observed that, in uniting the theories of exchange and production, a complicated double adjustment takes place in the quantities of commodity involved. Each party adjusts not only its consumption of articles in accordance with their ratio of exchange, but it also adjusts its production of them. The ratio of exchange governs the production as much as the production governs the ratio of exchange. For instance, since the Corn Laws have been abolished in England, the effect has been, not to destroy the culture of wheat, but to lessen it. The land less suitable to the growth of wheat has been turned to grazing or other purposes more profitable comparatively speaking. Similarly the importation of hops or eggs or any other article of food does not even reduce the quantity raised here, but prevents the necessity for resorting to more expensive modes of increasing the supply. It is not easy to express in words how the ratios of exchange are finally determined.[46] They depend upon a general balance of producing power and of demand as measured by the final degree of utility. Every additional supply tends to lower the the degree of utility; but whether that supply will be forthcoming from any country depends upon its comparative powers of producing different commodities.

Any very small tract of country cannot appreciably affect the comparative supply of commodities: it must therefore adjust its productions in accordance with the general state of the market. The county of Bedford, for instance, would not appreciably affect the markets for corn, cheese or cattle, whether it devoted every acre to corn or to grazing. Therefore the agriculture of Bedfordshire will have to be adapted to circumstances, and each field will be employed for arable or grazing land according as prevailing prices render one employment or the other more profitable. But any large country will affect the markets as well as be affected. If the whole habitable surface of Australia, instead of producing wool, could be turned to the cultivation of wine, the wool market would rise, and the wine market fall. If the Southern States of America abandoned cotton in favour of sugar, there would be a revolution in these markets. It would be inevitable for Australia to return to wool and the American States to cotton. These are illustrations of the reciprocal relation of exchange and production.

Relations of Economic Quantities

I hope that I may sometime be able, in a future and much larger work, to explain in detail the results which can be derived from the mathematical theory expounded in the previous pages. This essay gives them only in an implicit manner. But, before leaving the subject of exchange, it may be well without delay to point out how the results so far set forth connect themselves with the recognized doctrines of political economy. For the sake of accuracy I have avoided the use of the word *value*; the expression *cost of production*, so continually recurring in most economical treatises, is also here conspicuous by its absence. The reader then, unless he be very careful, may be thrown into some perplexity, when he proceeds to compare my results with those familiar to him elsewhere. I will therefore proceed to trace out the connexions between the several quantitative expressions, which most commonly occur in discussions concerning value, exchange and production.

In the first place, the ratio of exchange is the actual numerical ratio of the quantities given and received. Let X and Y be the names of the commodities; x and y the quantities of them respectively exchanged. Then the ratio of exchange is that of y to x. But the value of a commodity in exchange is greater as the quantity received is less, so that the ratio of the quantities dealt with must be the reciprocal of the ratio of the values of the substances, meaning by value the value per unit of the commodity. Thus we may say

$$\frac{y}{x} = \frac{\text{Value of X per unit}}{\text{Value of Y per unit}}.$$

Value is of course very frequently estimated by *price*, that is, by the quantity of legal money for which the commodity may be exchanged. Price is indeed ambiguous in the same way as value; it means either the *price of the whole quantity*, or the *pri per unit of the quantity.* Let p_1 be the price per unit of X, and p_2 the similar price of Y. Then it is apparent that $y \times p_2$ will be the whole price of y, and $x \times p_1$ will be the whole price of x. These two must be equal to each other, so that we get

$$\frac{y}{x} = \frac{p_1}{p_2}.$$

Thus we find that, when price means price per unit, the quantities exchanged are reciprocally as the prices. When price means price of the whole quantity, the quantities given and received are always of equal price.

Turning now to the production of commodity, it is sufficiently obvious that the cost of production, so far as this expression can be accurately interpreted, varies as the reciprocal of the degree of productiveness. The rate of wages remaining constant, the cost per unit of commodity must of course be lower as the quantity produced in return for a certain amount of wages is greater. Thus we may lay down the equation

$$\frac{\text{Degree of productiveness of Y[47]}}{\text{Degree of productiveness of X}} = \frac{\text{Cost of production of X}}{\text{Cost of production of Y}}.$$

Now, it was shown in pp. 201–2 that the quantities exchanged are directly proportional to the degrees of productiveness,

$$\text{or} \quad \frac{y}{x} = \frac{\text{Degree of productiveness of Y}}{\text{Degree of productiveness of X}}.$$

But the ratio of the values is the reciprocal of $\frac{y}{x}$, and the ratio of the costs of production is the reciprocal of the other member of the above equation. Thus it follows that

$$\frac{\text{Value per unit of X}}{\text{Value per unit of Y}} = \frac{\text{Cost of production per unit of X}}{\text{Cost of production per unit of Y,}}$$

or, in other words, *value is proportional to cost of production.* As, moreover, the final degrees of utility of commodities are inversely as the quantities exchanged, it follows that the values per unit are directly proportional to the final degrees of utility.

As it is quite indispensable that the student of political

economy should keep the relations of these quantities before his mind with perfect clearness, I repeat the results in several forms of statement. Thus we may group the ratios together –

$$\text{Ratio of exchange} = \frac{y}{x} = \frac{\text{Quantity of Y given or received}}{\text{Quantity of X received or given}}$$

$$= \frac{\text{Value per unit of X}}{\text{Value per unit of Y}} = \frac{\text{Price per unit of X}}{\text{Price per unit of Y}}$$

$$= \frac{\text{Final degree of utility of X}}{\text{Final degree of utility of Y}}$$

$$= \frac{\text{Cost of production per unit of X}}{\text{Cost of production per unit of Y}}$$

$$= \frac{\text{Degree of productiveness of Y}}{\text{Degree of productiveness of X}}.$$

We may state the matter more briefly in the following words: *The quantities of commodity given or received in exchange are directly proportional to the degrees of productiveness of labour applied to their production, and inversely proportional to the values and prices of those commodities and to their costs of production per unit, as well as to their final degrees of utility.* I will even repeat the same statements once more in the form of a diagram –

Quantities of Commodity exchanged vary

directly as the quantities produced by the same labour.

inversely as their
(1) Values
(2) Prices
(3) Costs of production
(4) Final degrees of utility.

Various Cases of the Theory

As we have now reached the principal question in economics, it will be well to consider the meaning and results of our equations in some detail.

It will, in the first place, be apparent that the absolute facility of producing commodities will not determine the character and amount of trade. The ratio of exchange $\frac{y_1}{x_1}$ is not determined by ω_1, nor by ω_2 separately, but by their comparative magnitudes.

If the producing power of a country were doubled, no direct effect would be produced upon the terms of its commerce provided that the increase were equal in all branches of production. This is a point of great importance, which was correctly conceived by Ricardo, and has been fully explained by J. S. Mill.

But though there is no such direct effect, it may happen that there will be an indirect effect through the variation in the degree of utility of different articles. When an increased amount of every commodity can be produced, it is not likely that the increase will be equally desired in each branch of consumption. Hence the degree of utility will fall in some cases more than in others. An alteration of the ratios of exchange must result, and the production of the less needed commodities will not be extended so much as in the case of the more needed ones. We might find in such instances new proofs that value depends not upon labour but upon the degree of utility.

It will also be apparent that nations possessing exactly similar powers of production cannot gain by mutual commerce, and consequently will not have any such commerce, however free from artificial restrictions. We get this result as follows: Taking ω_1 ω_2, as before, to be the final ratios of productiveness[48] in one country, and μ_1 μ_2 in a second, then, if the conditions of production are exactly similar, we have

$$\frac{\omega_2}{\omega_1} = \frac{\mu_2}{\mu_1}.$$

But when a country does not trade at all, its labour and consumption are distributed according to the condition

$$\frac{\varphi x}{\psi y} = \frac{\omega_2}{\omega_1}.$$

Now, from these equations, it follows necessarily that

$$\frac{\varphi x}{\psi y} = \frac{\mu_2}{\mu_1};$$

that is to say, the production and consumption already conform to the conditions of production of the second country, and will not undergo any alteration when trade with this country becomes possible.

This is the doctrine usually stated in works on political economy, and for which there are good grounds. But I do not think the statement will hold true if the conditions of consumption be very different in two countries. There might be two countries exactly similar in regard to their powers of producing beef and corn, and if their habits of consumption were also exactly similar, there would be no trade in these articles. But suppose that the first country consumed proportionally more beef, and the second more corn; then, if there were no trade, the powers of the soil would be differently taxed, and different ratios of exchange would prevail. Freedom of trade would cause an interchange of corn for beef. Thus I conclude that it is only where the habits of consumption, as well as the powers of production, are alike, that trade brings no advantage.

The general effect of foreign commerce is to disturb, to the advantage of a country, the mode in which it distributes its labour. Excluding from view the cost of carriage, and the other expenses of commerce, we must always have true

$$\frac{\omega_2}{\omega_1} = \frac{y_1}{x_1} = \frac{\mu_2}{\mu_1}.$$

If, then, ω_2 was originally less in proportion to ω_1 than is in accordance with these equations, some labour will be transferred from the production of y to that of x until, by the increased magnitude of ω_2, and the lessened magnitude of ω_1, equality is brought about.

As in the theory of exchange, so in the theory of production, any of the equations may fail, and the meaning is capable of interpretation. Thus, if the equation

$$\frac{\omega_2}{\omega_1} = \frac{y_1}{x_1}$$

cannot be established, it is impossible that the production of both commodities, y and x, can go on. One of them will be produced at an expenditure of labour constantly out of proportion to that at which it may be had by exchange. If we could not, for instance, import oranges from abroad, part of the labour of the country would probably be diverted from its present employment to raise them; but the cost of production would be always above that of getting them indirectly by exchange, so that free trade necessarily destroys such a wasteful branch of industry. It is on this principle that we import the whole of our wines, teas, sugar, coffee, spices and many other articles from abroad.

The ratio of exchange of any two commodities will be determined by a kind of struggle between the conditions of consumption and production; but here again failure of the equations may take place. In the all-important equations

$$\frac{\varphi(x + x_1)}{\psi(y - y_1)} = \frac{\omega_2}{\omega_1} = \frac{y_1}{x_1},$$

ω_2 expresses the ease with which we may make additions to y. If we find any means, by machinery or otherwise, of increasing y without limit, and with the same ease as before, we must, in all probability, alter the ratio of exchange $\frac{y_1}{x_1}$ in a corresponding degree. But if we could imagine the existence of a large population, within reach of the supposed country, whose desire to consume the quantity y_1 never decreased, however large was the quantity available, then we should never have $\frac{y_1}{x_1}$ equal to $\frac{\omega_2}{\omega_1}$, and the producers of y would make large gains of the nature of rent.

Joint Production

In one of the most interesting chapters of his *Principles of Political Economy*, Book III, ch. XVI, John Stuart Mill has treated of what he calls 'Some peculiar Cases of Value'. Under this title he refers to those commodities which are not produced by separate processes, but are the concurrent or joint results of the same operations.

It sometimes happens, [he says] that two different commodities have what may be termed a joint cost of production. They are both products of the same operation, or set of operations, and the outlay is incurred for the sake of both together, not part for one and part for the other. The same outlay would have to be incurred for either of the two, if the other were not wanted or used at all. There are not a few instances of commodities thus associated in their production. For example, coke and coal-gas are both produced from the same material, and by the same operation. In a more partial sense, mutton and wool are an example; beef, hides, and tallow; calves and dairy produce; chickens and eggs. Cost of production can have nothing to do with deciding the values of the associated commodities relatively to each other. It only decides their joint value. . . . A principle is wanting to apportion the expenses of production between the two.

He goes on to explain that, since the cost of production principle fails us, we must revert to a law of value anterior to cost of production, and more fundamental, namely, the law of supply and demand.

On some other occasion I may perhaps more fully point out the fallacy involved in Mill's idea that he is reverting to *an anterior law of value*, the law of supply and demand, the fact being that in introducing the cost of production principle, he had never quitted the laws of supply and demand at all. The cost of production is only one circumstance which governs supply, and thus indirectly influences values.

Again, I shall point out that these cases of joint production, far from being 'some peculiar cases', form the general rule, to which it is difficult to point out any clear or important exceptions. All the great staple commodities at any rate are produced jointly with minor commodities. In the case of corn, for instance, there are the straw, the chaff, the bran and the different qualities of flour or meal, which are products of the same operations. In the case of cotton, there are the seed, the oil, the cotton waste, the refuse, in addition to the cotton itself. When beer is brewed the grains regularly return a certain price. Trees felled for timber yield not only the timber, but the loppings, the bark, the outside cuts, the chips, etc. No doubt the secondary products are often nearly valueless, as in the case of cinders, slag from blast furnaces, etc. But even these cases go to show all the more impressively that it is not cost of production which rules values, but the demand and supply of the products.

The great importance of these cases of joint production renders it necessary for us to consider how they can be brought under our theory. Let us suppose that there are two commodities, X and Y, yielded by one same operation, which always produces them in the same ratio, say of m of X to n of Y. It might seem at first sight as if this ratio would correspond to the ratio of the degrees of productiveness, as shown a few pages above, that we might say

$$\frac{m}{n} = \frac{\omega_2}{\omega_1} = \frac{y_1}{x_1},$$

and thus arrive at the conclusion that things jointly produced would always exchange in the ratio of productiveness. But this would be entirely false, because *that equation can only be established when there is freedom of producing one or the other*, at each application of a new increment of labour. It is the freedom of varying the quantities of each that allows of the produce being accommodated to the need of it, so that the ratio of the degrees of utility, of the degrees of productiveness, and of the quantities exchanged are brought to equality. But in cases of joint production there is no such freedom; the one substance cannot be made without making a certain fixed proportion of the other, which may have little or no utility.

It will easily be seen, however, that such cases are brought under our theory by simply aggregating together the utilities of the increments of the joint products. If dx cannot be produced without dy, these being the products of the same increment of labour, dl, then the ratio of produce to labour cannot be written otherwise than as

$$\frac{dx + dy}{dl}.$$

It is impossible to divide up the labour and say that so much is expended on producing X, and so much on Y. But we must estimate separately the utilities of dx and dy, by multiplying by their degrees of utility $\frac{du_1}{dx}$ and $\frac{du_2}{dy}$, and we then have the aggregate ratio of utility to labour as

$$\frac{du_1}{dx} \cdot \frac{dx}{dl} + \frac{du_2}{dy} \cdot \frac{dy}{dl}.$$

It is plain that we have no equation arising out of these conditions of production, so that the ratio of exchange of X and Y will be governed only by the degrees of utility. But if we compare X and Y with a third commodity Z, as regards its production, we shall arrive at the equation

$$\frac{du_1}{dx} \cdot \frac{dx}{dl} + \frac{du_2}{dy} \cdot \frac{dy}{dl} = \frac{du_3}{dz} \cdot \frac{dz}{dl}.$$

In other words, the increment of utility obtained by applying an increment of labour to the production of Z, must equal the sum of the increments of utility which would be obtained if the same increment of labour were applied to the joint production of X and Y. It is evident that the above equation taken alone gives us no information as to the ratios existing between the quantities dx, dy and dz. Before we can obtain any ratios of exchange we must have the further equation between the degrees of utility of X and Y, namely,

$$\frac{du_1}{du_2} = \frac{dy}{dx}.$$

As a general rule, however, any two processes of production will both yield joint products, so that the equation of productiveness will take the form of a sum of increments of utility on both sides, which we may thus write briefly –

$$du_1 + du_2 + \ldots = du_n + du_{n+1} + \ldots$$

Such an equation becomes then a kind of equation of condition of which the influence may be very slight regarding the ratio of exchange of any two of the commodities concerned. And if in some cases the terms on one side of such an equation are reduced to one or two, it is probably because the other increments of produce are nearly or quite devoid of utility. As in the cases of cinders, chips, sawdust, spent dyes, potato stalks, chaff, etc., almost every process of industry yields refuse results, of which the utility is zero or nearly so. To solve the subject fully, however, we should have to admit negative utilities, as elsewhere explained, so that the increment of utility from any increment dl of labour would really take the form

$$du_1 \pm du_2 \pm du_3 \pm \ldots$$

The waste products of a chemical works, for instance, will some-times have a low value; at other times it will be difficult to get rid of them without fouling the rivers and injuring the neigh-bouring estates; in this case they are discommodities and take the negative sign in the equations.

Over-production

The theory of the distribution of labour enables us to perceive clearly the meaning of *over-production* in trade. Early writers on economics were always in fear of a supposed *glut*, arising from the powers of production surpassing the needs of consumers, so that industry would be stopped, employment fail, and all but the rich would be starved by the superfluity of commodities. The doctrine is evidently absurd and self-contradictory. As the acquirement of suitable commodities is the whole purpose of industry and trade, the greater the supplies obtained the more perfectly industry fulfils its purpose. To bring about a universal glut would be to accomplish completely the aim of the economist, which is to maximize the products of labour. But the supplies must be *suitable* – that is, they must be in proportion to the needs of the population. Over-production is not possible in all branches of industry at once, but it is possible in some as com-pared with others. If, by miscalculation, too much labour is spent in producing one commodity, say silk goods, our equations will not hold true. People will be more satiated with silk goods than cotton, woollen or other goods. They will refuse, therefore, to purchase them at ratios of exchange corresponding to the labour expended. The producers will thus receive in exchange goods of less utility than they might have acquired by a better distribution of their labour.

In extending industry, therefore, we must be careful to extend it proportionally to all the requirements of the population. The more we can lower the degree of utility of all goods by satiating the desires of the purchasers the better; but we must lower the degrees of utility of different goods in a corresponding manner, otherwise there is an apparent glut and a real loss of labour.

Limits to the Intensity of Labour

I have mentioned (p. 190) that labour may vary either in duration or intensity, but have yet paid little attention to the latter circumstance. We may approximately measure the intensity of labour by the amount of physical force undergone in a certain time, although it is the pain attending that exertion of force which is the all-important element in economics. Interesting laws have been or may be detected connecting the amount of work done with the intensity of labour. Even where these laws have not been ascertained, long experience has led men, by a sort of unconscious process of experimentation and inductive reasoning, to select that rate of work which is most advantageous.

Let us take such a simple kind of work as digging. A spade may be made of any size, and if the same number of strokes be made in the hour, the requisite exertion will vary nearly as the cube of the length of the blade. If the spade be small the fatigue will be slight, but the work done will also be slight. A very large spade, on the other hand, will do a great quantity of work at each stroke, but the fatigue will be so great that the labourer cannot long continue at his work. Accordingly, a certain medium-sized spade is adopted, which does not overtax a labourer and prevent him doing a full day's work, but enables him to accomplish as much as possible. The size of a spade should depend partly upon the tenacity and weight of the material, and partly upon the strength of the labourer. It may be observed that, in excavating stiff clay, navvies use a small strong spade; for ordinary garden purposes a larger spade is employed; for shovelling loose sand or coals a broad capacious shovel is used; and a still larger instrument is employed for removing corn, malt, or any loose light powder.

In most cases of muscular exertion the weight of the body or of some limb is of great importance. If a man be employed to carry a single letter, he really moves a weight of say a hundred and sixty pounds for the purpose of conveying a letter weighing perhaps half an ounce. There will be no appreciable increase of labour if he carries twenty letters, so that his efficiency will be multiplied twenty times. A hundred letters would probably prove a slight burden, but there would still be a vast gain in the work done. It is obvious, however, that we might go on loading a postman with letters until the fatigue became excessive; the maximum useful effect would be obtained with the largest load which does not severely fatigue the man, and trial soon decides the weight with considerable accuracy.

The most favourable load for a porter was investigated by Coulomb,[49] and he found that most work could be done by a man walking upstairs without any load, and raising his burden by means of his own weight in descending. A man could thus raise four times as much in a day as by carrying bags on his back with the most favourable load. This great difference doubtless arises from the muscles being perfectly adapted to raising the human body, whereas any additional weight throws irregular or undue stress on them. Charles Babbage, also, in his admirable *Economy of Manufactures*, has remarked on this subject, and has pointed out that the weight of some limb of the body is an element in all calculations of human labour.

The fatigue produced on the muscles of the human frame, [says Babbage] does not altogether depend on the actual force employed in each effort, but partly on the frequency with which it is exerted. The exertion necessary to accomplish every operation consists of two parts: one of these is the expenditure of force which is necessary to drive the tool or instrument; and the other is the effort required for the motion of some limb of the animal producing the action. In driving a nail into a piece of wood, one of these is lifting the hammer, and *propelling* its head against the nail; the other is *raising* the arm itself, and moving it in order to use the hammer. If the weight of the hammer is considerable, the former part will cause the greatest portion of the exertion. If the hammer is light, the exertion of *raising* the arm will produce the greatest part of the fatigue. It does therefore happen that operations requiring very trifling force, if frequently repeated, will tire more effectually than more laborious work. There is also a degree of rapidity beyond which the action of the muscles cannot be pressed.*

It occurred to me, some time since, that this was a subject admitting of interesting inquiry, and I tried to determine, by

*Babbage, *On the Economy of Machinery and Manufactures*, sec. xxxii, p. 30.

several series of experiments, the relation between the amount of work done by certain muscles and the rate of fatigue. One series consisted in holding weights varying from one pound to eighteen pounds in the hand while the arm was stretched out at its full length. The trials were two hundred and thirty-eight in number, and were made at intervals of at least one hour, so that the fatigue of one trial should not derange the next. The average number of seconds during which each weight could be sustained was found to be as follows:

Weight in pounds	18	14	10	7	4	2	1
Time in seconds	15	32	60	87	148	219	321.

If the arm had been thus employed in any kind of useful work, we should have estimated the useful effect by the product of the weight sustained and the time. The results would be as follows, in pound-seconds:

Weight	.	.	18	14	10	7	4	2	1
Useful effect	.	.	266	455	603	612	592	438	321.

The maximum of useful effect would here appear to be about seven pounds, which is about the weight usually chosen for dumbbells and other gymnastic instruments. Details of the other series of experiments are described in an article in *Nature* (30 June 1870, vol. II, p. 158).

I undertook these experiments as a mere illustration of the mode in which some of the laws forming the physical basis of economics might be ascertained. I was unaware that Professor S. Haughton had already, by experiment, arrived at a theory of muscular action, communicated to the Royal Society in 1862. I was gratified to find that my entirely independent results proved to be in striking agreement with his principles, as was pointed out by Professor Haughton in two articles in *Nature*.*

I am not aware that any exact experiments upon walking or

*Vol. II, p. 324; vol. III, p. 289. See also Haughton's *Principles of Animal Mechanics*, 1873, pp. 444–50. The subject has since been followed up with much care and ability by Professor Francis E. Nipher, of the Washington University, St Louis, Missouri, U.S.A. Details of his experiments will be found in the *American Journal of Science*, vol. IX, pp. 130–7; vol. X, etc.; *Nature*, vol. XI, pp. 256, 276, etc.

marching have been made, but, as Professor Haughton has remarked to me, they might easily be carried out in the movements of an army. It would only be necessary, on each march which is carried up to the limits of endurance, to register the time and distance passed over. Had we a determination of the exact relations of time, space and fatigue, it would be possible to solve many interesting problems. For instance, if one person has to overtake another, what should be their comparative rates of walking? Assuming fatigue to increase as the square of the velocity multiplied by the time, we easily obtain an exact solution, showing that the total fatigue will be least when one person walks twice as quickly as he whom he wishes to overtake.

In different cases of muscular exertion we shall find different problems to solve. The most advantageous rate of marching will greatly depend upon whether the loss of time or the fatigue is the most important. To march at the rate of four miles an hour would soon occasion enormous fatigue, and could only be resorted to under circumstances of great urgency. The distance passed over would bear a much higher ratio to the fatigue at the rate of three, or even two and a half miles an hour. But, if the speed were still further reduced, a loss of strength would again arise, owing to that expended in merely sustaining the body, as distinguished from that of moving it forward.

The economics of labour will constantly involve questions of this kind. When a work has to be completed in a brief space of time, workmen may be incited by unusual reward to do far more than their usual amount of work; but so high a rate would not be profitable in other circumstances. The fatigue always rapidly increases when the speed of work passes a certain point, so that the extra result is far more costly in reality. In a regular and constant employment the greatest result will always be gained by such a rate as allows a workman each day, or each week at the most, to recover all fatigue and recommence with an undiminished store of energy.

CHAPTER VI

Theory of Rent

———

Accepted Opinions concerning Rent

THE general correctness of the views put forth in preceding chapters derives great probability from their close resemblance to the theory of rent, as it has been accepted by English writers for nearly a century. It has not been usual to state this theory in mathematical symbols, and clumsy arithmetical illustrations have been employed instead; but it is easy to show that the fluxional calculus is the branch of mathematics which most correctly applies to the subject.

The theory of rent was first discovered and clearly stated by James Anderson in a tract published in 1777, and called *An Inquiry into the Nature of the Corn Laws, with a view to the Corn Bill proposed for Scotland.* An extract from this work may be found in MacCulloch's edition of the *Wealth of Nations,* p. 453, giving a most clear explanation of the effect of the various fertility of land, and showing that it is not the rent of land which determines the price of its produce, but the price of the produce which determines the rent of the land. The following passage must be given in Anderson's own words: *

. . . In every country there is a variety of soils, differing considerably from one another in point of fertility. These we shall at present suppose arranged into different classes, which we shall denote by the letters A, B, C, D, E, F, etc., the class A comprehending the soils of the greatest fertility, and the other letters expressing different classes of soils, gradually decreasing in fertility as you recede from the first. Now, as the expense of cultivating the least fertile soil is as great or greater than that of the most fertile field, it necessarily follows that if an equal quantity of corn, the produce of each field, can be sold at the same price, the profit on cultivating the most fertile soil must be much greater than

* *Inquiry,* etc., p. 45, note.

217

that of cultivating the others; and as this continues to decrease as the sterility increases, it must at length happen that the expense of cultivating some of the inferior soils will equal the value of the whole produce.

The theory really rests upon the principle, which I have called the law of indifference, that for the same commodity in the same market there can only be one price or ratio of exchange. Hence, if different qualities of land yield different amounts of produce to the same labour, there must be an excess of profit in some over others. There will be some land which will not yield the ordinary wages of labour, and which will, therefore, not be taken into cultivation, or if, by mistake, it is cultivated, will be abandoned. Some land will just pay the ordinary wages; better land will yield an excess, so that the possession of such land will become a matter of competition, and the owner will be able to exact as rent from the cultivators the whole excess above what is sufficient to pay the ordinary wages of labour.

There is a secondary origin for rent in the fact that if more or less labour and capital be applied to the same portion of land, the produce will not increase proportionally to the amount of labour. It is quite impossible that we could go on constantly increasing the yield of one farm without limit, otherwise we might feed the whole country upon a single farm. Yet there is no definite limit; for, by better and better culture, we may always seem able to raise a little more. But the last increment of produce will come to bear a smaller and smaller ratio to the labour required to produce it, so that it soon becomes, in the case of all land, undesirable to apply more labour.

MacCulloch has given, in his edition of the *Wealth of Nations*, * a supplementary note, in which he explains, with the utmost clearness and scientific accuracy, the nature of the theory. This note contains by far the best statement of the theory, as it seems to me, and I will therefore quote his recapitulation of the principles which he establishes.

1. That if the produce of land could always be increased in proportion to the outlay on it, there would be no such thing as rent.
2. That the produce of land cannot, at an average, be increased in

* New edition, 1839, p. 444.

proportion to the outlay, but may be indefinitely increased in a less proportion.

3. That the least productive portion of the outlay, which, speaking generally, is the last, must yield the ordinary profits of stock. And

4. That all which the other portions yield more than this, being above ordinary profits, is rent.

A most satisfactory account of the theory is also given in James Mill's *Elements of Political Economy*, a work which I never read without admiring its brief, clear and powerful style. James Mill constantly uses the expression *dose of capital*. 'The time comes,' he says, 'at which it is necessary either to have recourse to land of the second quality, or to apply a second dose of capital less productively upon land of the first quality.' He evidently means by a *dose of capital* a little more capital, and though the name is peculiar, the meaning is simply that of an *increment of capital*. The number of doses or increments mentioned is only three, but this is clearly to avoid prolixity of explanation. There is no reason why we should not consider the whole capital divided into many more doses. The same general law which makes the second dose less productive than the first, will make a hundredth dose, speaking generally, less productive than the preceding ninety-ninth dose. Theoretically speaking, there is no need or possibility of stopping at any limit. A mathematical law is in theory always continuous, so that the *doses* considered are indefinitely small and indefinitely numerous. I consider, then, that James Mill's mode of expression is exactly equivalent to that which I have adopted in earlier parts of this book. As mathematicians have invented a precise and fully recognized mode of expressing *doses or increments*, I know not why we should exclude language from economics which is found convenient in all other sciences. It is mere pedantry to insist upon calling that a *dose* in economics, which in all the other sciences is called by the perfectly established and expressive term *increment*.

The following are James Mill's general conclusions as to the nature of rent.[50]

In applying capital, either to lands of various degrees of fertility, or in successive doses to the same land, some portions of the capital

so employed are attended with a greater produce, some with a less
That which yields the least yields all that is necessary for reimbursin
and rewarding the capitalist. The capitalist will receive no more tha
this remuneration for any portion of the capital which he employs
because the competition of others will prevent him. All that is yielde
above this remuneration the landlord will be able to appropriate. Ren
therefore, is the difference between the return yielded to that portio
of the capital which is employed upon the land with the least effec
and that which is yielded to all the other portions employed upon
with a greater effect.

Symbolic Statement of the Theory

The accepted theory of rent, as given above, needs little or n
alteration to adapt it to expression in mathematical symbols. Fo
doses or increments of capital I shall substitute increments c
labour, partly because the functions of capital remain to b
considered in the next chapter, and partly because James Mil
J. S. Mill and MacCulloch hold the application of capital to b
synonymous with the application of labour. This assumption i
implied in James Mill's statement (p. 13); it is expressly state
in J. S. Mill's *First Fundamental Proposition concerning the Natur
of Capital*,* and MacCulloch adds a footnote† to make it clea
that as all capital was originally produced by labour, the applica
tion of additional capital is the application of additional labour
'Either the one phrase or the other may be used indiscriminately
This doctrine is in itself altogether erroneous, but it will not b
erroneous to assume as a mode of simplifying the problem tha
the increments of labour applied are equally assisted by capita
It is a separate and subsequent problem to determine how ren
or interest arises when the same labour is assisted by differen
quantities of capital.

I shall suppose that a certain labourer, or, what comes t
exactly the same thing, a body of labourers, expend labour o
several different pieces of ground. On what principle will the
distribute their labour between the several pieces? Let us imagin
that a certain amount has been spent upon each, and tha
another small portion, Δl, is going to be applied. Let there b

* Book I, ch. V, sec. i.   † *Wealth of Nations*, p. 445.

two pieces of land, and let Δx_1, Δx_2, be the increments of produce to be expected from the pieces respectively. They will naturally apply the labour to the land which yields the greatest result. So long as there is any advantage in one use of labour over another, the most advantageous will certainly be adopted. Therefore, when they are perfectly satisfied with the distribution made, the increment of produce to the same labour will be equal in each case; or we have

$$\Delta x_1 = \Delta x_2.$$

To attain scientific accuracy, we must decrease the increments infinitely, and then we obtain the equation –

$$\frac{dx_1}{dl} = \frac{dx_2}{dl}.$$

Now $\frac{dx}{dl}$ represents the ratio of produce, or the productiveness of labour, as regards the last increment of labour applied. We may say, then, that whenever a labourer or body of labourers distribute their labour over pieces of land with perfect economy, the *final ratios of produce to labour will be equal.*

We may now take into account the general law, that when more and more labour is applied to the same piece of land, the produce ultimately does not increase proportionately to the labour. This means that the function $\frac{dx}{dl}$ diminishes without limit towards zero after x has passed a certain quantity. The whole produce of a piece of land is x, the whole labour spent upon it is l; and x varies in some way as l varies, never decreasing when l increases. We may say, then, that x is a function of l; let us call it Pl. When a little more labour is expended, the increment of produce dx is dPl, and $\frac{dPl}{dl}$ is the final rate of production, the same as was previously denoted by $\frac{dx}{dl}$.[51]

In the theory of labour it was shown that no increment of labour would be expended unless there was sufficient recompense in the produce, but that labour would be expended up to the point at which the increment of utility exactly equals the increment of pain incurred in acquiring it. Here we find an exact definition of the amount of labour which will be profitably applied.

It was also shown that the last increment of labour is the most painful, so that if a person is recompensed for the last increment of labour which he applies to land by the rate of production $\frac{dx}{dl}$, it follows that all the labour he applies might be recompensed sufficiently at the same rate. The whole labour is l, so that if the recompense were equal over the whole, the result would be $l \cdot \frac{dx}{dl}$. Consequently, he obtains more than the necessary return to labour by the amount

$$Pl - l \cdot \frac{dx}{dl};$$

or, as we may write it,

$$Pl - l \cdot P'l,$$

in which $P'l$ is the differential coefficient of Pl, or the final rate of production. This expression represents the advantage he derives from the possession of land in affording him more profit than other methods of employing his labour. It is therefore the rent which he would ask before yielding it up to another person, or equally the rent which he would be able and willing to pay if hiring it from another.

The same considerations apply to every piece of land cultivated. When the same person or body of labourers cultivate several pieces, $P'l$ will be of the same magnitude in each case, but the quantities of labour, and possibly the functions of labour, will be different. Thus with two pieces of land the rent may be represented as

$$P_1l_1 + P_2l_2 - (l_1 + l_2)P_1'l_1;$$

or, speaking generally of any number of pieces, it is the sum of the quantities of the form Pl, *minus* the sum of the quantities of the form $l.P'l$.

Illustrations of the Theory

It is very easy to illustrate the theory of rent by diagrams. For, let distances along the line ox denote quantities of labour, and let the curve *apc* represent the variation of the rate of production, so that the area of the curve will be the measure of the produce. Thus when labour has been applied to the amount *om*, the produce will correspond to the area *apmo*. Let a small new increment of labour, *mm'*, be applied, and suppose the rate of production

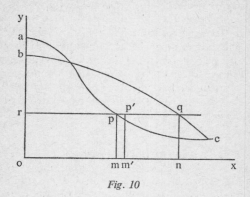

Fig. 10

equal over the whole of the increment. Then the small parallelogram, *pp'm'm*, will be the produce. This will be proportional in quantity to *pm*, so that the height of any point of the curve perpendicularly above a point of the line *ox* represents the rate of production at that point in the application of labour.

If we further suppose that the labourer considers his labour, *mm'*, repaid by the produce *pm'*, there is no reason why any other part of his labour should not be repaid at the same rate. Drawing, then, a horizontal line, *rpq*, through the point *p*, his whole labour, *om*, will be repaid by the produce represented by the area *orpm*. Consequently, the overlying area, *rap*, is the excess of produce which can be exacted from him as rent, if he be not himself the owner of the land.

Imagining the same person to cultivate another piece of land, we might take the curve, *bqc*, to represent its productiveness. The same rate of production will repay the labourer in this case as in the last, so that the intersection of the same horizontal line, *rpq*, with the curve, will determine the final point of labour, *n*.

The area, *rn*, will be the measure of the sufficient recompense to the whole labour, *on*, spent upon the land; and the excess of produce, or rent, will be the area, *rbq*. In a similar manner, any number of pieces of land might be considered. The figure might have been drawn so that the curves would rise on leaving the initial line *oy*, indicating that a very little labour will have a poor rate of production; and that a certain amount of labour is requisite to develop the fertility of the soil. This may often or always be the case, as a considerable quantity of labour is generally requisite in first bringing land into cultivation, or merely keeping it in a fit state for use. The laws of rent depend on the undoubted principle that the curves always *ultimately* decline towards the base line *ox*, that is, the final rate of production always *ultimately* sinks towards zero.

CHAPTER VII

Theory of Capital

The Function of Capital

IN considering the nature and principles of capital, we enter a distinct branch of our subject. There is no close or necessary connexion between the employment of capital and the processes of exchange. Both by the use of capital and by exchange we are enabled vastly to increase the sum of utility which we enjoy; but it is conceivable that we might have the advantages of capital without those of exchange. An isolated man like Alexander Selkirk might feel the benefit of a stock of provisions, tools and other means of facilitating industry, although cut off from traffic, with other men. Economics, then, is not solely the science of exchange or value: it is also the science of capitalization.

The views which I shall endeavour to establish on this subject are in fundamental agreement with those adopted by Ricardo; but I shall try to put the theory of capital in a more simple and consistent manner than has been the case with some later economists. We are told, with perfect truth, that capital consists of wealth employed to facilitate production; but when economists proceed to enumerate the articles of wealth constituting capital, they obscure the subject. 'The capital of a country,' says Mac-Culloch, 'consists of those portions of the produce of industry existing in it which may be directly employed either to support human beings, or to facilitate production.'* Professor Fawcett again says:† 'Capital is not confined to the food which feeds the labourers, but includes machinery, buildings, and, in fact, every product due to man's labour which can be applied to assist his industry; but capital which is in the form of food does not perform its functions in the same way as capital that is in the form

* *Principles of Political Economy*, p. 100.
† *Manual of Political Economy*, 2nd ed., p. 47.

of machinery: the one is termed circulating capital, the other fixed capital.'

The notion of capital assumes a new degree of simplicity as soon as we recognize that what has been called a part is really the whole. Capital, as I regard it, consists merely in the *aggregate of those commodities which are required for sustaining labourers of any kind or class engaged in work*. A stock of food is the main element of capital; but supplies of clothes, furniture, and all the other articles in common daily use are also necessary parts of capital. The *current means of sustenance constitute capital in its free or uninvested form*. The single and all-important function of capital is to enable the labourer to await the result of any long-lasting work – to put an interval between the beginning and the end of an enterprise.

Not only can we, by the aid of capital, erect large works which would otherwise have been impossible, but the production of articles which would have been very costly in labour may be rendered far more easy. Capital enables us to make a great outlay in providing tools, machines or other preliminary works, which have for their sole object the production of some important commodity, and which will greatly facilitate production when we enter upon it.

Capital is concerned with Time

Several economists have clearly perceived that the time elapsing between the beginning and end of a work is the difficulty which capital assists us to surmount. Thus James Mill has said:

If the man who subsists on animals cannot make sure of his prey in less than a day, he cannot have less than a whole day's subsistence in advance. If hunting excursions are undertaken which occupy a week or a month, subsistence for several days may be required. It is evident, when men come to live upon those productions which their labour raises from the soil, and which can be brought to maturity only once in the year, that subsistence for a whole year must be laid up in advance.*

* *Elements of Political Economy*, 3rd ed., 1826, p. 9.

Much more recently, Professor Hearn has said, in his admirable work entitled *Plutology*: *

The first and most obvious mode in which capital directly operates as an auxiliary of industry is to render possible the performance of work which requires for its completion some considerable time. In the simplest agricultural operations there is the seed-time and the harvest. A vineyard is unproductive for at least three years before it is thoroughly fit for use. In gold mining there is often a long delay, sometimes even of five or six years, before the gold is reached. Such mines could not be worked by poor men unless the storekeepers gave the miners credit, or, in other words, supplied capital for the adventure. But, in addition to this great result, capital also implies other consequences which are hardly less momentous. One of these is the steadiness and continuity that labour thus acquires. A man, when aided by capital, can afford to remain at his work until it is finished, and is not compelled to leave it incomplete while he searches for the necessary means of subsistence. If there were no accumulated fund upon which the labourer could rely, no man could remain for a single day exclusively engaged in any other occupation than those which relate to the supply of his primary wants. Besides these wants, he should also from time to time search for the materials on which he was to work.

These passages imply, as it seems to me, a clear insight into the nature and purposes of capital, except that the writers have not with sufficient boldness followed out the consequences of their notion. If we take a comprehensive view of the subject, it will be seen that not only the chief but the sole purpose of capital is as above described. Capital simply allows us *to expend labour in advance*. Thus, to raise corn we need to turn over the surface of the soil. If we proceed straight to the work, and use the implements with which nature has furnished us – our fingers – we should spend an enormous amount of painful labour with very little result. It is far better, therefore, to spend the first part of our labour in making a spade or other implement to assist the rest of our labour. This spade represents so much labour which has been invested, and so far spent; but if it lasts three years, its cost may be considered as repaid gradually during those three

* *Plutology; or The Theory of the Efforts to Satisfy Human Wants*, 1864, Macmillan, p. 139.

years. This labour, like that of digging, has for its object the raising of corn, and the only essential difference is that it has to precede the production of corn by a longer interval. The average interval of time for which labour will remain invested in the spade is half of the three years. Similarly, if we possess a larger capital, and expend it in making a plough, which will last for twenty years, we invest at the beginning a great deal of labour which is only gradually repaid during those twenty years, and which is therefore, on the average, invested for about ten years.

It is true that in modern industry we should seldom or never find the same man making the spade or plough, and afterwards using the implement. The division of labour enables me, with much advantage, to expend a portion of my capital in purchasing the implement from someone who devotes his attention to the manufacture, and probably expends capital previously in facilitating the work. But this does not alter the principles of the matter. What capital I give for the spade merely replaces what the manufacturer had already invested in the expectation that the spade would be needed. Exactly the same considerations may be applied to much more complicated applications of capital. The ultimate object of all industry engaged with cotton is the production of cotton goods. But the complete process of producing those goods is divided into many parts; and it is necessary to begin the spending of labour a long time before any goods can be finished.

In the first place, labour will be required to till the land which is to bear the cotton plants, and probably two years at least will elapse between the time when the ground is first broken and the time when the cotton reaches the mills. A cotton mill, again, must be a very strong and durable structure, and must contain machinery of a very costly character, which can only repay its owner by a long course of use. We might spin and weave cotton goods as in former times, or as it is done in Cashmere, with a very small use of capital; but then the labour required would be enormously greater in proportion to the produce. It is far more economical in the end to spend a vast amount of labour and capital in building a substantial mill and filling it with the best machinery, which will then go on working with unimpaired efficiency for thirty years or more. This means that, in addition to the labour spent in superintending the machines at the moment when goods are produced, a great quantity of labour has been spent from one to thirty years in advance, or, on the average, fifteen years in advance. This expenditure is repaid by an annuity of profit extending over those thirty years.

The interval elapsing between the first exertion of labour and the enjoyment of the result is further increased by any time during which the raw material may lie in warehouses before reaching the machines; and by the time employed in distributing the goods to retail dealers, and through them to the consumers. It may even happen that the consumer finds it desirable to keep a certain stock on hand, so that the time when the real object of the goods is fulfilled becomes still further deferred. During this time, also, capital seems to me to be invested, and only as actual utilization takes place is expenditure repaid by corresponding utility enjoyed.

I would say, then, in the most general manner, that *whatever improvements in the supply of commodities lengthen*[52] *the average interval between the moment when labour is exerted and its ultimate result or purpose accomplished, such improvements depend upon the use of capital*. And I would add that this is the sole use of capital. Whenever we overlook the irrelevant complications introduced by the division of labour and the frequency of exchange, all employments of capital resolve themselves into the fact of time elapsing between the beginning and the end of industry.

Quantitative Notions concerning Capital

One main point which has to be clearly brought before the mind in this subject is the difference between the *amount of capital invested* and the *amount of investment of capital*. The first is a quantity of one dimension only – the quantity of capital; the second is a quantity of two dimensions, namely, the quantity of capital and the length of time during which it remains invested. If one day's labour remains invested for two years, the capital is only that equivalent to one day; but it is locked up twice as long as if it were invested for only one year. Now all questions in which we consider the most advantageous employment of capital turn upon the length of investment quite as much as upon the amount. The same capital will serve for twice as much industry if it be absorbed or invested for only half the time.

The amount of investment of capital will evidently be determined by multiplying each portion of capital invested at any moment by the length of time for which it remains invested. One pound invested for five years gives the same result as five pounds invested for one year, the product being *five pound-years*. Most commonly, however, investment proceeds continuously or at intervals, and we must form clear notions on the subject. Thus, if a workman be employed during one year on any work, the result of which is complete, and enjoyed at the end of that time, the absorption of capital will be found by multiplying each day's wages by the days remaining till the end of the year, and adding all the results together. If the daily wages be four shillings, then we have

$$4 \times 364 + 4 \times 363 + 4 \times 362 \ldots + 4 \times 1;$$

or, $4 \times \dfrac{365 \times 364}{2}$, or 265,720 *shilling-days*.

We may also represent the investment by a diagram such as figure 11. The length along the line *ox* indicates the duration of

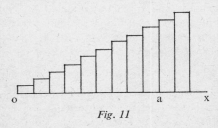

Fig. 11

investment, and the height attained at any point, *a*, is the amount of capital invested. But it is the whole area of the rectangles up to any point, *a*, which measures the amount of investment during the time *oa*.

The whole result of continued labour is not often consumed and enjoyed in a moment; the result generally lasts for a certain length of time. We must then conceive the capital as being progressively *uninvested*. Let us, for sake of simple illustration, imagine the labour of producing the harvest to be continuously and equally expended between the first of September in one year and the same day in the next. Let the harvest be then completely gathered, and its consumption begin immediately and continue equally during the succeeding twelve months. Then the amount of investment of capital will be represented by the area of an isosceles triangle, as in figure 12, the base of which corresponds to two

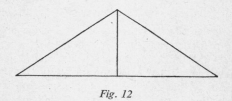

Fig. 12

years of duration. Now the area of a triangle is equal to the height multiplied by half the base; and as the height represents the greatest amount invested, that upon the first of September, when the harvest is gathered; half the base, or one year, is the *average time of investment of the whole amount.*

In the 37th proposition of the first book of Euclid it is proved that all triangles upon the same base and between the same parallels are equal in area. Hence we may draw the conclusion that, provided capital be invested and uninvested continuously and in simple proportion to the time, we need only regard the greatest amount invested and the greatest time of investment. Whether it be all invested suddenly, and then gradually withdrawn; or gradually invested and suddenly withdrawn; or gradually invested and gradually withdrawn; the amount of investment will be in every case the greatest amount of capital multiplied by half the time elapsing from the beginning to the end of the investment.

Expression for Amount of Investment

To render our notions of the subject still more exact and general, let us resort once more to mathematical symbols.

Let $\Delta p =$ amount of capital supposed to be invested in the time Δt; let $t =$ time elapsing before its result is enjoyed, the enjoyment taking place in an interval of time Δt, which may be disregarded in comparison with t. Then $t \cdot \Delta p$ is the amount of investment; and if the investment is repeated, the sum of the quantities of the nature of $t \cdot \Delta p$, or, in the customary mode of expression, $\Sigma t \cdot \Delta p$ is the total amount of investment. But it will seldom be possible to assign each portion of result to an exactly corresponding portion of labour. Cotton goods are due to the aggregate industry of those who tilled the ground, grew the cotton, plucked, transported, cleaned, spun, wove and dyed it; we cannot distinguish the moment when each labourer's work is separately repaid. To avoid this difficulty, we must fix on some moment of time when the whole transaction is closed, all labour upon the ground repaid, the mill and machinery worn out and sold, and the cotton goods consumed. Let t now denote the time elapsing from any moment up to this final moment of closing the accounts. Let Δp be as before an increment of capital invested, and let Δq be an increment of capital uninvested by the sale of the products and their enjoyment by the consumer. Thus it will be pretty obvious that the sum of the quantities $t \cdot \Delta p$, less by the sum of the quantities $t \cdot \Delta q$, will be the total investment of capital, or expressed in symbols $\Sigma t \cdot \Delta p - \Sigma t \cdot \Delta q$.

Dimensions of Capital, Credit and Debit

As the subject presents itself to me at present, I apprehend that capital is to be regarded simply as commodity. If so, the dimension of capital will be represented by M, and the *amount of investment of capital*, possessing the additional dimension of time, will have the symbol MT. How then are we to determine the quantitative nature of what Senior called *Abstinence*, that temporary sacrifice of enjoyment which is essential to the existence of capital? Senior thus explicitly defined what he meant by the word: * 'By the word Abstinence, we wish to express that agent, distinct from labour and the agency of nature, the concurrence of which is necessary to the existence of capital, and which stands in the same relation to profit as labour does to wages.' He goes on to explain that abstinence, though usually accompanying labour, is distinct from it. A careful consideration of Senior's remarks shows that in reality abstinence is the endurance of want, the abstaining from the enjoyment of utility which might be enjoyed. Now the degree or intensity of want is measured by the degree of utility of commodity if it were consumed. Great degree of utility simply means great want, so that one dimension of abstinence must be U, and time being also obviously an element of abstinence, the required symbolic statement of its dimensions will be UT. This result satisfactorily corresponds with Senior's definition, for he says that abstinence is to profit as labour is to wages. Now profit or interest is clearly symbolized by M, and wages also by M, both consisting simply of quantities of commodity. Thus UT bears just the same relation to M that ET does to M, for E signifies the degree of painfulness of labour, and can barely be distinguished from U, except in sign.

The relation of abstinence, UT, to total utility, MU, also confirms our result. For if we convert *abstinence* into *satisfaction*, by giving a supply of commodity for consumption, this action is symbolically represented by multiplying UT into MT^{-1}, which yields MU, or utility.

It will need no argument to show that the dimension of *debit* and *credit*, having regard only to what is borrowed and owed, will be the dimension of commodity simply, or M. According to the practice of commerce, a contract of debt is a contract to return a certain physically defined quantity of a specified substance, such as an ounce of gold, a ton of pig-iron, a hogshead of palm oil. No attempt is made to define quantities of utility, so that the debt when repaid shall yield utility equal to what it possessed when lent. The borrower and lender either take their chance about this, or provide for it in the rate of interest to be paid. It is equally obvious that in another sense the *amount of credit or*

* *Political Economy*, by Nassau W. Senior, 5th ed., 1863, p. 59.

debit will be proportional to the duration of the operation, and will have the dimensions MT.

Effect of the Duration of Work

Perhaps the most interesting point in the theory of capital is the advantage arising from the rapid performance of work, if it is capable of being done with convenience and with the same ultimate result. To investigate this point, suppose that $w =$ the whole amount of wages which it is requisite to pay in building a house, and that this does not alter when we vary, within certain limits, the time employed in the work, denoted by t. If the work goes on continuously, we shall, during each unit of time, have an amount invested equal to the tth part of w. The whole amount of investment of capital will therefore be represented by the area of a triangle whose base is t and height w; that is, the investment is $\frac{1}{2} t w$. Thus when the whole expenditure is ultimately the same, the amount of investment is simply proportional to the time. The result would be more serious if the accumulation of compound interest during the time were taken into account; but the consideration of compound interest would render the formulae very complex, and is not requisite for the purpose in view.

We must clearly distinguish the case treated above, in which the amount of labour is the same, but spread over a longer time, from other cases where the labour increases in proportion to the time. The investment of capital, then, grows in an exceedingly rapid manner. Neglecting the first cost of tools, materials and other preparations, let the first day's labour cost a; during the second day this remains invested, and the amount of capital a is added; on each following day a like addition is made. The amount of capital invested is evidently

> At beginning of second day . . $a,$
>   ,,   ,,   third   ,,   . . $a + a,$
>   ,,   ,,   fourth ,,   . . $a + a + a;$

and so on. If the work lasts during $n + 1$ days, the total amount of investment of capital will be

$$a + 2a + 3a + 4a + \ldots na.$$

The sum of the series is

$$a\left(\frac{n}{2}+\frac{n^2}{2}\right),$$

which increases by a term involving the square of the time. The employment of capital thus grows in proportion to the triangular numbers

1, 3, 6, 10, 15, 21, etc.

If we regard the investment as taking place continuously, the whole absorption of capital is represented by the area of a right-angled triangle (figure 13), in which ob_1, b_1b_2, b_2b_3, etc., are the successive units of time. The heights of the lines a_1b_1, a_2b_2 represent the amounts invested at the ends of the times. The daily investment being a, the total amount of investment will be $a\frac{n^2}{2}$, increasing as the square of the time.

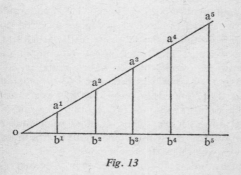

Fig. 13

Cases of this kind continually occur, as in sinking a deep mine, of which the requisite depth cannot be previously known with accuracy. Any large work, such as a breakwater, an embankment, the foundations of a great bridge, a dock, a long tunnel, the dredging of a channel, involves a problem of a similar nature; for it is seldom known what amount of labour and capital will be required; and if the work lasts much longer than was expected, the result is usually a financial disaster.

Illustrations of the Investment of Capital

The time during which capital remains invested, and the circumstances of its investment and reproduction, are exceedingly various in different employments. If a person plants cabbages, they will be ready in the course of a few months, and the labour of planting and tending them, together with a part of the labour of preparing and manuring the soil, yields its results with very little delay. In planting a forest tree, however, a certain amount of labour is expended, and no result obtained until after the lapse of thirty, forty or fifty years. The first cost of enclosing, preparing and planting a plantation is considerable; and though, after a time, the loppings and thinnings of the trees repay the cost of superintendence and repairs, yet the absorption of capital is great, and we may thus account for the small amount of planting which goes on. The ageing of wine is a somewhat similar case. A certain amount of labour is expended without result for ten or fifteen years, and the cost of storage is incurred during the whole time. To estimate the real cost of the articles at the end of the time, we must, in all such cases, add compound interest, and this grows in a rapid manner. Every pound invested at the commencement of a business becomes 1·63 pounds at the end of ten years, 11·47 pounds at the end of fifty years, and no less than 131·50 pounds at the end of a century, the rate of interest being taken at five per cent. Thus it cannot be profitable to store wine for fifty years, unless it become about twelve times as valuable as it was when new. It cannot pay to plant an oak and let it live a century, unless the timber then repays the cost of planting 132 times.

If an annual charge, however small, has to be incurred (for instance, the cost of storage and superintendence), the expense mounts up in a still more alarming manner. Thus, if the cost of any investment is one pound per annum, the amount invested, with compound interest at five per cent, becomes 12·58 pounds at the end of ten years, 209·35 pounds at the end of fifty years, and the enormous amount of 2,610·03 at the end of a century. We shall almost always have to take into account both the original and continuous cost of an investment. Thus if a stock of wine worth £100 be laid by for fifty years, and the cost of storage be £1 per annum, the total cost at the end of the time will be £1,147·0 on account of original cost, and £209·35 for storage, or in all £1,356·35.

It is to be feared that the rapid accumulation of compound interest is often overlooked in estimating the cost of public works and other undertakings of considerable duration. A great fort, breakwater or canal (the Caledonian Canal, for instance) is often not completed for twenty years after its commencement, and in the meantime it may be of little or no use. Suppose that its cost has been £10,000 each year; then the aggregate cost would seem to be £200,000, but allowing for interest at five per cent it is really £330,000. The French engineer and economist, Minard,[*] fully understood this point of finance, and showed that in the case of some public works, such as the great *digue* of Cherbourg harbour, and canals, the execution of which is allowed sometimes to drag on for half a century before any adequate result is returned, the real cost is incomparably greater than it is represented to be by merely stating the sums of money expended. In some cases, such as the first canal of Saint Quentin, a work, after being long prosecuted, is abandoned, and the loss by first cost and interest becomes enormous. The Guernsey harbour is a case in point, and the English dockyards would supply abundance of similar facts.

An interesting example of the investment of capital occurs in the case of gold and silver, a large stock of which is maintained either in the form of money, or plate and jewellery. Labour is spent in the digging or mining of the metals, which is gradually repaid by the use or satisfaction arising from the possession of the metals during the whole time for which they continue in use. Hence the investment of capital extends over the average duration of the metals. Now, if the stock of gold requires one per cent of its amount to maintain it undiminished, it will be apparent that each particle of gold remains in use 100 years on the average;

[*] Minard, *Annales des ponts et chaussées*, 1850, 1er semestre, p. 57.

if $\frac{1}{2}$ per cent is sufficient, the average duration will be 200 years.
We may state the result thus:

Loss of gold or silver annually	Average duration of each particle in use
1 per cent	100 years
$\frac{1}{2}$,,	200 ,,
$\frac{1}{4}$,,	400 ,,
$\frac{1}{10}$,,	1,000 ,,

The wear and loss of the precious metals in a civilized country
is probably not more than $\frac{1}{200}$ part annually, including plate,
jewellery and money in the estimate, so that the average investment will be for 200 years. It is curious that, if we regard a
quantity of gold as wearing away annually by a fixed percentage
of what remains, the duration of some part is infinite, and yet
the average duration is finite. Some of the gold possessed by the
Romans is doubtless mixed with what we now possess; and some
small part of it will be handed down as long as the human race
exists.

Fixed and Circulating Capital

Economists have long been accustomed to distinguish capital
into the two kinds, fixed and circulating. Adam Smith called that
circulating which passes from hand to hand, and yields a revenue
by being parted with. The fact of being frequently exchanged is,
however, an accidental circumstance which leads to no results of
importance. Ricardo altered the use of the terms, applying the
name *circulating* to that which is frequently destroyed and has
to be reproduced. He says unequivocally: * 'In proportion as
fixed capital is less durable, it approaches to the nature of circulating capital. It will be consumed, and its value reproduced in a
shorter time, in order to preserve the capital of the manufacturer.'
Accepting this doctrine, and carrying it out to the full extent,
we must say that no precise line can be drawn between the two
kinds. The difference is one of amount and degree. The duration

* *On the Principles of Political Economy and Taxation*, ch. I, sec. v, 3rd
ed., p. 36.

of capital may vary from a day to several hundred years; the most circulating is the least durable; the most fixed the most durable.

Free and Invested Capital

I believe that the clear explanation of the doctrine of capital requires the use of a term *free capital*, which has not been hitherto recognized by economists. By free capital I mean the wages of labour, either in its transitory form of money, or its real form of food and other necessaries of life. The ordinary sustenance requisite to support labourers of all ranks when engaged upon their work is really the true form of capital. It is quite in agreement with the ordinary language of commercial men to say, not that a factory, or dock, or railway, or ship, *is capital*, but that *it represents so much capital sunk in the enterprise*. To invest capital is to spend money, or the food and maintenance which money purchases, upon the completion of some work. The capital remains invested or sunk until the work has returned profit, equivalent to the first cost, with interest.

Much clearness would result from making the language of economics more nearly coincident with that of commerce. Accordingly, I would not say that a railway *is fixed capital*, but that *capital is fixed in the railway*. The capital is not the railway, but the food of those who made the railway. Abundance of free capital in a country means that there are copious stocks of food, clothing and every article which people insist upon having – that, in short, everything is so arranged that abundant subsistence and conveniences of every kind are forthcoming without the labour of the country being much taxed to provide them. In such circumstances it is possible that a part of the labourers of the country can be employed on works of which the utility is distant, and yet no one will feel scarcity in the present.

Uniformity of the Rate of Interest

A most important principle of this subject is that *free capital can be indifferently employed in any branch or kind of industry*. Free capital, as we have just seen, consists of a suitable assortment

of all kinds of food, clothing, utensils, furniture and othe
articles which a community requires for its ordinary sustenance
Men and families consume much the same kind of commodities
whatever may be the branch of manufacture or trade by whicl
they earn a living. Hence there is nothing in the nature of fre
capital to determine its employment to one kind of industr
rather than another. The very same wages, whether we regar
the money wages, or the real wages purchased with the money
will support a man whether he be a mechanic, a weaver, a coa
miner, a carpenter, a mason or any other kind of labourer.

The necessary result is that the rate of interest for free capita
will tend to and closely attain uniformity in all employments
The market for capital is like all other markets: *there can be bu
one price for one article at one time*. It is a case of the law o
indifference (p. 137). Now the article in question is the same, s
that its price must be the same. Accordingly, as is well known
the rate of interest, when freed from considerations of risk
trouble and other interfering causes, is the same in all trades
and every trade will employ capital up to the point at which i
just yields the current interest. If any manufacturer or trade
employs so much capital in supporting a certain amount of labou
that the return is less than in other trades, he will lose; for he migh
have obtained the current rate by lending it to other traders.

General Expression for the Rate of Interest

We may obtain a general expression for the rate of interes
yielded by capital in any employment provided that we ma
suppose the produce for the same amount of labour to vary a
some continuous function of the time elapsing between th
expenditure of the labour and the enjoyment of the result. Le
the time in question be t, and the produce for the same amoun
of labour the function of t denoted by Ft, which may be suppose
always to increase with t. If we now extend the time to $t + \Delta t$, th
produce will be $F(t + \Delta t)$, and the increment of produc
$F(t + \Delta t) - Ft$. The ratio which this increment bears to th
increment of investment of capital will determine the rate o
interest. Now, at the end of the time t, we might receive the pro

duct Ft, and this is the amount of capital which remains invested when we extend the time by Δt. Hence the amount of increased investment of capital is $\Delta t \cdot Ft$; and, dividing the increment of produce by this last expression, we have

$$\frac{F(t + \Delta t) - Ft}{\Delta t} \times \frac{1}{Ft}.$$

When we reduce the magnitude of Δt infinitely, the limit of the first factor of the above expression is the differential coefficient of Ft, so that we find the rate of interest to be represented by

$$\frac{dFt}{dt} \cdot \frac{1}{Ft} \text{ or } \frac{F't}{Ft}.$$

The interest of capital is, in other words, *the rate of increase of the produce divided by the whole produce*; but this is a quantity which must rapidly approach to zero, unless means can be found of continually maintaining the rate of increase. Unless a body moves with a rapidly increasing speed, the space it moves over in any unit of time must ultimately become inconsiderable compared with the whole space passed over from the commencement. There is no reason to suppose that industry, generally speaking, is capable of returning any such vastly increasing produce from the greater application of capital. Every new machine or other great invention will usually require a fixation of capital for a certain average time, and may be capable of paying interest upon it; but when this average time is reached, it fails to afford a return to more prolonged investments.

To take an instance, let us suppose that the produce of labour in some case is proportional to the interval of abstinence t; then we have say $Ft = a \cdot t$, in which a is an unknown constant. The differential coefficient $F't$ is now a; and the rate of interest $\frac{a}{Ft}$ or $\frac{a}{at}$ or $\frac{1}{t}$; or the rate of interest varies inversely as the time of investment.

Dimension of Interest

The formula which we obtained in the preceding section has been subjected to close criticism by an eminent mathematician, who proposed several alternative formulae, but finally accepted my solution of the question as correct. As Professor Adamson, however, has also raised some objections to the formula, it seems desirable to explain its meaning and mode of derivation more fully than was done in the first edition. [53]

In the first place, as regards the theory of dimensions the formula is clearly correct. The rate of interest expresses the ratio which the sum paid per annum for the loan of capital bears to the capital. The interest and the capital are quantities of the same nature, their ratio being an abstract number. Dividing by length of time *rate of interest* will have the dimension T^{-1}.

Or we may put it in this way: interest is paid per annum, or per month, or per other unit of time, and the less the magnitude of this unit, the less must be the numerical expression of the rate of interest. Simple interest at five per cent per annum is $0·416 \ldots$ per cent per month, and so on. Hence time enters negatively, and the dimension of the rate of interest will be T^{-1}. Or, again, we may state it thus symbolically: the capital advanced may be taken as having the dimension M; the annual return has the dimensions MT. Dividing the former by the latter we obtain [54]

$$\frac{M}{MT} = T^{-1}.$$

Now the formula $\frac{F't}{Ft}$ clearly agrees with this result; for the denominator is a certain unknown function of the time of advance of the capital t. We may assume that it can be expressed in a finite series of the powers of t, and the numerator, being the differential coefficient of the same function, will be of one degree of power less than Ft. Hence the dimensions of the formula will be

$$\frac{T^{n-1}}{T^n}, \text{ or } \frac{1}{T}, \text{ or } T^{-1}.$$

It must be carefully remembered that it is the *rate of interest* which has the dimension T^{-1}, not interest itself, which, being simply commodity of some kind, has the dimension of commodity, namely M, of the same nature, and having the same dimensions.

The function of capital is simply this, that labour which would produce certain commodity m_1, if that commodity were needed immediately for the satisfaction of wants, is applied so as to produce m_2 after the lapse of the time t. The reason for this deferment is that m_2 usually exceeds m_1, and the difference or *interest* $m_2 - m_1$ is commodity having the same dimensions as m_1. Hence the *rate of interest*, apart from the question of time, would be $m_2 - m_1$ divided by m_1, and the quantities being of the same nature, the ratio will be an abstract number devoid of dimensions. But the time for which the results of labour are foregone is as important a matter as the quantity of commodity. The amount of deferment is m_1t, so that the rate of interest is $m_2 - m_1$ divided by m_1t, which will have the dimension T^{-1}.

Exactly the same result would be obtained, however, if we regarded the use of capital from a different point of view. Capital and deferment of consumption are not needed only in order to increase production, that is to say, the manufacture of goods; they are needed also to equalize consumption, and to allow commodity to be consumed when its utility is at the highest point. Now, when certain commodity is consumed within an interval of time, the utility produced will, as we have seen, possess the dimensions $MUT^{-1}T$, or MU. Suppose that instead of being consumed within that interval, the commodity is held in hand for a time before being consumed at all. Then the amount of deferment of utility will be proportional both to the interval of time over which it is deferred, and to the utility which is deferred. Thus the amount of deferment will have the dimensions MUT. The increase of utility due to deferment will clearly have the same dimensions as were previously determined, namely MU. Hence the ratio of this increase to the amount of deferment will have the dimensions $\dfrac{MU}{MUT}$ or T^{-1}, and this result corresponds with the dimension of the rate of interest as otherwise reached.

Peacock on the Dimensions of Interest

The need of some care in forming our conceptions of these quantities is strikingly illustrated by the fact that not quite fifty years ago so profound and philosophic a mathematician as the late Dean Peacock completely misapprehended the matter. In the first edition of his celebrated and invaluable *Treatise on Algebra*, published in 1830, he gives (§ 111, p. 91) the interest of money as an example of a quantity of *three dimensions*, and one which may be represented by a solid. He says:

If *p* represent the principal or sum of money lent or forborne, *r* the rate of interest (of £1 for one year), and *t* the number of years, then the interest accumulated or due will be represented by *prt*; for if *r* be the interest of £1 for one year, *pr* will be the interest of a sum of money denoted by *p* for one year, and therefore *prt* will be the amount of this interest in *t* years, no interest being reckoned upon interest due such would be the result according to the principles of Arithmetical Algebra.

If we now suppose *prt* represented respectively by lines which form the adjacent edges of a parallelopipedon, the solid thus formed will represent the interest accumulated or due: in other words, it will represent whatever is represented by the general formula *prt* when specific values and significations are given to its symbols: for in whatever manner we may suppose any one of the symbols of *prt* to vary the solid will vary in the same proportion.

The lines which we assume to represent units of *p*, *r* and *t*, are perfectly arbitrary, whether they are made equal to each other or not: this is clearly the case with *p* and *t*, which are quantities of a different nature: and the third quantity is likewise different from the other two being an abstract numerical quantity: for it expresses the relation between the interest of £1 and £1, or between the interest of £100 and £100, which is the quotient of the division of one quantity by another of the same nature: thus, if the interest be five per cent, then $r = \frac{5}{10}$ or $\frac{1}{20}$: if four per cent, then $r = \frac{4}{100}$ or $\frac{1}{25}$: and similarly in other cases the line, therefore, which is assumed to represent the abstract unit to which *r* is referred, is independent of the lines which represent units of *p* and of *t*, and may therefore be assumed at pleasure, equally with those lines.

The lines which represent *p* and *t* form a rectangular area, which is the geometrical representation of their product: the third quantity *r* being merely numerical, may either be represented by a line, as in the case just considered, when a solid parallelopipedon is made the representative of *prt*: or we may consider the area *pt* as representing the product *prt* when *r* = 1, and that this product in any other case is represented by a rectangle which bears to the rectangle *pt* the ratio of *r* to 1: this may be effected by increasing or diminishing one of the sides of the rectangle in the required ratio: the product *prt* may there-fore be correctly represented either by a solid or an area, when one of the factors is an abstract number.

The conclusion at which he arrives is a lame one, for he thinks that the same kind of quantity may be represented indifferently by a solid or an area. The fact is that Peacock confused a product of three factors with a quantity of three dimensions. He took these dimensions as if they were, say M = money, R = rate of interest and T = time. If we simply multiply these together, as Peacock first does, we get a quantity apparently of three dimen-sions, MRT. If, according to Peacock's subsequent idea, we take R to be an abstract numerical quantity, then we have two dimensions left, namely, MT. He overlooks the fact that the rate of interest involves time negatively, although he describes r as 'the rate of interest (of £1 for one year)'. Correctly stated, the dimensions of *prt*, the quantity of *interest* are $M \times T^{-1} \times T$ or M, that is simply the dimension of the money advanced.

If you say, for instance, that the simple interest of £300 at five per cent per annum for five years is £75, there remains no reference in this result to time: £75 is simply £75, and is of exactly the same nature as the £300 which bore the interest.

That Peacock subsequently discovered error, or at least diffi-culty, in this section, is rendered probable by the fact that he omitted the illustration altogether in his second edition; but he does not, so far as I have observed, give any explanation.

Tendency of Profits to a Minimum

It is one of the favourite doctrines of economists since the time of Adam Smith, that as society progresses and capital accumu-lates, the rate of profit, or more strictly speaking, the rate of interest, tends to fall. The rate will always ultimately sink so low, they think, that the inducements to further accumulation will cease. This doctrine is in striking agreement with the result of the somewhat abstract analytical investigation given above. Our formula for the rate of interest shows that unless there be con-stant progress in the arts, the rate must tend to sink towards zero, supposing accumulation of capital to go on. There are sufficient statistical facts, too, to confirm this conclusion historically. The only question that can arise is as to the actual cause of this tendency.

Adam Smith vaguely attributed it to the competition of capitalists, saying: 'The increase of stock which raises wages, tends to lower profit. When the stocks of many rich merchants are turned into the same trade, their mutual competition naturally tends to lower its profit; and when there is a like increase of stock in all the different trades carried on in the same society, the same competition must produce the same effect in them all.' *

Later economists have entertained different views. They attributed the fall of interest to the rise in the cost of labour. The produce of labour, they said, is divided between capitalists and labourers, and if it is necessary to give more to labour, there must be less left to capital, and the rate of profit will fall. I shall discuss the validity of this theory in the final chapter, and will only remark, here, that it is not in agreement with the view which I have ventured to take concerning the origin of interest. I consider that interest is determined by the increment of produce which it enables a labourer to obtain, and is altogether independent of the total return which he receives for this labour. Our formula (p. 241) shows that the rate of interest will be greater as the whole produce Ft is less, if the advantage of more capital, measured by $F't$, remains unchanged. In many ill-governed countries, where the land is wretchedly tilled, the average produce is small, and yet the rate of interest is high, simply because the want of security prevents the due supply of capital: hence more capital is urgently needed, and its price is high. In America and the British colonies the produce is often high, and yet interest is high, because there is not sufficient capital accumulated to meet all the demands. In England and other old countries the rate of interest is generally lower because there is an abundance of capital, and the urgent need of more is not actually felt.

I conceive that the returns to capital and labour are independent of each other.[55] If the soil yields little, and capital will not make it yield more, then both wages and interest will be low,

* *Wealth of Nations*, Book I, ch. IX., second paragraph. [Cannan's ed. vol. I, p. 89.]

provided that the capital be not attracted away to more profitable employment. If the soil yields much, and capital will make it yield more, then both wages and interest will be high; if the soil yields much, and capital will not make it yield more, then wages will be high and interest low, unless the capital finds other investments. But the subject is much complicated by the interference of rent. When we speak of the soil yielding much, we must distinguish between the *whole yield* and the *final rate of yield*. In the western states of America the land yields a large total, and all at a high final rate, so that the labourer enjoys the result. In England there is a large total yield, but a small final yield, so that the landowner receives a large rent and the labourer small wages. The more fertile land having here been long in cultivation, the wages of the labourer are measured by what he can earn by cultivating sterile land which it only just pays to take into cultivation.

Advantage of Capital to Industry

We must take great care not to confuse the rate of interest on capital with the whole advantage which it confers on industry. The rate of interest depends on the advantage of the last increment of capital, and the advantages of previous increments may be greater in almost any ratio. In considering the laws of utility, we found that an article possessing an immensely great total utility, for instance corn or water, might have a very low final degree of utility, because our need of it was almost entirely satisfied; yet the ratio of exchange always depends upon the final, not the previous degree of utility. The case is the same with capital. Some capital may be indispensable to a manufacture; hence the benefit conferred by the capital is indefinitely great, and were there no more capital to be had, the rate of interest which could be demanded, assuming the article manufactured to be necessary, would be almost unlimited. But as soon as ever a larger supply of capital becomes available, the prior benefit of capital is overlooked. As free capital is always the same in quality, the second portion may be made to replace the first if needful; hence capitalists can never exact from labourers the whole

advantages which their capital confers – they can exact only a
rate determined by the advantage of the last increment. A lender
of capital cannot say to a borrower who wants £3,000: 'I know
that £1,000 is indispensable to your business, and therefore will
charge you 100 per cent interest upon it; for the second £1,000,
which is less necessary, I will charge twenty per cent; and as
upon the third £1,000 you can only earn the common profit,
I will only ask five per cent.' The answer would be, that there are
many people only earning five per cent on their capital who
would be glad to lend enough at a small advance of interest;
and it is a matter of indifference who is the lender.

The general result of the tendency to uniformity of interest is
that employers of capital always get it at the lowest prevailing
rate; they always borrow the capital which is least necessary to
others, and either the labourers themselves, or the public generally as consumers, gather all the excess of advantage. To illustrate
this result, let distances along the line *ox*, in figure 14, mark

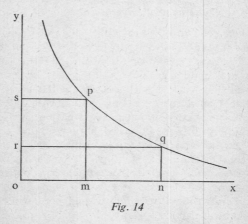

Fig. 14

quantities of capital employing in any branch of industry a
fixed number of labourers. Let the area of the curve denote the
whole produce of labour and capital. Thus to the capital, *on*,
results a produce measured by the area of the curvilinear figure
between the upright lines *oy* and *qn*. But the amount of increased

produce which would be due to an increment of capital would be measured by the line qn, so that this will represent $F't$ (p. 241).[56] The interest of the capital will be its amount, on, multiplied by the rate qn, or the area of the rectangle oq. The remainder of the produce, $pqry$, will belong to the labourer. But had less capital been available, say not more than om, its rate of interest would have been measured by pm, the amount of interest by the rectangle op, while the labourer must have remained contented with the smaller share, psy. I will not say that the above diagram represents with strict accuracy the relations of capital, produce, wages, rate of interest and amount of interest; but it may serve roughly to illustrate their relations. I see no way of representing exactly the theory of capital in the form of a diagram.

Are Articles in the Consumers' Hands Capital?

The views of the nature of capital expressed in this chapter generally agree with those entertained by Ricardo and various other economists; but there is one point in which the theory leads me to a result at variance with the opinions of almost all writers. I feel quite unable to adopt the opinion that the moment goods pass into the possession of the consumer they cease altogether to have the attributes of capital. This doctrine descends to us from the time of Adam Smith, and has generally received the undoubting assent of his followers. The latter, indeed, have generally omitted all notice of such goods, treating them as if no longer under the view of the economist. Adam Smith, although he denied the possessions of a consumer the name of capital, took care to enumerate them as part of the *stock* of the community. He divides into three portions the general stock of a country, and while the second and third portions are fixed and circulating capital, the first is described as follows: *

The first is that portion which is reserved for immediate consumption, and of which the characteristic is, that it affords no revenue or profit. It consists in the stock of food, clothes, household furniture, etc., which have been purchased by their proper consumers, but which

* *Wealth of Nations*, Book II, ch. I, twelfth paragraph. [Cannan's ed., vol. I, p. 263.]

are not yet entirely consumed. The whole stock of mere dwelling-houses too subsisting at any one time in the country make a part of this first portion. The stock that is laid out in a house, if it is to be the dwelling-house of the proprietor, ceases from that moment to serve in the function of a capital, or to afford any revenue to its owner. A dwelling-house, as such, contributes nothing to the revenue of its inhabitant; and though it is, no doubt, extremely useful to him, it is as his clothes and household furniture are useful to him, which, however, make a part of his expense, and not of his revenue.

MacCulloch, indeed, in his edition of the *Wealth of Nations*, p. 121, has remarked upon this passage, that 'the capital laid out in building houses for such persons is employed as much for the public advantage as if it were vested in the tools or instruments they make use of in their respective businesses'. He appears, in fact, to reject the doctrine, and it is surprising that economists have generally acquiesced in Adam Smith's view, though it leads to manifest contradictions. It leads to the absurd conclusion that the very same thing fulfilling the very same purposes will be capital or not according to its accidental ownership. To procure good port wine it is necessary to keep it for a number of years, and Adam Smith would not deny that a stock of wine kept in the wine merchant's possession for this purpose is capital, because it yields him revenue. If a consumer buys it when new, and keeps it to improve, it will not be capital, although it is evident that he gains the same profit as the merchant by buying it at a lower price. If a coal merchant lays in a stock of coal when cheap, to sell when dear, it is capital; but if a consumer lays in a stock, it is not.

Adam Smith's views seem to be founded upon a notion that capital ought to give an annual revenue or increase of wealth like a field yields a crop of corn or grass. Speaking of a dwelling-house, he says:

If it is to be let to a tenant for rent, as the house itself can produce nothing, the tenant must always pay the rent out of some other revenue, which he derives either from labour, or stock, or land. Though a house, therefore, may yield a revenue to its proprietor, and thereby serve in the function of a capital to him, it cannot yield any to the public, nor serve in the function of a capital to it, and the revenue of the whole body of the people can never be in the smallest degree increased by it. Clothes and household furniture, in the same manner, sometimes yield a revenue, and thereby serve in the function of a capital to particular persons. In countries where masquerades are common, it is a trade to let out masquerade dresses for a night. Upholsterers frequently let furniture by the month or by the year. Undertakers let the furniture of funerals by the day and by the week. Many people let furnished houses, and get a rent, not only for the use of the house, but for that of the furniture. The revenue, however, which is derived from such things, must always be ultimately drawn from some other source of revenue.*

This notion that people live upon a kind of net revenue flowing in to them appears to be derived from the old French economists, and plays no part in modern economics.[57] Nothing is more requisite than a dwelling-house, and if a person cannot hire a house at the required spot, he must find capital to build it. I think that no economist would refuse to count among the fixed capital of the country that which is sunk in dwelling-houses. Capital is sunk in farming that we may have bread, in cotton mills that we may be clothed, and why not in houses that we may be lodged? If land yields an annual revenue of corn and wool, milk, beef and other necessaries, houses yield a revenue of shelter and comfort. The sole end of all industry is to satisfy our wants; and if capital is requisite to supply shelter, and furniture and useful utensils, as it undoubtedly is, why refuse it the name which it bears in all other employments?

Can we deny that the property of a hotel-keeper is capital and yields a revenue to its owner? Yet it is invested in pots and pans and beds and all kinds of common furniture. In America it is not uncommon for people to live all their lives in hotels or boarding-houses; and we might readily conceive the system to advance until no one would undertake housekeeping except as a profession. Now if we allow to what is invested in hotels, hired furnished houses, lodgings and the like, the nature of capital, I do not see how we can refuse it to common houses. We should thus be led into all kinds of absurdities.

For instance, if two people live in their own houses, these are

* *Wealth of Nations*, Book II, ch. I, twelfth paragraph continued.

251

not, according to present opinion, capital; if they find it convenient to exchange houses and pay rent each to the other, the houses are capital. At great watering-places like Brighton it is a regular business to lease houses, fill them with furniture, and then let them for short periods as furnished houses: surely it is capital which is embarked in the trade. If a private individual happens to own a furnished house which he does not at the time want, and lets it, can we refuse to regard his house and furniture as capital? Whenever one person provides the articles and another uses them and pays rent, there is capital. Surely, then, if the same person uses and owns them, the nature of the things is not fundamentally different. There is no need for a money payment to pass; but every person who keeps accurate accounts should debit those accounts with an annual charge for interest and depreciation on what he has invested in house and furniture. House-keeping is an occupation involving wages, capital and interest, like any other business, except that the owner consumes the whole result.

By accepting this view of the subject, we shall avoid endless difficulties. What, for instance, shall we say to a theatre? Is it not the product of capital? Can it be erected without capital? Does it not return interest, if successful, like any cotton mill or steam vessel? If the economist agrees to this, he must allow, on similar grounds, that a very large part of the aggregate capital of the country is invested in theatres, hotels, schools, lecture rooms and institutions of various kinds which do not belong to the industry of the country, taken in a narrow sense, but which none the less contribute to the wants of its inhabitants, which is the sole object of all industry.

I may add that even the food, clothes and many other possessions of extensive classes are often indubitable capital; they are bought upon credit, and interest is undoubtedly paid for the capital sunk in them by the dealers. There is hardly, I suppose, a man of fashion in London who walks in his own clothes; and the tailors find in the practice of giving credit a very profitable investment for capital. Except among the poorer classes, and often among them, food is seldom paid for until after it is consumed. Interest must be paid one way or another upon the capital thus absorbed. Whether or not these articles in the consumers' hands are *capital*, at any rate they have capital invested in them – that is, labour has been spent upon them of which the whole benefit is not enjoyed at once.

I might also point out at almost any length that the stock of food, clothing and other requisite articles of subsistence in the country are a main part of capital according to the statements of J. S. Mill, Professor Fawcett and most other economists. Now what does it really matter if these articles happen to lie in the warehouses of traders or in private houses, so long as there is a stock? At present it is the practice for farmers and corn merchants to hold the produce of the harvest until the public buys and consumes it. Surely the stock of corn is capital. But if it were the practice of every housekeeper to buy up corn in the autumn and keep it in a private granary, would it not serve in exactly the same way to subsist the population? Would not everything go on exactly the same, except that every one would be his own capitalist in regard to corn in place of paying farmers and corn merchants for doing the business?

CHAPTER VIII

Concluding Remarks

The Doctrine of Population

IT is no part of my purpose in this work to attempt to trace out, with any approach to completeness, the results of the theory given in the preceding chapters. When the views of the nature of value, and the general method of treating the subject by the application of the fluxional calculus, have received some recognition and acceptance, it will be time to think of results. I shall therefore only occupy a few more pages in pointing out the branches of economic doctrine which have been passed over, and in indicating their connexion with the theory.

The doctrine of population has been conspicuously absent, not because I doubt in the least its truth and vast importance, but because it forms no part of the direct problem of economics. I do not remember to have seen it remarked that it is an inversion of the problem to treat labour as a varying quantity, when we originally start with labour as the first element of production, and aim at the most economical employment of that labour. The problem of economics may, as it seems to me, be stated thus: *Given, a certain population, with various needs and powers of production, in possession of certain lands and other sources of material: required, the mode of employing their labour which will maximize the utility of the produce*. It is what mathematicians would call a change of the variable, afterwards to treat that labour as variable which was originally a fixed quantity. It really amounts to altering the conditions of the problem so as to create at each change a new problem. The same results, however, would generally be obtained by supposing the other conditions to vary. Given, a certain population, we may imagine the land and capital at their disposal to be greater or less, and may then trace out the results which will, in many respects, be applicable respectively to a less or greater population with the original land and capital.

Relation of Wages and Profit

There is another inversion of the problem of economics which is generally made in works upon the subject. Although labour is the starting-point in production, and the interests of the labourer the very subject of the science, yet economists do not progress far before they suddenly turn round and treat labour as a commodity which is bought up by capitalists. Labour becomes itself the object of the laws of supply and demand, instead of those laws acting in the distribution of the products of labour. Economists have invented, too, a very simple theory to determine the rate at which capital can buy up labour. The average rate of wages, they say, is found by dividing the whole amount of capital appropriated to the payment of wages by the number of the labourers paid; and they wish us to believe that this settles the question. But a little consideration shows that this proposition is simply a *truism*. *The average rate of wages must be equal to what is appropriated to the purpose divided by the number who share it.* The whole question will consist in determining how much is appropriated for the purpose; for it certainly need not be the whole existing amount of circulating capital. Mill distinctly says, that because industry is limited by capital, we are not to infer that it always reaches that limit;* and, as a matter of fact, we often observe that there is abundance of capital to be had at low rates of interest, while there are also large numbers of artisans starving for want of employment. The wage-fund theory is therefore illusory as a real solution of the problem, though I do not deny that it may have a certain limited and truthful application, to be shortly considered.

Another part of the current doctrines of economics determines the rate of profit of capitalists in a very simple manner. The whole produce of industry must be divided into the portions paid as rent, taxes, profits and wages. We may exclude taxes as

* *Principles of Political Economy*, Book I, ch. V, sec. ii.

exceptional, and not very important. Rent also may be eliminated, for it is essentially variable, and is reduced to zero in the case of the poorest land cultivated. We thus arrive at the simple equation –

$$produce = profit + wages.$$

A plain result also is drawn from the formula; for we are told that if wages rise profits must fall, and vice versa. But such a doctrine is radically fallacious; *it involves the attempt to determine two unknown quantities from one equation.* I grant that if the produce be a fixed amount, then if wages rise profits must fall, and vice versa. Something might perhaps be made of this doctrine if Ricardo's theory of a natural rate of wages, that which is just sufficient to support the labourer, held true. But I altogether question the existence of any such rate.

The wages of working men in this kingdom vary from perhaps ten shillings a week up to forty shillings or more; the minimum in one part of the country is not the minimum in another. It is utterly impossible, too, to define exactly what are the necessaries of life. I am inclined, therefore, to reject altogether the current doctrines as to the rate of wages; and even if the theory held true of any one class of labourers separately, there is the additional difficulty that we have to account for the very different rates which prevail in different trades. It is impossible that we should accept for ever Ricardo's sweeping simplification of the subject, involved in his assumption, that there is a natural ordinary rate of wages for common labour, and that all higher rates are merely exceptional instances, to be explained away on other grounds.

The view which I accept concerning the rate of wages is not more difficult to comprehend than the current one. It is that *the wages of a working man are ultimately coincident with what he produces, after the deduction of rent, taxes and the interest of capital.* I think that in the equation

$$produce = profit + wages,$$

the quantity of produce is essentially variable, and that profit is the part to be first determined. If we resolve profit into wages of superintendence, insurance against risk, and interest, the first part is really wages itself; the second equalizes the result in different employments; and the interest is, I believe, determined as stated in the last chapter. The reader will observe the important qualification that wages are only *ultimately* thus determined – that is, in the long run, and on the average of any one branch of employment.

The fact that workmen are not their own capitalists introduces complexity into the problem. The capitalists, or entrepreneurs, enter as a distinct interest. It is they who project and manage a branch of production, and form estimates as to the expected produce. It is the amount of this produce which incites them to invest capital and buy up labour. They pay the lowest current rates for the kind of labour required; and if the produce exceeds the average, those who are first in the field make large profits. This soon induces competition on the part of other capitalists, who, in trying to obtain good workmen, will raise the rate of wages. Competition will proceed until the point is reached at which only the market rate of interest is obtained for the capital invested. At the same time wages will have been so raised that the workmen reap the whole excess of produce, unless indeed the price of the produce has fallen, and the public, as consumers, have the benefit. Whether this latter result will follow or not depends upon the number of labourers who are fitted for the work. Where much skill and education is required, extensive competition will be impossible, and a permanently high rate of wages will exist. But if only common labour is requisite, the price of the goods cannot be maintained, wages will fall to their former point, and the public will gain the advantage of cheaper supplies.

It will be observed that this account of the matter involves the temporary application of the wage-fund theory. It is the proper function of capitalists to sustain labour before the result is accomplished, and as many branches of industry require a large outlay long previous to any definite result being arrived at, it follows that capitalists must undertake the risk of any branch of industry where the ultimate profits are not accurately known. But we now have some clue as to the amount of capital which will be appropriated to the payment of wages in any trade. The amount of capital will depend upon the amount of anticipated profits, and the competition to obtain proper workmen will strongly tend to secure to the latter all their legitimate share in the ultimate produce.

For instance, let a number of schemes be set on foot for laying telegraphic cables. The ultimate profits are very uncertain, depending upon the utility of the cables as compared with their cost. If capitalists make a large estimate of those profits, they will apply much capital to the immediate manufacture of the cables. All workmen competent at the moment to be employed will be hired, and high wages paid if necessary. Every man who has peculiar skill, knowledge or experience, rendering his assistance valuable, will be hired at any requisite cost. At this point it is the wage-fund theory that is in operation. But, after a certain number of years, the condition of affairs will be totally different. Capitalists will learn, by experience, exactly what the profits of cables may be; that amount of capital will be thrown into the work which finds the average amount of profits, and neither more nor less. The cost of transmitting messages will be reduced by competition, so that no excessive profits will be made by any of the parties concerned; the rate of wages, therefore, of every species of labour will be reduced to the average proper to labour of that degree of skill. But if there be required in any branch of the work a very special kind of skilled and experienced labour, it will not be affected by competition in the same way, and the wages or salary will remain high.

I think that it is in this way quite possible to reconcile theories which are at first sight so different. The wage-fund theory acts in a wholly temporary manner. Every labourer ultimately receives the due value of his produce after paying a proper fraction to the capitalist for the remuneration of abstinence and risk. At the same time workers of different degrees of skill receive very different shares according as they contribute a common or a scarce kind of labour to the result.

Professor Hearn's Views

I have the more pleasure and confidence in putting forward these somewhat heretical views concerning the general problem of economics, inasmuch as they are nearly identical with those arrived at by Professor Hearn, of Melbourne University. It would be a somewhat long task to trace out exactly the co-incidence of opinions between us, but he certainly adopts the notion that the capitalist merely buys up temporarily the prospects of the concern he manages and the labourers he employs. Thus he says:

In place of having a share in the undertaking, the cooperator sells for a stipulated price his labour or the use of his capital. The case therefore comes within the ordinary conditions of exchange; and the price of labour and the price of capital are determined in the same manner as all other questions of price are determined. Yet the general character of the partnership is not destroyed. Although each particular transaction amounts to a sale, yet for the continuance of the business a nearer connexion arises. Although the whole loss of the undertaking, if the undertaking be unfortunate, falls upon the last proprietor, and the interests of the other parties have been previously secured, yet each such loss prevents a repetition of the transaction from which it arose. The capital which ought to have been replaced, and which if replaced would have afforded the means of employing labour and of defraying the interest upon other capital, has disappeared; and thus the market for labour and for capital is by so much diminished. Both the labourer and the intermediate capitalist are therefore directly concerned in the success of every enterprise towards which they have contributed. If it be successful, they feel the advantage; if it be not successful, they feel in like manner the loss. But this community of interest is no longer direct, but is indirect merely; and it arises not from the gains or the losses of partners, but from the increased ability, or the diminished demands, of customers.*

This passage really contains a statement of the views which I am inclined wholly to accept; but no passages which I can select will convey an adequate notion of the enlightened view which Professor Hearn takes of the industrial structure of society in his admirable work on *Plutology*.

Plutology: or The Theory of the Efforts to Satisfy Human Wants. By William Edward Hearn, LL.D., professor of history and political economy in the University of Melbourne. London, Macmillan and Co., 1864, p. 329.

The Noxious Influence of Authority

I have but a few lines more to add. I have ventured in the preceding pages to call in question not a few of the favourite doctrines of economists. To me it is far more pleasant to agree than to differ; but it is impossible that one who has any regard for truth can long avoid protesting against doctrines which seem to him to be erroneous. There is ever a tendency of the most hurtful kind to allow opinions to crystallize into creeds. Especially does this tendency manifest itself when some eminent author, enjoying power of clear and comprehensive exposition, becomes recognized as an authority. His works may perhaps be the best which are extant upon the subject in question; they may combine more truth with less error than we can elsewhere meet. But 'to err is human', and the best works should ever be open to criticism. If, instead of welcoming inquiry and criticism, the admirers of a great author accept his writings as authoritative, both in their excellences and in their defects, the most serious injury is done to truth. In matters of philosophy and science authority has ever been the great opponent of truth. A despotic calm is usually the triumph of error. In the republic of the sciences sedition and even anarchy are beneficial in the long run to the greatest happiness of the greatest number.

In the physical sciences authority has greatly lost its noxious influence. Chemistry, in its brief existence of a century, has undergone three or four complete revolutions of theory. In the science of light, Newton's own authority was decisively set aside, though not until after it had retarded for nearly a century the progress of inquiry. Astronomers have not hesitated, within the last few years, to alter their estimates of all the dimensions of the planetary system, and of the universe, because good reasons have been shown for calling in question the real coincidence of previous measurements. In science and philosophy nothing must be held sacred. Truth indeed is sacred; but, as Pilate said, 'What is truth?' Show us the undoubted infallible criterion of absolute truth, and we will hold it as a sacred inviolable thing. But in the absence of that infallible criterion, we have all an equal right to grope about in our search of it, and no body and no school nor clique must be allowed to set up a standard of orthodoxy which shall bar the freedom of scientific inquiry.

I have added these words because I think there is some fear of the too great influence of authoritative writers in political economy. I protest against deference for any man, whether John Stuart Mill, or Adam Smith, or Aristotle, being allowed to check inquiry. Our science has become far too much a stagnant one, in which opinions rather than experience and reason are appealed to.

There are valuable suggestions towards the improvement of the science contained in the works of such writers as Senior, Cairnes, Macleod, Cliffe-Leslie, Hearn, Shadwell, not to mention a long series of French economists from Baudeau and Le Trosne down to Bastiat and Courcelle Seneuil; but they are neglected in England, because the excellence of their works was not comprehended by David Ricardo, the two Mills, Professor Fawcett and others who have made the orthodox Ricardian school what it is. Under these circumstances it is a positive service to break the monotonous repetition of current questionable doctrines, even at the risk of new error. I trust that the theory now given may prove accurate; but, however this may be, it will not be useless if it cause inquiry to be directed into the true basis and form of a science which touches so directly the material welfare of the human race.

NOTES

═══

1. (p. 47) Henry Dunning Macleod (1821–1902), lecturer on political economy in the University of Cambridge. 'An economist of many merits who somehow failed to achieve recognition, or even to be taken quite seriously, owing to his inability to put his many good ideas in a professionally acceptable form.' (Schumpeter; *History of Economic Analysis*, p. 1115.)

Author of *Theory & Practice of Banking*, 1855–6, *A Dictionary of Political Economy*, vol. I, 1863, *The Principles of Economic Philosophy*, 1879, *Elements of Economics*, 1881, and *History of Economics*, 1896.

2. (p. 47) Harald Ludvig Westergaard (1853–1926), professor of political science and statistics at the University of Copenhagen 1886–1924 and one of the leading European statisticians of his time.

3. (p. 49) William Thomas Thornton (1813–80) was the author of a number of works on applied political economy; but those which Jevons had in mind here were almost certainly 'A New Theory of Supply and Demand', *Fortnightly Review*, vol. VII, 1866, pp. 420–34, and *On Labour: its wrongful claims and rightful dues*, London, 1869. The latter gave rise to a famous review article by J. S. Mill, 'Thornton on Labour and its Claims', *Fortnightly Review*, vol. XI, 1869, pp. 505–18, widely interpreted as a retraction of the wages-fund theory.

Thornton attacked classical ideas of supply and demand and the relation of cost and price, but his analysis was much inferior to that of Jevons. See below, p. 148, and, for Jevons's own statement and critique of the wages-fund theory, p. 255.

4. (p. 49) Thomas Edward Cliffe Leslie (1826–82) and John Kells Ingram (1823–1907) were among the leading exponents of the historical method in English economics. Both were Irishmen, and Leslie held the chair of jurisprudence and political economy at Queen's College, Belfast, from 1853 until his death. Ingram, a true polymath, held in succession the chairs of oratory, English literature and Greek at Trinity College, Dublin, but made a substantial reputation by his economic writings, of which his address on 'The Present Position & Prospects of Political Economy', here referred to by Jevons, was one of the best-known.

5. (p. 52) William Ballantyne Hodgson (1815–80) was Principal of the Mechanics Institute at Liverpool when Jevons was a pupil there. Hodgson was appointed first professor of political economy at Edinburgh in 1871 and retained the chair until his death.

Robert Adamson (1852–1902), Jevons's successor as professor of political economy at Owens College, Manchester, 1876–82. Also professor of philosophy there, 1876–93; later professor of philosophy in the University of Glasgow.

W. H. Brewer (1841–19??) served as a substitute lecturer for Jevons at

Owens College, Manchester, and seems to have had a strong interest in the bibliography of economics.

Johan Baron d'Aulnis de Bourouill (1850–1930) was awarded his doctorate by the University of Leiden in 1874 for a thesis (*Het Inkommen der Maatschappij*) in which he made use of Jevons's theory of value. He was for a time a lawyer in Amsterdam and a member of the Finance Department until 1878, when he was elected professor of political history, statistics and economics at the University of Utrecht, a post which he held until 1917.

Nicolass Gerard Pierson (1839–1909), Dutch economist, banker and statesman. Professor of economics at the University of Amsterdam. Appointed to the board of directors of the Netherlands Bank, 1860; president of the Bank 1885–91, Minister of Finance of the Netherlands 1891–4, Prime Minister and Minister of Finance 1897–1901.

'M. Vissering of Leiden' – presumably W. Vissering, son of Simon Vissering (1818–88), professor of political economy at Leiden, 1860–78, and Minister of Finance of the Netherlands 1879–81. Jevons's correspondence appears to have been with the younger Vissering.

Luigi Cossa (1831–96), professor of political economy at Pavia from 1858.

6. (p. 56) Jeremy Bentham, *A Table of the Springs of Action . . . to which are added, explanatory notes and observations.* London, R. & A. Taylor. The first printing was dated 1815.

7. (p. 57) Étienne Bonnot de Condillac, *Le commerce et le gouvernement, considérés rélativement l'un à l'autre.* Amsterdam and Paris, 1776. In fact, the work was first published in 1772; see *Catalogue of the Kress Library of Business & Economics*, Cambridge, Mass., 1940, entry 7200.

8. (p. 58) Antoine Augustin Cournot (1801–77), professor of analysis and mechanics at Lyons 1834; Rector of the Academy of Grenoble 1835; Inspector-General of studies 1838; Rector of the Academy of Dijon 1854; now probably the best known of early mathematical economists. His *Récherches* was published in 1838, but not translated into English until 1897. Jevons's claim that it 'remained for me among Englishmen to discover its value' was no doubt sincere, but not well founded: according to Keynes the book came into Marshall's hands between 1867 and 1870 and formed a starting point for his work. See *Memorials of Alfred Marshall*, p. 19.

9. (p.59) *Principes de la théorie des richesses.*

10. (p. 62) Marshall points out that while Jevons here criticizes Gossen for assuming linear functions, Jevons himself assumed that the function representing the investment of capital was of the first order. See note XIII in the Mathematical Appendix to Marshall's *Principles*, 9th ed., vol. I, p. 846.

11. (p. 65) Henry Charles Fleeming Jenkin (1833–85), professor of mechanical engineering at the University of Edinburgh. His papers, 'Trade Unions: how far legitimate?' and 'The Graphic Representation of the Laws of Supply and Demand' (1868), which had such strong in-

fluence on Jevons, are reprinted in his *Papers, Literary, Scientific, etc.* (2 vols, London, 1888). See Introduction, p. 14.

[Sir] George Howard Darwin (1845–1912), was the second son of Charles Darwin. His life was mainly devoted to the study of mathematics at Cambridge where, from 1883, he was Plummer Professor of Astronomy and Experimental Philosophy.

Simon Newcomb (1835–1909), American astronomer. Commissioned professor of mathematics in the American navy 1861, and served until 1897. Professor of mathematics and astronomy, Johns Hopkins University, 1884–94.

Newcomb published a *Principles of Political Economy* in 1886.

12. (p. 65) Giovanni Ceva (1647–1734), an engineer of Mantua who wrote on monetary questions and for whom Schumpeter claims the distinction of having anticipated the method of mathematical model-building in economics by two centuries (*History of Economic Analysis*, p. 301).

Cesare Bonesana, marchese di Beccaria (1738–94), best known for his work on penology and his work as an administrator in Milan, but also an able economist. He founded the periodical, *Il Caffè*, in which his 1765 article 'On Smuggling', cited in Jevons's list of mathematico-economic works, was published.

13. (p. 66) Henry Humphry Evans Lloyd (1720–83), captain in the 1745 expedition to Scotland, and later a major-general in the Austrian army, author of *History of the War between the King of Prussia and the Empress of Germany and Her Allies* (1766 and 1782) and *A Political and Military Rhapsody on the Defence of Great Britain* (1779).

The *Essay on the Theory of Money* is attributed to Lloyd in Higgs: *Bibliography of Economics* 1751–1775, item 5263, on the authority of Foxwell; the grounds for Cossa's attribution are not clear.

14. (p. 66) An English translation of Cossa's *Guido* was in fact published in 1880, with a preface by Jevons.

15. (p. 67) On Condillac, see above, note 7. Abbé Nicolas Baudeau (1730–92) and G. F. Le Trosne (1728–80) were both orthodox Physiocrats, followers of François Quesnay. J.-B. Say (1767–1832) is now best remembered for his law of markets, accepted, though not stressed, by Jevons. Antoine, comte Destutt de Tracy (1754–1836) published his *Traité d'économie politique* at Paris in 1823. He was not an original thinker in comparison with Say, but perhaps intellectually more distinguished than Frederic Bastiat (1801–50), now chiefly remembered for popularizing free trade doctrines. J. G. Courcelle-Seneuil (1813–92) was likewise an author of clarity rather than originality, but an early user of graphical method. For Storch's work, see below, note 17.

16. (p. 68) John Lancelot Shadwell, author of 'A Theory of Wages', *Westminster Review*, New Series, vol. XLI, Jan. 1872, pp. 184–203, – in which he argued that 'wages must be determined by the efficiency of labour' – and of *A System of Political Economy*, London, 1877.

W. E. Hearn, *Plutology; or the Theory of Efforts to supply Human Wants,*

London, 1864; 2nd ed. 1878. W. E. Hearn (1826–88), having been professor of Greek at University College, Galway, from 1849 to 1854, was appointed professor of political economy at Melbourne in 1854; he later became a member of the legislative council of Victoria, where he lived until his death. See D. B. Copland, *W. E. Hearn, First Australian Economist*, Melbourne, 1935.

17. (p. 69) Heinrich Friedrich von Storch (1766–1835), *Cours d'économie politique, ou exposition des principes qui déterminent la prospérité des nations . . . avec des notes explicatives et critiques par J. B. Say*. 5 vols., Paris, 1823–4. Storch was a German who made his career in Russia; his work in economics follows mainly Smithian lines.

18. (p. 72) W. S. Jevons: *Political Economy*, Science Primers Series, London, 1878. Paragraph 69, 'The Cause of Rent', p. 94, attributes rent entirely to differences in fertility and accessibility of land.

19. (p. 79) Pierre Simon, Marquis de Laplace (1749–1827), *Exposition du système du monde*, Paris 1796.

20. (p. 80) The article 'Tides and Waves' appeared in the *Encyclopaedia Metropolitana*, London, 1845, vol. V, pp. 241–394 and was also published as a separate volume.

Sir George Biddell Airy (1801–92) was Astronomer Royal from 1835 to 1881, having previously held the chairs of astronomy and mathematics at Cambridge.

21. (p. 83) Cf. Marshall: *Principles of Economics* Book I, ch. II, §1, 9th ed., vol. I, p. 15: 'It is essential to note that the economist does not claim to measure any affection of the mind in itself, or directly; but only indirectly through its effect.'

22. (p. 85) Jevons himself has not remained consistently on this pinnacle of solitude. It is abandoned by economists in general in the received theory of taxation, founded, as Mill says, 'on human wants and feelings', Edgeworth, 'The Theory of Distribution', *Papers relating to Political Economy*, London, 1925, vol. I, p. 58. Since Edgeworth's day economists in general have been striving to regain the Jevonian pinnacle.

23. (p. 86) This passage has relevance to the Jevonian concept of a 'trading body', developed on pp. 135–6. See below, note 35.

24. (p. 89) Jevons here cites some of the main exponents of the historical method outside Germany.

Richard Jones (1790–1855) was professor of political economy at King's College, London, from 1831 to 1833 and then moved to the East India Company's College at Haileybury. His best-known work was an *Essay on the Distribution of Wealth*, of which part 1, 'Rent', 1831, was all that was published.

Émile de Laveleye (1822–92) was a Belgian economist who wrote much on monetary questions, but his *De la propriété et ses formes primitives*, 1873, was a work on historist lines.

Leonce de Lavergne (1809–80) was a specialist in agricultural economics and wrote many comparative works in this field, notably his *Économie rurale de l'Angleterre, de l'Écosse et de l'Irlande*, 1854.

On Cliffe Leslie see above, note 4.

Sir Henry Maine (1822–88), the outstanding jurist and the only non-economist in Jevons's list here, used the historical method in his classic work on *Ancient Law*, 1861, and other writings.

James E. Thorold Rogers (1823–90) twice Drummond Professor of Political Economy at Oxford, author of *A History of Agriculture and Prices in England*, 7 vols., 1866–87, was one of the founders of economic history as a discipline in England.

25. (p. 91) Hume: *Essays and Treatises on Several Subjects*, vol. I, part II, London, 1752, essay I, 'Of Commerce', p. 265.

26. (p. 103, note 2) The reprint of the *Encyclopaedia Metropolitana* article to which Jevons here refers was, and is, more widely known as Senior's *Outline of the Science of Political Economy*. The fifth edition appeared in 1863; the page reference in the Library of Economics reprint, 1938, second impression 1951, is the same.

27. (p. 112) Marshall argued that while Jevons was correct in substituting the proposition that the satisfaction of a lower want permits a higher want to manifest itself, for Banfield's proposition that it *creates* a higher want, this undermined the claim which Jevons had made, and supported by reference to Banfield (see above pp. 104–5) 'that the scientific basis of economics is in a theory of consumption'. Marshall's view was that 'the science of wants' and 'the science of efforts and activities' supplement each other. It could be argued that this was Jevons's view also, but Marshall had some grounds for complaining that 'Jevons's delight in stating his case strongly' had led him to overstress the consumption side. Cf. Marshall, *Principles of Economics*, Book III, ch. II, § 4, 9th ed., vol. I, p. 90.

28. (p. 116) Compare the passage on composite demand which appeared in the first edition of Marshall's *Principles of Economics*: see 9th ed., vol. II, p. 402.

29. (p. 121) Reference to the lines in italics on p. 120 shows that this should read: 'MUT^{-1} means therefore so much pleasurable effect produced by *so much* commodity per unit of time' – H.S.J.

30. (p. 122) Over the Menai Straits, north Wales. This tubular bridge was considered a feat of engineering at the time of its completion in 1850, and for many years after – H.S.J.

31. (p. 123) In the first and second editions Jevons had here inserted a footnote giving a cross-reference to chapter VII, but as his son pointed out in the third and fourth editions, the terms 'mediate' and 'immediate utility' do not occur there or anywhere else in the book.

32. (p. 131) See the articles on Baudeau and Condillac in Macleod's *Dictionary of Political Economy*, vol. I, London, 1863. This was the only volume of the work published.

33. (p. 131) Correctly no dimensions; that is, mere number – H.S.J.

34. (p. 134) Professor Stigler has pointed out that Jevons's treatment here merges the concepts of competition and the market, an approach which he regards as 'unfortunate', arguing that 'a market may be perfect and

monopolistic or imperfect and competitive'; but he admits that 'Jevons's mixture of the two has been widely imitated by successors'. G. J. Stigler, 'Perfect Competition, Historically Contemplated', *Journal of Political Economy*, vol. LXV, 1957; reprinted in *Essays in the History of Economics*, Chicago, 1965, p. 245.

35. (p. 135) The concept of the 'trading body' has been frequently criticized as a vague and unsatisfactory concept by means of which Jevons tried to generalize his equation of exchange, developed first for the case of two-party two-commodity barter trade, without clearly realizing that contract in such a case is indeterminate – a point which it was left to Edgeworth to bring out and clear up.

However, this was not the view which Edgeworth himself took when he wrote: 'It must be carefully remembered that Prof. Jevons's Formulae of Exchange apply not to bare individuals, an isolated couple, but (as he himself sufficiently indicates) to individuals clothed with the properties of a market, a typical couple.' (*Mathematical Psychics*, p. 31.)

The first view perhaps does rather less than justice to Jevons, the second rather more. For, as examination of the text will show, Jevons does not try to generalize the equations of exchange after having analyzed two-person two-commodity barter trade. The concept of a trading body as a general one covering any group of buyers or sellers is developed before the theory of exchange is set out, and Jevons's 'A' and 'B' are 'bodies', not necessarily persons.

But are they then a typical couple operating under the influence of market competition, as Edgeworth suggested? There are indeed certain passages which admit of this interpretation, but equally there are others which do not (cf. the various cases treated on pp. 151 and 152). A careful reading of this section *Definition of Trading Body* suggests a possible explanation: Jevons developed the concept in an attempt to treat all cases as if they displayed that 'precise and continuous variation' which he realized to exist in the case of 'large aggregates'. Hence he argues that 'the general principles will be the same, whatever the extent of the trading body considered' – but in fact they will not. It might be legitimate in the general case of exchange, as Edgeworth suggested, to assume that the trading bodies operate with a class of competitors in the background – 'But in dealing with exceptional cases, a reference to first principles and the presupposition of competition would have introduced greater precision and suggested the distinction submitted in these pages, namely, that exchange is indeterminate, if either (1) one of the trading bodies (*qua* individual or *qua* union) or (2) the commodity supplied by one of the dealers, be *indivisible or not* perfectly divisible' (*Mathematical Psychics*, p. 109).

36. (p. 144) These objections came from T. Barker, a senior wrangler of Cambridge, who was professor of mathematics at Owens College from 1865 to 1885.

37. (p. 144) Sir Philip Magnus; *Lessons in Elementary Mechanics, introductory to the study of physical science, etc.*, London, 1875.

Jevons and Magnus were contemporaries as undergraduates at University College, London.

38. (p. 148) Cf. above, note 3, and references there cited.

39. (p. 169) Strictly: 'on the functions of final degree of utility', i.e. the shapes of the curves – H.S.J.

40. (p. 170) Since, in equilibrium, final degrees of utility are proportional to market prices, the 'certain' equality of utility here said to exist between different commodities is that between marginal portions of such relative size that they are purchasable with the same small sum of money; e.g. between a 'shilling's worth' of one and of other commodities – H.S.J.

Professor R. S. Howey has criticized Jevons's use of the concept of 'acquired utility' in this section as involving the 'basic error' that 'exchange value enters as a factor determining exchange value' and points out that 'the use of indirect utility would put a kink in every utility curve at the value at which the utility of the money received for the good was greater than further units of the good itself'. (*Rise of the Marginal Utility School*, pp. 43–4.) But this argument assumes that a good can possess both direct and indirect utility, whereas Jevons specifically says that 'things which have *no* direct utility may be the means of procuring us such by exchange, and they may therefore be said to have indirect utility' (above, p. 123).

41. (p. 174) In relation to this and the preceding section, the comment made by Marshall to J. N. Keynes (in a letter dated 26 November 1889) is relevant: 'I hold that Jevons' great error was that of applying to utility propositions that are only true of price. It was here that he thought himself most profound: and it is because I think he was wrong in this one point in which he differed from his predecessors von Thünen and Cournot that I consider his claims to greatness do not to any considerable extent rest on his *Theory of Political Economy*.' In a later letter Marshall referred to 'Jevons's systematic confusion ... of hedonics and economics' and stressed his own desire 'to make clear that economic statistics have nothing to do with utility but only with its rough money measure' (*Principles of Economics*, 9th ed., vol. II, pp. 260–1).

Marshall in fact was anxious to break the link with utilitarianism which was so strong in Jevons; and undoubtedly Jevons, by such procedures as here attempting to determine the 'laws of utility' rather than the 'laws of demand' was moving away from his ideal of a quantitative economics towards a dubious psychology, which his successors realized was not essential for the logic of value analysis.

42. (p. 180) This edition of Chalmers' *Estimate* was first published in London, 1802.

43. (p. 186) This statement has been justified by the fact. *The Great Eastern* steamship, built to the design of Brunel and Russell in 1858, with six masts and a displacement of 32,160 tons, proved a white elephant, being irremediably slow for passenger traffic, and too great in draft and general unwieldiness for cargo. She was sold two or three years ago [1888] for her value as old iron, and broken up at Glasgow. – H.S.J.

44. (p. 198) George Berkeley, Bishop of Cloyne, *The Querist*, 1st ed. in 3 parts, Dublin, 1735–7, Query no. 20.

45. (p. 200) Edgeworth drew attention to this passage as refuting those who claimed that Jevons, because of his assertion that 'value depends entirely upon utility', was in effect putting forward a doctrine of opportunity cost akin to the Austrian. His comment on this sentence was: 'In other words, and as the symbols of the context suggest, utility and disutility are independent variables in that expression, the maximum of which determines economic equilibrium. Among the important lessons which the world owes to the Austrian school, this is not one'. (*Papers relating to Political Economy*, London, 1925, vol. III, p. 32.) This seems fair comment in relation to the passage cited and indeed to the whole of Jevons's theory of labour; the apparent inconsistency between this view of his theory of costs and Jevons's presentation of an alternative cost doctrine in his preface to the second edition (p. 71) could be explained on the ground that here Jevons is considering varying inputs of a factor, whereas in the preface he is treating the allocation of an existing total of a factor between different uses.

46. (p. 202) The difficulty of expressing the determination of ratios of exchange in words is indeed manifest throughout this section. In his anxiety to avoid the terms *value*, *price* and *cost of production* Jevons inevitably imposed some difficulties on himself and his readers. The ensuing section on relations of economic quantities does much to clear these up, but the reader acquainted with modern elementary economics will inevitably feel that these passages cry out to be translated into diagrams using demand and cost curves.

47. (p. 204) 'Degree of productiveness of Y' is to be understood as meaning 'degree of productiveness of labour in producing Y', and similarly for X. – H.S.J.

48. (p. 206) Rather, *final productiveness*, or *rates of production*, to be consistent with the nomenclature adopted on p. 201 – H.S.J.

49. (p. 214) Charles Augustin de Coulomb (1736–1806): *Théorie des machines simples. . . . Nouvelle édition, à laquelle on a ajoûté les mémoires du même auteur. . . . 3º – Sur la force des hommes, ou les quantités d'action qu'ils peuvent fournir*, Paris, 1821. The original memoirs date from 1779.

50. (p. 219) James Mill, *Elements of Political Economy*, 2nd ed.,London, 1824, p. 31.

51. (p. 221) The final rate of production $\frac{dx}{dl}$ is now generally known as marginal *productiveness* or *productivity*. – H.S.J.

52. (p. 229) Meaning *involve a lengthening of*. – H.S.J.

53. (p. 242) The 'eminent mathematician' here referred to was G. H. Darwin (see above note 11). In correspondence with Jevons during the winter of 1873–4, Darwin had proposed a more complicated interest formula allowing for the fact that 'the value of the *expectation* of the produce must reimburse outgoings and return the current interest on each of them, irrespectively of the rates actually earned by them or of the rates at which

I may have borrowed.' Jevons preferred the simplicity of his own formula and Darwin finally conceded its correctness 'in a certain point of view'.

Adamson found difficulty in the idea of expressing the amount of investment as a function of time, and particularly the amount of increased investment as $\Delta t . Ft$ (p. 241). He contended against Jevons's idea 'that if the labourer defers it for time Δt the capital which enables him to do so is $\Delta t . Ft$'. This appeared to him to involve identifying the produce due to investment with the increment in the amount of capital invested. Such an identification was, however, perfectly possible and legitimate under the special assumptions Jevons was making which gave what was virtually a one-commodity economy.

Again Jevons was apparently able to convince Adamson of the general validity of his formula. However, he did make considerable modifications to the chapter on the theory of capital between the first and second editions. A number of these, for example the section headed 'Dimensions of Capital, Credit and Debit', seem to have owed their introduction to points raised by Adamson.

54. (p. 242) The text is printed here as it stands in the second edition, but a little consideration shows that it should read: Capital advanced has the dimension M; the annual return has the dimensions MT^{-1}. Dividing the *latter* by the *former* we have $\frac{M}{MT^{-1}} = T^{-1}$. – H.S.J.

55. (p. 246) It is evident that in any process of joint production the returns to capital and labour are not independent of each other, and Jevons clearly does not intend to deny this but only to controvert propositions such as Ricardo's 'as wages rise, profits fall'.

56. (p. 249) A slip, or unconscious error, in the author's explanation of figure 14 should be noticed. On p. 249, lines 1–2, he says that the increased produce 'due to an increment of capital would be measured by the line qn, so that this will represent $F't$.' He must have intended to write 'will represent $\frac{F't}{t}$' instead of '$F't$', for a few lines farther on he says clearly that when the capital is om the *rate of interest* is 'measured by pm', which equals qn, and in a previous section (p. 241), he has most clearly stated that the rate of interest is represented by $\frac{F't}{Ft}$. – H.S.J.

57. (p. 251) Jevons's approach to this question is as characteristically neo-classical as Smith's is classical. To Jevons, concentrating on consumer satisfaction, the important point is the shelter and comfort, in other words the utility, which the house can provide, and will provide equally to owner or tenant. To Smith, concentrating on the production of real wealth, 'the house itself can produce nothing', i.e. it does not add to the economy's capacity to produce and so any payment made for its services must be derived from some other productive source. This distinction, which for Jevons 'played no part in modern economics', has come back into recent economic thinking, concerned as it is with the problems of increasing

production in less-developed societies. Cf. Hla Myint, *Theories of Welfare Economics*, London, 1948.

On the question dealt with in this section, we may accept Marshall's judgement that 'Jevons, regarding the problem from a purely mathematical point of view, was justified in classing all commodities in the hands of consumers as capital.' (*Principles of Economics*, Book II, iv, § 4; 9th ed., vol. I, p. 77.) Nevertheless, as Marshall pointed out also, such a classification is not in accordance with common usage and is too broad to be convenient. Economists have generally preferred to restrict the term capital to goods used for further production.

NOTE ON THE TEXT
AND ON BIBLIOGRAPHY

THERE have been four previous editions of *The Theory of Political Economy*. Of these, the first (1871) and second (1879) were published during the author's lifetime. The third edition (1888) was prepared by his widow, Harriet A. Jevons; the fourth (1911) by his son Herbert Stanley Jevons.

In the second edition Jevons made numerous changes and added a long preface and two appendices – one a 'List of Mathematico-Economic Writings' and the other a list of his own writings. In the third edition Mrs Jevons brought the 'List of Mathematico-Economic Writings' up to date, but otherwise left the text unchanged.

H. S. Jevons, in the fourth edition, made a number of notes and corrections to his father's text, and added three further appendices – a reprint of Jevons's first 'Brief Account of a General Mathematical Theory of Political Economy', read to the British Association in 1862, a 'Fragment on Capital Intended to Form Part of Chapter XXV of the Author's *Principles of Economics*', and a commentary of his own on his father's theory of interest.

The present edition includes the prefaces which Jevons wrote for the first and second editions and the full text of the *Theory* as revised and printed in the fourth edition, without abridgement. All the appendices have been omitted, but the notes which H. S. Jevons added to his father's text have been retained. These are distinguished from other notes by the addition of the initials – H.S.J.

* * *

Jevons's *Theory of Political Economy* is referred to, at greater or less length, in every general history of economic thought, but has received comparatively little specific and detailed attention. The only complete monograph, E. W. Eckard's *Economics of W. S. Jevons*, Washington D.C., 1940, is now out of print.

Among works on economic thought which gave more attention to Jevons and his period, reference may be made to T. W. Hutchison, *A Review of Economic Doctrines 1870–1929*, London, 1953; R. S. Howey, *The Rise of the Marginal Utility School, 1870–1889*, Laurence Kansas, 1960; M. Blaug, *Economic Theory in Retrospect*, 2nd ed. London, 1968; G. J. Stigler, *Production and Distribution Theories* New York, 1941.